Strategic Cultural Center Management

Strategic Cultural Center Management focuses on private cultural centers and their operational preconditions. The aim is to illustrate how to strategically manage a cultural center in varied external environments.

Analyzing processes of organizational change, the author uses institutional and resource dependence theories alongside concepts such as business models, profitability, mission focus and quality management. The book examines theoretical and managerial implications, highlighting that cultural managers lean towards different strategies that diversify resource streams, facilitating agile strategic responses to institutional pressures.

Offering valuable theoretical, empirical and conceptual analysis, this book serves as an incomparable reference for researchers, postgraduate students, civic leaders and arts managers involved in the creative and cultural industries.

Tomas Järvinen is CEO and Principal of Folkhälsan Education, Finland. He holds a PhD in Arts Management (Sibelius Academy, University of the Arts, Helsinki).

Routledge Research in the Creative and Cultural Industries

Series Editor: Ruth Rentschler

This series brings together book-length original research in cultural and creative industries from a range of perspectives. Charting developments in contemporary cultural and creative industries thinking around the world, the series aims to shape the research agenda to reflect the expanding significance of the creative sector in a globalized world.

Music Business Careers
Career Duality in the Creative Industries
Cheryl Slay Carr

Racial and Ethnic Diversity in the Performing Arts Workforce
Tobie S. Stein

Understanding Audience Engagement in the Contemporary Arts
Stephanie E. Pitts and Sarah M. Price

Access, Diversity, Equity and Inclusion in Cultural Organizations
Insights from the Careers of Executive Opera Managers of Color in the US
Antonio C. Cuyler

Digital Transformation in the Cultural and Creative Industries
Production, Consumption and Entrepreneurship in the Digital and Sharing Economy
Edited by Marta Massi, Marilena Vecco and Yi Lin

Researching Art Markets
Past, Present and Tools for the Future
Edited by Elisabetta Lazzaro, Nathalie Moureau and Adriana Turpin

Strategic Cultural Center Management
Tomas Järvinen

Strategic Cultural Center Management

Tomas Järvinen

Routledge
Taylor & Francis Group
NEW YORK AND LONDON

First published 2021
by Routledge
52 Vanderbilt Avenue, New York, NY 10017

and by Routledge
2 Park Square, Milton Park, Abingdon, Oxon OX14 4RN

Routledge is an imprint of the Taylor & Francis Group, an informa business

Library of Congress Cataloging-in-Publication Data
A catalog record for this title has been requested

ISBN: 978-0-367-51024-4 (hbk)

ISBN: 978-0-367-51023-7 (pbk)

ISBN: 978-1-003-05213-5 (ebk)

Typeset in Times
by Newgen Publishing UK

Contents

Illustration

Figures

Tables

Pictures

Preface

It seems as if nearly everyone has a notion of what a cultural center is. Yet, these centers differ a lot and have vast differences in their operational possibilities. Although the concept of a cultural center is somewhat self-explanatory, there is an immense need for mapping existing centers and exploring new ways of managing these organizations. But as you will find out when reading this book, there is very little prior studies on cultural centers. Deciphering the enigma of these multi-purpose centers with generally vast turnovers should have been done years ago. But there is no virtue in dwelling in the past, rather to change the current status by writing one more book about the subject. There is much to learn about the existing centers and the outcome can, as often is the case, be applied to a versatility of organizations – be they of the same or different kinds.

This book focuses on private cultural centers and their operational preconditions within the fields of both private and public cultural centers. It not only examines processes of change within organizational fields, using institutional theory (IT) and resource dependence theory (RDT), but it also involves concepts such as business models, profitability, mission focus and quality management. The aim is to present how to strategically manage a cultural center through different external pressures that an organization may – and most likely will – be subject for, as well as to introduce the differing organizational premises the management must take into account whilst leading the cultural center through miscellaneous trials.

Theoretically, the aim is inter alia to examine the ways resource dependence encourages heterogeneity among cultural centers, or reverse institutional isomorphism, transforming the change agents of private cultural centers into driven institutional entrepreneurs. This happens in practice by developing new insights into theories by problematizing the empirical work this book leans on. Although cultivating different assumptions than those in the applied literature and problematizing the empirical work are considered to be two disconnected methods, this book put these approaches into interplay to produce contributions on a theoretical level.

Why and under which situations does an organization accept or resist institutional pressures? Using IT and RDT literature as well as a framework that connects environmental pressures to distinct organizational strategies, this book analyzes how the type and level of resource dependence affect cultural centers in different ways. Private centers, which likely are dependent on diverse revenue sources, likely will exhibit a higher degree of diversity, whereas public centers, which likely are dependent primarily on one revenue source, likely will exhibit a higher degree of conformity. A central theme is therefore to explore the effects of isomorphic pressures in the context of cultural centers. Isomorphism, a central concept within IT, refers to a shift towards homogenization among organizations within a particular field. Some have nevertheless suggested the opposite: isomorphic pressures can lead to isomorphism in reverse. In this book, you will have the opportunity to see how an institutional change due to resource dependence leads not to isomorphism but to isomorphism in reverse.

How do such institutional contradictions arise? By focusing on knowledgeable change agents, we will examine change in a field-level setting by examining IT and RDT, interviews on the cases of four private cultural centers, as well as a questionnaire sent to all cultural centers in Finland. We will then explore how microlevel organizational behavior influences macrolevel field changes.

We will also aim attention on mission focus. A mission statement defines what line of business an organization is in, as well as why it exists or what purpose it serves. Mission drift, on the other hand, in which an organization deviates from its mission, is commonly defined as a process of organizational change. It may occur due to commercial activities and dependence on any dominant funder, such as foundations and the state. Mission drift is defined as a focus on profits instead of social goods. While trying to manage diverse revenue sources, private cultural centers may become more resource- than mission-oriented. We will explore the connection between perceived resource dependence and mission focus or drift.

This is the basic plan of the book. The paradox of historical knowledge is nevertheless, that once it is out there, the actions for the future can be corrected and the theories of the past become obsolete. Where science often is supposed to predict the future relying on the past, it fails to do so because things change. The past cannot be copied into the future. But there are still things to be learned from the past. People are often afraid of change even if they know it is constant. But you cannot welcome any true changes if you do not first admit to yourself that it is needed.

Paradoxically, the very power of succeeding will increase the danger of failing, as everyone start to mimic your model and you become one in a crowd before you know it. That is, unless you reinvent yourself constantly and stay a step ahead all the time, which is quite hard, if not to say impossible in the long run. It is also unclear whether organizations will be able to reinvent themselves in such a manner needed to stay ahead of the game. Still, once the scientific insights are adapted by everyday routine activities as well as economic systems, there is no limit to the success. When people come together and form a common story, or at least find a mutual red thread in their network of stories, meaning is created. Belief is grounded in that community and can stop to exist or be recreated whenever. So, create your own story!

Writing this book has been an interesting experience, not in any way made easier by the Covid-19 spring we all suffered in 2020. I still managed to make ends meet, and I would like to thank everyone involved – since this was not in any way a one man's job. I wish to thank all the contributing centers for their input of knowledge and expertise in this book. This book is based on my PhD thesis and I would therefore furthermore like to thank Sibelius Academy of Uniarts Helsinki for the permission to use existing text in this book. I would also like to thank my former professor Tanja Johansson for all her contribution in my journey into the world of science. Lastly, my family, who has supported me throughout this process. My beautiful wife Sofia Eriksson and my lovely children Tilde and Tyra.

Tomas Järvinen

1 Introduction to cultural centers

The aim with this first chapter is to frame the essence of a cultural center, why they initially were built and for what purpose. Some differences between different countries will also be presented. What is the idea behind connecting citizens with their culture as well as allowing them to learn from each other? Why build stages for multiple use, with restaurants and libraries and other services, all for a usually quite small entrance fee? Let us start by finding out the backdrop to the cultural centers.

This chapter will also present a conceptual framework for the whole book, as well as a short overview of the study in the form of a brief methodological introduction.

1.1 What is a cultural center?

What exactly is a cultural center other than a big building with a palette of artistic activities? Well, cultural centers are venues in public use that create a platform for people to both practice and take part in cultural activities (Stenlund, 2010). They may for instance provide commercial concerts, theatre productions, standup comedy, musicals, or even be the home of the city's symphony orchestra (Lambert & Williams, 2017). In this book, we refer to cultural centers as houses in versatile use for cultural activities. The concept also includes cultural institutions and cultural halls, although venues used for a single purpose (e.g. theatres) are not taken into account (Statistics Finland, 2017). The cultural center may also have differing names in different countries, such as the performing arts centers in North America (Lambert & Williams, 2017). Any big venue arguably could function as a cultural center, and that most likely was the case earlier. Generally, cultural centers do not have any artistic personnel of their own and mostly focus on productions (Silvanto, et al., 2008). Public cultural centers commonly describe their primary mission as to producing (by prioritizing and coordinating) exclusive cultural offerings to the community (Ruusuvirta, et al., 2012). Cultural centers are often seen as a tool for the municipality's cultural planning and development efforts (Lambert & Williams, 2017). A vast majority of cultural centers are located in urban areas (Bogen, 2018; Kangas & Ruokolainen, 2012). The buildings of the centers vary a lot, and can cover both renovated former industrial, religious,

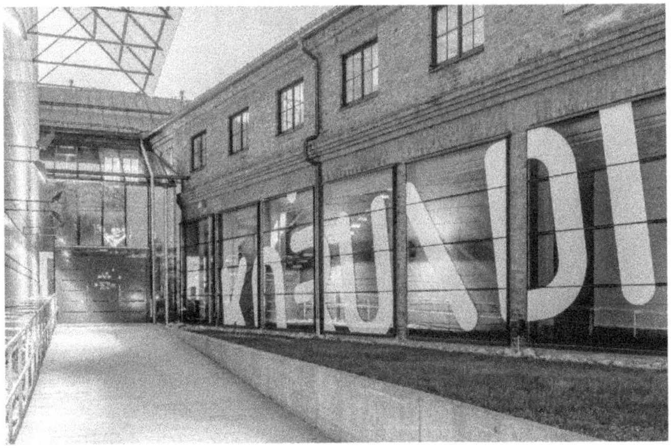

Picture 1.1 The entrance of cultural center Korundi in Rovaniemi, Finland.

commercial and military buildings, but also new buildings (Bogen, 2018). They are not even limited to buildings, as some centers are boats or barges.

The concept of arts facilities in residential areas in Finland was proposed during the Finnish cultural debates in the 1960s, followed by the expression 'democratization of culture' in the 1970s (Silvanto, et al., 2008). The main objective of cultural democracy was to highlight citizens' activities, needs and understandings of culture (Kangas, 1988). During this ongoing debate, Finnish municipalities began to produce cultural services (Silvanto et al., 2008). Helsinki was the first city to plan a multipurpose center, and in 1984, Stoa, the first public cultural center, was opened. In Finland, the idea was to establish such a center in every part of the country, or at least every big city (Silvanto et al., 2008), which why cultural centers are mostly found in cities (Kangas & Ruokolainen, 2012). There, of course, were venues, such as the Turun VPK (2018) house in Finland built in 1892, that were used in the same manner before 1984 but simply were not called cultural centers then. Other similar examples of early arts or cultural centers' in the larger parts of Europe that can be traced back to initiatives founded by labor movements as long ago as in the late 19th and early 20th centuries, are, for instance, the People's Palaces and Union facilities in United Kingdom, Folkets hus in Scandinavia and Ateneos or Casa del Pueblo's in Spain (Bogen, 2018).

Nevertheless, there are some substantial differences between countries which should be acknowledged. The majority of the private cultural centers in Finland were founded after the state initiative in the 1980s (Statistics Finland, 2017). In western Europe, the opposite seems to have taken place. States began to build their own centers in the 1990s, after the private initiative of the art labs in the 1960s, which became private cultural centers in the 1970s and 1980s (Fitzgerald, 2010). The North American equivalent, the Performing arts centers (PAC), were also founded in the 1960s (Wolff, 2017).

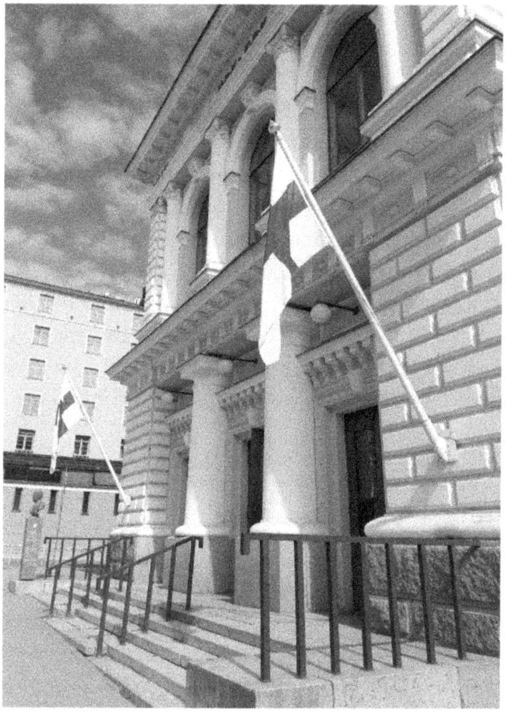

Picture 1.2 The front of Turun VPK with flags, in Turku, Finland.

In 2017, there were 185 cultural centers in Finland, including 71 (38,37%) private cultural centers (Statistics Finland, 2017). Statistics Finland's list is not comprehensive but gives an adequate picture of the situation. Of the 71 private centers, 28 are maintained by non-government organizations (NGOs), 26 by joint-stock companies, 7 by university fraternities, 4 by foundations, 3 by private citizens, 2 by parishes and 1 by a cooperative (Statistics Finland, 2017). Regarding management, 105 are maintained by municipalities directly, 6 by joint-stock companies owned by municipalities and 3 by the state. Interestingly, of the eight hybrid centers (both private and public), this study could identify four joint-stock companies, two NGOs, one foundation and one fraternity.

In a survey to 50 arts or cultural centers in Europe, Paul Bogen (2018) concluded that 93% of the respondents have private as opposed to public legal structures. A total of 27 were associations, 11 limited companies, 9 foundations, 1 co-operative, 1 partnership and 1 registered charity. European Network of Cultural Centres (ENCC) represents 3000 centers via their 14 national networks in 12 countries (Bogen, 2018). In order to get exact figures of the centers in Europe, we would have to take into account that not all European countries have national networks, and not all are members of ENCC. As a result, there could easily be more than twofold the number of centers in Europe than that of the members in ENCC. Thus, the numbers presented above of the legal structures of centers in Europe are not of course adequate but does give a sort of general impression about the status in Europe (Bogen, 2018).

According to a survey by the Finnish Cultural Foundation (2013), the Finnish think it is important to have opportunities to exercise and take part in local cultural activities, with an emphasis on venues, such as cultural centers. According to Kangas and Ruokolainen (2012), the majority of municipalities think that the cultural sector develops the community's image and cultural heritage, economic development, citizens' wellbeing and children's cultural skills. On the Nordic level, researchers in Sweden and Norway indicate that cultural centers have the same impact on society (Ambrecht, 2012; Storstad, 2010). In North America, cultural centers, called performing arts centers, are seen as a part of the '*creative and cultural industries, significantly influencing the cultural and economic vitality of communities*' (Lambert & Williams, 2017, p. 1).

1.2 The jungle of organizational types

Beside the question on how to frame the mission of the cultural centers, as well as their financing as in subchapter 1.3, there is also the question of how to define their organizational types. Some are for instance joint-stock companies, some NGO's, others are maintained by municipalities or by the state. Some may even be joint ventures between private and public owners. The two fundamental categories seem nevertheless to be private and public, with some alternative combinations.

Organizations are often divided into private or public (Bozeman, 1987; Rainey, 2003). Bozeman (1987) offered three dimensions of public character that define organizations: 1) ownership, 2) funding and 3) control. Different organizations fall differently within these dimensions, which is why categorization is difficult. Bozeman (1987) defined *ownership* as the maintainer of the organization, whether private organizations or the state. *Funding* refers to how the money generated by the activities of the maintainer, whether subsidies, tax revenues or sales of products or services. An organization, of course can have diverse ways of getting funding. The last dimension, *control*, concerns the question of who inspects the organization's activities. Generally, the stakeholders carry through the inspection; the owner supervises the production, the customer (renter) the product (event) and society ensures that laws and regulations are followed (Bozeman, 1987). Many other dimensions have been presented throughout the years, but according to Boyne (2002), these three core definitions are the most used. They are mostly used in a simplified manner, and when significant differences are identified, it is not uncommon that only the ownership dimension is used to distinguish organizational publicity. In Table 1.1, the four cultural center groups are divided according to ownership and control.

Many types of cultural centers serve different community functions, which makes it difficult to study them (Lambert & Williams, 2017). According to

Table 1.1 Ownership and control

		Ownership	
		Public	*Private*
Control	*Public*	b) The public centers	d) The centers maintained by governmental companies
	Private	c) The hybrid centers	a) The private centers

Statistics Finland's (2017) list of the maintainers of cultural centers in Finland, there seem to be three main groups of cultural centers in the country at hand: (1) the private centers; (2) the public centers; and (3) the combination private and public centers (the hybrid model). Also, some private centers are maintained by the municipalities that founded them, which would therefore present a fourth type of cultural centers, a group where the private centers are maintained by government agency. The same division applies in North America amongst the performing arts centers, even if Lambert and Williams (2017) do group hybrid arts centers under the public centers and some other smaller differences.

There may be different kind of entities involved in ownership, governance, management and operations that are not fully depicted here, but the following figure presents how the groups of cultural centers are situated in relation to each other, in a Finnish context.

The field of cultural centers seem to be swiftly changing as these different types of cultural centers emerge (Statistics Finland, 2017). It is therefore important to take into account the differing premises of the centers, especially when taking into account the emerging hybrid center types. Lambert and Williams (2017) emphasized the need to address the '*hybrid mix of public administration, non-profit management, and for-profit entrepreneurship competencies required of these leaders*' (p. 8).

1.2.1 The private center

When the initiative to found cultural centers and maintain them is on a non-governmental basis, cultural centers are called private (Fitzgerald, 2010). Private centers can be divided into several subgroups: (1) a collective with no formal structure and no legal entity; (2) a collective with a structure and a legal entity; (3) a non-profit organization; (4) a for-profit organization; (5) an organization operating under the legal auspices of a local authority, such as a joint-stock company owned by the municipality (though this example is problematized in subsection 1.2.4); (6) a partnership between two or more organizations; (7) a social business, which is run like a business but with a non-profit motive; (8) an educational institution, either public or private; (9) a foundation, which in Finland are seen as non-profit organizations (Manninen, 2005).

According to Sandy Fitzgerald (2014), with Trans Europe Halles, the activities of the private cultural centers

> *take place in the vacuum that often exists between citizens and the state, between vested interests and communities, between cultural development and consumerism ... where the political or social status quo has failed to take responsibility, failed to act or is actively opposed to cultural democracy.*
>
> (p. 6)

Private cultural centers seem to rely on many different private subsidies and thereby do not have the same steady income from the state or the municipality as their public peers do. These private institutions are a very heterogeneous collection of actors that usually have modest balance sheets, making them unattractive for investors – which, in turn, usually prevents them from expanding (Kangas & Pirnes, 2015).

1.2.2 The public center

Of the administrative bodies in Finland, both the state and municipalities maintain public cultural centers (Statistics Finland, 2017). The latter maintains the most. The idea to maintain a public cultural center is to '*ensure both equal abilities to both produce and experience art regardless of one's residential area or social background*' (Silvanto et al., 2008, p. 170). The same applies to North America, where even some NGOs with governmental boards are considered public centers (Lambert & Williams, 2017).

The offering of public services can be arranged in different ways by municipalities (Kangas & Ruokolainen, 2012). Public cultural centers are mostly part of municipalities' cultural services and thus funded by municipalities (Silvanto et al., 2008; Ruusuvirta & Saukkonen, 2014). In a survey in 20 Finnish cities, public funding accounts for 17% of the total annual turnover of public cultural centers, sales and payment revenues 40%, rent income 28% and other incomes 14% (Ruusuvirta & Saukkonen, 2014). A later survey finds that it is mostly impossible to gather information about public grants for public centers as the costs are divided among many areas of the municipality's spending (Ruusuvirta & Saukkonen, 2014). For example, the costs of maintaining the venue itself are often not counted in the turnover of a public cultural center.

Furthermore, according to Kangas and Pirnes (2015), the current system of accounting for state subsidies includes only expenditures and the amount of personnel, which does not give adequate information for assessing the content of activities or societal influence of the public centers. State subsidies, though, do offer economic security. At the moment, the municipalities have no sufficient efficiency or quality requirements or any aims of cultural policy that must be met. Neither is there an incentive system to reward organizations that have succeeded in achieving the aims of the current cultural policy (Kangas & Pirnes, 2015).

1.2.3 The hybrid model center

The model in which both private organizations and the municipality maintain a cultural center, or '*the open hybrid model of an institution based on civil-public partnership*' (Fitzgerald, 2010, p. 63), seems to vary in funding sources and the share of ownership the various entities hold (Ruusuvirta et al., 2012; Ruusuvirta & Saukkonen, 2014). Hybrid organizations appear at the interface of the state, market and civil society (Thornton & Ocasio, 2008). These are organizational forms involving government bureaucracy, business firms and non-profit organizations. Although studies indicate the establishment of such public–private cooperation in Finland (Kangas & Pirnes, 2015), there are rather few practical examples of it within the cultural field, according to Kangas and Ruokolainen (2012). According to the quantitative findings of this study, there are 11 such hybrid centers in Finland, of a total of 189.

Public funding is a commonality between this model and publicly funded private centers (Ruusuvirta & Saukkonen, 2014). In Finland, the funding of public cultural centers and publicly funded private centers varies but generally is a substantial part of municipalities' budget for cultural services (Ruusuvirta & Saukkonen, 2014). Directly involving the municipality as a co-maintainer of the cultural center gives it direct responsibility for both the mission and the financial sustainability of the center (Fitzgerald, 2010). The main idea in this collaboration is that the municipality presents an equal, not a dominant partner.

1.2.4 The center maintained by government agencies

The goal of privatization among public cultural organizations has been to lighten the economic burden of municipalities (Kangas & Pirnes, 2015). The idea is that organizations themselves will find alternative private funding. The art industry, though, is different than the market and commercialism (Chong, 2008), so it is to be seen who will gain from the privatization of cultural centers.

The support the government distributes to private organizations can have both direct and indirect forms (Kangas & Ruokolainen, 2012; Kangas & Pirnes, 2015). The most common support mechanisms are subsidies or grants, and the reported values of these are often used to summarize government funding to, for instance, to non-profits (Rushton & Brooks, 2007). Publicly funded private centers enjoy tax money, which, according to Chris Torch (2010), artistic director of Intercult in Stockholm, Sweden, builds their sense of responsibility as it is '*money from my neighbors and from the school teachers of my children, and it is also my own*' (p. 17).

Public authorities every so often endure financial crisis, which seem to be a result of a weak functional and structural organization. Therefore, a paradigm shift called 'New Public Management' is applied in public administration with an array of innovative reforms. It is an attempt to profit from progresses in the private sector. With new public management, they aim attention at decentralization, focus on core competencies (Prahalad & Hamel, 1990), outsourcing and lastly, a closer relationship between supplier and buyer (Loeffler, 2003).

1.2.5 Positioning private cultural centers in relation to public centers

While interviewing people from different cultural centers, it became clear that there is not much collaboration or contact between the public centers and the private centers. Some respondents mention working on a few productions at public centers, and some centers share artists on tour. Organizations still tend to mold their organizational identities in relation to other organizations in their field (Strandgaard Pedersen & Dobbin, 2006), and seem to apply to private cultural centers as well.

The vast majority of the interview respondents think private entrepreneurs are responsible for the majority of cultural offerings in their community. Some consider the municipality to be the main cultural provider, a few feels that private entrepreneurs and the municipality share equal amounts of responsibility, and one sees no differences at all between private actors and the municipality in providing culture. The respondents all share the opinion that the municipality has an important role in supporting cultural activities. There are differences in this role; some stress the responsibility of the municipality to take the lead in cultural offerings, whereas some propose municipalities should merely act as facilitators.

> *I see the role of the city [...] as a facilitator. (...) The creation of opportunities is included in facilitation activities. That could mean spaces or resources. I do not see the city as a commissioner. I do not see that a city subscribes to a certain type of culture, let alone as the producer itself.*
>
> (Respondent C)

Most respondents nevertheless think the municipality has a role in offering cultural activities to the community on a smaller level. Some opinions hold that the cultural offerings of a community might be jeopardized if they rested solely on the shoulders of the private entrepreneurs: '*I think it should be as it is now. To say that the fundament would ... be at risk if it were to be run private as they can stop doing it at any time*' (Respondent R).

Furthermore, the respondents seem to share a view that the municipality mostly offers culture due to the national strategy. The underlying opinion here is that even if the municipal cultural department emphasizes the importance of offering diverse art to its community, regulations on a national level still dictate what is to be offered. This changes the foundation of what is to be offered, in a way not in balance with the actual needs of a specific local society. This dictating of the municipal cultural departments as to what is to be offered is in stark contrast to private cultural centers, which foremost offer what they think is needed in their particular region. As one respondent puts it:

> *Well, municipal institutions have to offer art, to … to be able to say on a national scale that art is offered equally to children and adolescents and adults, and drama and comedy, for example, on the theatre side. We do not in any way have any obligation to provide certain types of software or certain types of events.*
>
> (Respondent N)

Most respondents emphasize that their role as private organizations enables them to analyze their local society and plan their cultural offerings accordingly. If there is another cinema in the same town, the private cultural center may aim to show movies that cannot be seen in that cinema. If there is another theatre, it does other plays. If there is a music hall, it offers other sorts of concerts. Their goal is to fill a void, not to duplicate what is offered elsewhere.

> *We perceive ourselves that we play a significant role in the fact that we do [it] differently and from different starting points than these big municipal cultural institutions here.*
>
> (Respondent N)

Most respondents see their mission as filling a void as the current situation of public cultural offerings in their society has left large areas of culture blank. The idea is not merely to act as a supplement to public cultural offerings but to present an alternative culture to customers, a slight difference the respondents highlight.

1.3 Cultural centers through an economic lens

According to Lambert & Williams (2017), the cultural centers are multimillion-dollar institutions that many take for granted. But just how much is their turnover? Without some comparative numbers, it is a little hard to grasp the economic and social significance of the cultural centers in different countries.

To use the numbers of one cultural center in Finland as an example, the public cultural center Savoy in Helsinki had a turnover of 1,624,894 euros in 2016, including 808,301 euros from subsidies from the city of Helsinki (Helsingin kaupunki, 2017). Overall, it had 415 events in 2016, of which 17 were its own productions, 250 joint ventures and 148 external renters. It aimed to have an audience of 60,000 in 2016 and ended up with an audience of 89,451 people (Helsingin kaupunki, 2017).

According to Renko and Ruusuvirta (2018), there were 105 public cultural centers in Finland in 2016. They received a total of approximately 43 million euros in municipal funding. The amount varied among municipalities from 0 to 9,8 million euros. The mean was 1,8 million euros, and the median 0,6 million euros. Helsinki gave the highest funding, subsidizing its 9 cultural centers with 9,8 million euros (Renko & Ruusuvirta, 2018).

Drawing on data from 45 private cultural centers in 27 countries, Trans Europe Halles, a Europe-based network of cultural centers, notes that the mean turnover in Europe is 1,25 million euros (Schiuma et al., 2015). Nonetheless, differences arise among centers depending on which area of Europe they represent: '*The Scandinavian and western European organizations budgets averaged over €2 million, while the annual budgets of the organizations based in southern and Eastern Europe were only just under €200,000*' (Schiuma et al., 2016, p. 25). According to Schiuma et al. (2016), Scandinavia has the highest amount of public funding, 100% according to the report, whereas southern European centers get 70% of the total turnover. Ten per cent of all centers studied received no public funding. The average number of annual events is 200, with 295 in western Europe, 273 in Scandinavia and 105 in eastern and southern Europe. The centers in Scandinavia have an annual average attendance of 166,000 people, western European centers 114,000, eastern Europeans 24,000 and southern Europeans 14,000 (Schiuma et al., 2016).

According to a newer study on private cultural centers in Europe it could be concluded that:

> *the average or 'typical' non-governmental Arts/Cultural Centre has a building of 2,500 square metres located in an urban area, presents 200 mainly performing arts, public events a year covering eight art form areas to an audience of 75,000, curates 50% of their programme, earns more from renting out space than from any other income source, has 19 staff, a budget of €1.25 million, earns 80% of their total income and has a bar of café that produces as much income as they receive in public funding!*
>
> (Bogen, 2018, p. 13)

Mulcahey (2000) noted that government funding for arts organization in United States, France, Norway and Canada, has decreased since the 1990s. This has led to a need to diversify the palette of funding sources, for instance, through corporate and private philanthropy (Froelich, 1999). In Finland, municipal funding to cultural centers and subsidies grew over 2006–2016, from 106,310,000 euros to 116,313,000 euros. In total, an increase of 10,003,000 euro or about 8,6% (Statistics Finland, 2017b). Renko and Ruusuvirta (2018), in a study on 24 Finnish cities in 2016, found that the public centers received a total of 37,148,000 euros in 2010 and 43,218,000 euros in 2016, an increase of 6,070,000 euros, or about 14%.

These numbers are not absolutely comparable, but they still imply that most of the municipal funding reserved for subsidies to cultural centers other than those run by municipalities has decreased. This can also be seen in the number of subsidies from private funds (The Swedish Cultural Foundation in Finland, 2017; Konstsamfundet; 2016) and the diversification in private centers' revenue sources (Anonymous, 2016c).

Not all municipalities have the resources to maintain cultural centers, and the future seems to promise even fewer opportunities for public funding. In fact, already the pre-corona European financial crisis in 2008 resulted in a dramatic decrease in public funding and support for arts and culture (Schiuma et al., 2016). How Covid-19 will change the field is yet to be seen. Arts and cultural institutions and organizations find themselves at a turning point where new ways of managing and funding culture need to be explored

A survey indicated that public officials in Finland believe that cultural centers will not be a public service in 10 years, as external producers were assumed to take over this service (Kangas & Ruokolainen, 2012). There has been criticism of the number of public cultural institutions due to decreasing possibilities for public funding and the inability of centers to meet the changing demands of artistic content (Kangas & Pirnes, 2015). Whereas decreasing the numbers of these public institutions very well could solve the economic problems, it would also inevitably lead to a decrease in public services. Since 2010, there has been a movement to privatize governmental and municipal institutions. According to Kangas and Pirnes (2015), the main reason for this is to decrease cultural expenditures and to encourage and oblige these institutions to raise money from elsewhere. Still, in most of these cases, municipalities have retained their authority to monitor and control the activities and the economy of the centers, conveyed, for instance, by municipal board members (Ruusuvirta & Saukkonen, 2015). Furthermore, there are not many such private institutions operating under the legal auspices of a local authority.

People in Finland as well as in rest of Europe are looking for experiences and find cultural centers to be important providers of such (Silvanto et al., 2008; Eriksson et al., 2018). This could be a sign of growing interest in founding new private cultural centers even in smaller cities, where there are no public centers. I, therefore, assume that private centers will likely become an alternative to public centers in the future. Assuming that private centers aim to have the same mission as their public peers, what possibilities and tools do the managers of private centers have to actualize this mission? As legal entities, the private centers have the sole liability for their activities. With less steady income, they might overemphasize renting the venue to external producers of cultural events. One can assume that the market for such cultural venues is restricted in smaller communities. With less external producers (renters) to choose among, the question becomes whether private centers can commit to a mission to produce versatile offerings of cultural activities in their venues, as their public peers do? The private centers simply may not be able to influence the program content of the external producer (the renter). In addition, a focus on acquiring more revenue can lead to mission drift.

However, the economic uncertainty among the private centers, created by the lack of steady public funding, generates a natural flexibility towards a changing environment (Eikenberry & Klover, 2004). Consequently, the lack of competition, as would seem to be the case with the public peers, leads to decreased innovation, efficiency and productivity (Sherer & Lee, 2002). Without competing forces, organizations have no need to change. In addition, private centers do not have to endure a public scrutiny and demands for insight, transparency and control of information and resources, which inevitably create time-consuming administrative work.

1.4 Decentralized organizations

As noted in new public management (see subsection 1.2.4), public authorities focus on decentralization, and not without good reasons. Decentralization happens when especially the activities regarding decision making of an organization are distributed or delegated away from an authoritative body (Merriam-Webster Dictionary, 2020). The process of decentralization can be executed by privatization of public owned activities, as shortly described in subsection 1.2.4. Another option is deregulation, the elimination of restrictions on organizations contending with government services (Falleti, 2005).

1.4.1 Deregulation

According to Hillman, Cannella and Paetzold (2000), one environmental change that highlights resource dependence (see Chapter 6) is the balance between regulation and deregulation. By regulation, Hillman, Cannella and Paetzold (2000) mean government economic regulations that affect the competitive dynamics of a particular industry, for instance, by setting prices and services and imposing rivalry and constraints. Governments generally use the power acquired from resource dependence to influence organizational operations, such as acquisitions, staffing and reporting (Froelich, 1999; Tolbert, 1985). This, in turn, leads to governments assuming an active role in the governance of organizations depending on the government's resources. Regulations thus result in limited strategical availability for the organization. According to Stigler (2003), government intervention, in some cases, can be more harmful than, for instance, market failures. Stigler (2003) argued that regulations can interrupt innovation and progress. Deregulation, in turn, is commonly connected to market transitions, such as privatization, or the transfer of public ownership and management to the private sector (Vickers & Yarrow, 1991). Privatization is usually focused on finding suitable boundaries between the public and private sectors. Amid deregulation, organizations face new sources of uncertainty as they are not protected from competition anymore and are confronted with a need for strategic change (Stigler, 2003, Vickers & Yarrow, 1991).

Stigler (2003) emphasized two perspectives on whether the government should intervene or regulate markets. First, regulations may be established to protect or benefit the public or a large part of it. Second, regulations may benefit industry. These two perspectives are not necessarily antagonistic as the impact of the perspectives most likely varies over time. However, even if the initial motivation was the public benefit, industry might ultimately take charge and demand a regulation be continued. Vickers and Yarrow (1991) highlighted two factors affecting the efficiency of organizations: ownership and the force from the competitive market. Privatization can be a greater force if it leads to greater competition, but with a large public organization, competition might be as strong or stronger.

DiMaggio and Powell (1983) emphasized that coercive isomorphism (see Chapter 5) '*is most likely to occur where there is financial dependence, centralized resources with limited alternatives*' (p. 264), suggesting public cultural centers with their limited authority and sole dependence on municipal funding. Resource Dependence Theory (RDT) explains that the primary duty of the board of a regulated organization is to supply organization-specific information to the regulatory agency (Pfeffer & Salancik, 2003). In this book, this applies to publicly funded public cultural centers. In the case of deregulated organizations, the information recipient usually is the board itself, as in the case of private cultural centers.

Economic viability, like legitimacy, is a prerequisite for organizational survival (Pfeffer & Salancik, 2003). According to classical economics, low-cost production and meeting market demand better than one's competitors are imperative for economic viability. Again, this assumption does not apply to state regulation and intervention into the marketplace. As there are pros and cons with both competition and state regulation, there are also signs of these two replacing and becoming intertwined with each other over time, as in the example of new public management. Nonetheless, state regulations are more common in times of crisis and less helpful for the market as a whole during prosperity (Pfeffer & Salancik, 2003).

> *When organizations are regulated by the state, the economic environment diminishes in importance as the importance of the political and administrative environment increases. Both attention and behavior shift accordingly. The decisions of consumers become less important than the decisions of lawmakers and government agents.*
>
> (Pfeffer & Salancik, 2003, p. 203)

Organizations seem to struggle to attain stability in the provision of a resource or consumption of an output if they also need steady resource transactions to operate (Pfeffer & Salancik, 2003; Froelich, 1999). Some organizations need stability more than profitability or growth. Here, again, a situation with acceptable supply of resources might easily turn into one of insufficiency. Stability does not only facilitate administration but is also in the interest of all the allied groups that gain benefits if the organization survives. Instability casts the shadow of doubt on the organization, and those relying on its resources either try to stabilize it or seek a more stable organization (Pfeffer & Salancik, 2003). As management's duty is to guarantee access to resource, the continuation of alliances is of upmost importance (Hillman et al., 2009).

The type of external demands depends on the ownership of the organization (Bozeman, 1987; Vickers & Yarrow, 1991). Public organizations owned by a municipality or the state experience both political and common interests in their administration (Silvanto et al., 2008). Political governance fluctuates depending on the political balance in society. In addition, public organizations do not have to tolerate the pressure of competition, at least in the short-term (Boyne, 2002). They do not have to struggle for their existence in the same manner as private organizations, which negatively affects innovation, efficiency and productivity. Furthermore, public organizations, including public cultural centers, have to endure a public scrutiny and demands for insights, transparency and control of information and resources (Jennergren, 1981; Metcalfe, 1993; Rainey, 2003). Whereas Pfeffer and Salancik (2003) emphasized that firms may gain certain benefits from their board members (e.g. expertise, advice, access to resources, legitimacy), Hillman (2005) noted that heavily regulated organizations have more former politicians on their boards than less-regulated organizations. Hillman (2005) furthermore demonstrated that having more former politicians on their board's correlates to lower financial performance for regulated organizations, and higher financial performance for less-regulated organizations.

1.4.2 The cultural centers take on deregulation

An interesting viewpoint on the topic of deregulation would be what the cultural centers have to say about the state of regulations and deregulations. As the empirical data collected for this specific study were done in a Finnish context, the answers will less surprising be restricted to Finland.

Private cultural centers in Finland generally state that they are less exposed to municipal regulations and control. However, according to the respondents, several regulations still apply to them, especially those centers that get municipal or state funding.

> *One problem is a relation to ... an indirect reliance on [...] [the] city. However, it is completely different than if politicians or officials would come and sit in our board. I am much more comfortable with this model.*
>
> (Respondent G)

All the centers in focus are nevertheless self-governing and give priority to an open dialogue within the center. The board or the director makes the decisions, with a lot less external interference. The centers are naturally aware that they need to carry out some rules and regulations, but otherwise, it is up to them how to proceed in every issue at hand.

> *It is the kind of a democratic organization where anybody can basically come to suggest or say anything. It consists of a few companies owned by a supportive association.*
>
> (Respondent O)

As stated, private cultural centers would like to collaborate more with the municipalities, but most centers see collaboration with municipal institutions as somewhat problematic. The obstacles for such cooperation can be too many. As one respondent concludes:

> *I would hope that this number of regulations and the way to work together with the public sector could be advanced, and then we could look for a*

> *common goal. That such fears should be reduced, and in addition to enthusiasm to work together, both parties should also strive to focus on solutions.*
> (Respondent A)

This is very much in line with the weak functional and structural organization of the municipalities, as noted in new public management. The state of Finland has many regulations that apply even to private organizations, according to the respondents. Laws, for instance, set the opening hours for restaurants, govern alcohol sales and establish specific rules for employment. These laws can hinder motivations to carry out activities in the private sector. Some respondents even state that some things do not get done due to regulation: '*I know really many things that fall because people have not had the strength to cope with that bureaucracy when they start something*' (Respondent E).

Most centers have designated individuals who are responsible for various issues and work very independently. They typically make their own decisions in their area of responsibility and attempt to streamline all the cultural offerings to have unity and not to obstruct the other activities happening in the center.

> *I'm responsible for that program, so I do it completely independently. [...] So if I decide something, a show gets booked. Then I only check the electronic calendar that there is not anything overlapping [...]. As I just said, everybody has their own areas of responsibility they are responsible for. [...] We, so to speak, play Tetris. The square meters are limited, so we just need to [...] adjust so there will be no overlapping and noise in order to not spoil each other's stuff.*
> (Respondent O)

The centers' boards make all the bigger decisions, as legislation in Finland requires. The employees nonetheless make decisions about running errands but report to the board. A dominant theme arising during the interviews is that all the centers believe in giving freedom to act and make decisions at almost every level of their organizations.

> *We believe very strongly in our director. To have free hands. And we have underlined what things we want to be aware of. As for financial... major financing, they all come to the board. (...) The board is not unaware of any major investments or staff appointments, or ... [...] we can talk very openly, and she also reports pretty well.*
> (Respondent J)

Furthermore, most respondents emphasize the courage of private actors. Their decisions are made quickly and are often bold, which is how they differ quite substantially from public institutions. The possibility to be at the surface of current trends vastly favors private actors, according to the respondents. This is a sort of discretion public centers do not have.

1.5 Conceptual framework

Some core terms should be defined before we unravel the mysteries of cultural centers in the upcoming chapters. In this subchapter, we will define the concept of an organization, an institution and an organizational field.

1.5.1 What is an organization?

Organizations are defined as social structures created by individuals with the objective to support the collaborative pursuit of stated goals (Scott, 2002): '*an organized collection of individuals working interdependently within a relatively structured, organized, open system to achieve common goals*' (Richmond & McCroskey, 2009, p. 1). Organizations vary in shape and size, but usually, every organization has a structure, participants, technologies, a set of goals and physical limits that frame and constrain its actions. It is assumed by Scott (2014) that organizations can respond to changes in their environment as they are open systems. Organizations are social arrangements but follow collective goals within their institutional frameworks (Scott, 2014). Even if organizations encounter the same or similar institutional environments, they experience and respond to these influences in different ways. In other words, organizations are influenced by their institutional environment and react to it differently. As Child (1976, p. 2) highlighted, '*no organization operates in a vacuum*'.

Scott (2002) emphasized that organizations are systems with rational, natural and open features. As rational systems, organizations are defined structures seeking to achieve goals. As natural systems, organizations are entities competing to survive within their environment. Lastly, as open systems, organizations exist to establish relationships with their environment. In other words, there is no point in studying organizations outside their environment, the very thing that explains their behavior and efficiency (Scott, 2002).

Within the creative industries, where cultural centers are positioned, the work carried out is symbolic and produces experiential goods of nonutilitarian value (Townley et al., 2009). Arts organizations work with '*expressive or aesthetic tastes rather than utilitarian needs; their meaning and significance determined by the consumer's coding and decoding of value*' (Townley et al., 2009, p. 942). Creative cultural offerings are used and consumed differently than traditional goods, so there is uncertainty about their response to a presumed market. In fact, according to Chong (2008, p. 14), an arts organization should '*be in the business of helping to shape taste, which suggests leading rather than merely reacting*'. Furthermore, arts organizations do not consider economic equity to be as important as cultural equity, whereas institutions in the business of mass production have an opposite view on the matter (Halonen, 2011). As Baumol and Bowen pointed out in 1966, the creation of artwork is not correlated with productivity gains, the costs always grow over time, and revenue increases are limited by market forces, so the arts organization are likely to fall behind (Webb, 2017). Nevertheless, arts organizations need to be cost-effective and aim to diversify their funding sources and achieve efficiency in management structures in order to ensure financial stability without being guided by money (Chong, 2008). Quality and profitability, however, not mutually exclusive.

1.5.2 What is an institution?

In management studies, institutions are commonly analyzed in the context of organization (Scott, 2014). It, therefore, is important to distinguish between institutions and organizations. There are many definitions of institutions, and there is no general agreement on how to conceptualize institutions (North, 1990). Nevertheless, institutions are durable, versatile social structures built upon symbolic elements, material resources and social activities. They display unique characteristics, such as resistance to change and reproduction, and are nongeneration-specific (Scott, 2014). Actors usually accept and recreate beliefs and practices that have become institutionalized (Meyer & Rowan, 1977; Zucker, 1977). Streeck and Thelen (2005) described institutions on a general level as '*building-blocks of social order: they represent socially sanctioned, that is, collectively enforced expectations with respect to the behavior of specific categories of actors or to the performance of certain activities*' (p. 9). The institutions are furthermore distinguished between appropriate and inappropriate and between possible and impossible actions (Streeck & Thelen, 2005).

Institutions generate behavioral predictability and reliability (Streeck & Thelen, 2005). Regardless of what the actors independently want to accomplish, they are expected to adjust themselves to the institution. The actors themselves, as well as society, hold these expectations. Douglass North (1990) proclaimed that institutions '*are the rules of the game in a society, or more formally, are the humanly devised constraints that shape human interaction*' (pp. 4–5). Institutions '*reduce uncertainty by providing a structure to everyday life*' (p. 3). They incorporate both formal rules (laws and constitutions) and informal constraints (conventions and norms). According to Greenwood et al. (2008), an institution is a:

> *more or less taken for granted repetitive social behavior that is underpinned by normative systems and cognitive understandings that give meaning to social exchange and thus enable self-producing social order.*
>
> (Greenwood et al., 2008, pp. 4–5)

Institutions reinforce each other and:

> *on the one hand, organizations inculcate, and reflectively manifest norms, values, and meanings drawn from the institutions that surround and support them; and, on the other hand, institutions are reproduced through the actions of organizations*
>
> (Suddaby & Greenwood, 2009, p. 177).

Institutions are considered to be an answer to a problem (Berger & Luckmann, 2008). However, they are challenged if the answer changes. Equally, institutions can succeed if they are seen as answering a problem, even if it is no longer the original one.

There are at least three academic schools that define institutions in different ways (Scott, 2014). These are: (1) historical, (2) economic and (3) sociological institutionalism. Albeit they share some similarities, they have evolved in quite differently. Historical institutionalists: (1) usually examine the state, which is not considered to be a neutral player, but rather a network of institutions able to interfere in group conflicts (Hall & Taylor, 1996). This school sees '*institutions as providers of moral or cognitive templates for interpretation and action*' (Hall & Taylor, 1996, pp. 6–8). Institutional economics: (2) in turn aim attention on understanding the function of the evolutionary process and the role of institutions in forging economic behavior. They give priority to an extensive study of institutions and they see markets as a result of the complicated interaction of these distinct institutions (Hall & Taylor, 1996). There are quite a few versions of sociological institutionalism (3) (Friedland & Alford, 1991). Still, all of them are interested in institutions as social systems that adjust social interactions. According to sociological intuitionalists, institutions are composed of 'patterns of activity', where actors conduct their material lives (e.g. rules, routines, habits, roles, etc.), and furthermore 'symbolic' or meaning systems (e.g. beliefs, values, principles, paradigms, ideologies, theories, etc.) through which they make sense of the world. Sociological institutionalism usually sees institutions as social constructions that shape the understandings and preferences of actors (Scott, 2014).

This book focuses on, among other things, the interplay between homogeneity and heterogeneity, and institutions have an active role in disseminating institutional norms within an organizational field. This study does not aim to define whether a private cultural center is considered an institution but does view public cultural centers as such. It does apply a sociological institutionalist approach to investigating responses to institutional pressures on organizations, as the empirical study foremost investigates perceptions, not behavior.

1.5.3 Organizational fields

Researchers studying organizations occasionally use the term *field* to describe a set of organizations linked together, either as collaborators or competitors, within a social space with the purpose of accomplishing a distinct action (DiMaggio & Powell, 1983; Meyer & Rowan, 1977). The literature includes various similar concepts, such as interorganizational field (Aiken & Alford, 1970), institutional field (Meyer & Rowan, 1977) and organizational field (DiMaggio & Powell, 1983; Scott & Meyer, 1983). Bourdieu (1984) presented a related but distinct concept of field as the setting where agents and their social positions are situated. Whereas Bourdieu (1984) concentrates on power and class relations, this study adopts the concept of a field defined by organizational researchers. Mazza and Strandgaard Pedersen (2004, p. 876) summarized the definition of the *field* in the literature as '*a social space [that] identifies a number of nodes, points of observation or positions and their mutual relations in the analysis*'.

The definition of an organizational field is still somewhat ambiguous in the literature (Machado-da-Silva, et al., 2006). Organizational fields are commonly viewed as

> *sets of organizations that, in the aggregate, constitute a recognized area of institutional life; key suppliers, resource and product consumers, regulatory agencies, and other organizations that produce similar services or products.*
> (DiMaggio & Powell, 1983, p. 48)

Scott and Meyer's (1991) concept of a societal sector is similar. It includes both organizations that offer comparable services or products in a given domain and other organizations that '*critically influence their performance*' (Scott, 2014, p. 83), where the concept of a field is emphasized as practical interrelation over geographical proximity. Scott (1994, 2002) identified funding sources and regulators as patterns in a functional field. Hoffman (1999) suggested that: '*the field should be thought of as the center of common channels of dialogue and discussion [...] which bring together various field constituents with disparate purposes*' (p. 352).

A field can exist at various levels (Emirbayer & Johnson, 2008). It can be a distinct organization consisting of a group of departments or individuals or a network of organizations functioning in the same environment, market or subsector. In addition, organizations can be seen as functioning as both as-fields and in-fields (Emirbayer & Johnson, 2008).

According to DiMaggio and Powell (1983), the actors in an organizational field interact through diverse exchanges and through competition. The authors also described the environment as a socially constructed field (DiMaggio & Powell, 1983). In this book, an organizational field consists of the arenas (e.g. cultural centers) for producing cultural offerings for the local community.

Institutional analyses commonly pay attention to field-level processes as these are happening at the organizational field level (Suddaby, 2010). As Scott (1994) put it:

> *a community of organizations that partakes of a common meaning system and whose participants interact more frequently and fatefully with one another than with actors outside the field.*
> (pp. 207–208)

The following three important components reinforce organizational fields: (1) actors, both individuals and organizations; (2) logics; and (3) governance arrangements (Scott et al., 2000). Hoffmann and Ventresca (2002) broadened this perception of an organizational field by recognizing two supplementary field elements: (4) intermediary institutions; and (5) local sense-making activities. These components can both inhibit and enable action within fields and thus mold the behavior and characteristics of organizational participants (DiMaggio & Powell, 1983; Meyer & Rowan, 1977; Scott & Meyer, 1991). Hoffman and Ventresca (2002) described the concept of a field as an empirical trace, which can be beneficial as it defines the borders for the shaping processes (e.g. competition, influence, coordination and innovation) (DiMaggio & Powell, 1991).

The field concept is relevant to the present research as it provides a method to study organizations both in combination and in interplay with their institutional contexts. Based on the foregoing, this study interprets the concept of an organizational field as a platform for interactions among all the cultural centers and their stakeholders. The institutional pressures exerted on private cultural centers are defined by this organizational field.

1.6 Overview of the study

The key objective of this book was to empirically assess the operational preconditions of cultural centers. In order to do this, the conclusions of this book are deduced from both interviews with and a questionnaire sent to managers in cultural centers in Finland. There will naturally also be referring's to results from other studies to get a more substantial width to the positioning of this book. This subchapter will illustrate how the data were collected.

1.6.1 Qualitative case studies

The results presented in this book draws on 20 semi-structured interviews with 5 interviewees each at 4 cultural centers in Finland. The four cases chosen for this case study were Grand in Porvoo, Korjaamo in Helsinki, Telakka in Tampere and Ritz in Vaasa.

The respondents were kept anonymous and given a label from Respondent A to T. The respondents from Kulttuuritehdas Korjaamo were labeled Respondents A–E, Kulturföreningen Grand Respondents F–J, Kulttuuritalo Telakka Respondents K–O and Skafferiet Ritz Respondents P–T.

As the main focus is on private cultural centers, I wanted to choose cases that were completely private. In some cases, this was not that clear, such as a joint-stock company owned by the municipality or a joint venture of some sort. Consequently, these four cases were chosen, as they were also geographically widespread throughout the country.

Kulturföreningen Grand

Background: The joint-stock company Aktiebolaget Svenska Gården i Borgå was established in 1919 (Björklund, 2010). The aim was to build a Swedish building in Porvoo as there was a need for a place for Swedish NGOs to meet and enjoy culture. These local actors started raising money

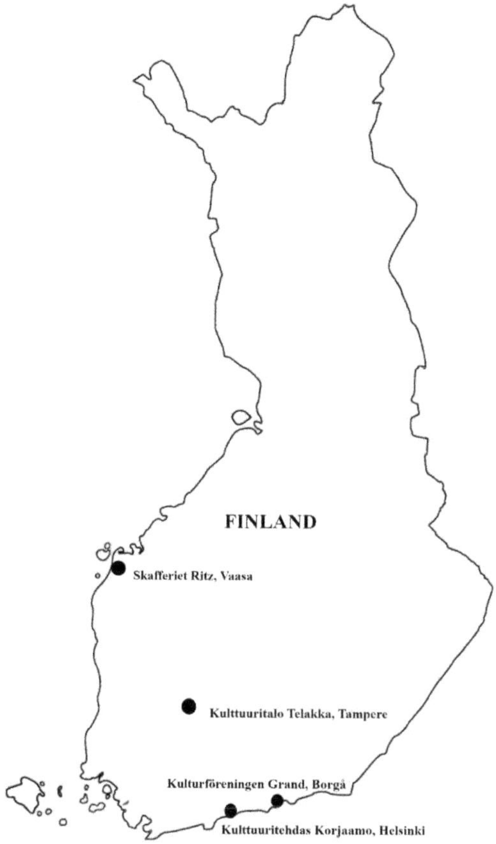

Figure 1.1 Geographical locations of the cases in Finland.

for the company build the house, and in 1934, they had the money they needed. The house was ready by the end of 1935. It was built for cultural performances and is situated by the town square in the center of Porvoo. In 2009, a large extension was built for the restaurant in the cultural center. Over the years, the house has served versatile uses, with various bars, restaurants, movie theatre and such in the focus (Björklund, 2010).

Organizational structure: In 1998, the NGO Kulturföreningen Grand was founded, and it started its activities as a cultural center in 1999 (Björklund, 2010).

Mission: The purpose in clause the charter states that the aim of Grand is to develop and support the cultural activities of Fastighet Ab Svenska Gården i Borgå (the joint-stock company that owns the house) and otherwise develop different sorts of NGOs in the eastern part of Uusimaa (Björklund, 2010). To fulfil these purposes, the NGO Kulturföreningen

Grand rents appropriate spaces from Fastighet Ab Svenska Gården i Borgå to rent, in turn, to NGOs, companies, private citizens and such. The spaces are rented for cultural activities.

Activities: Kulturföreningen Grand maintains the Luckan information point, serving the population of Porvoo and representing the Finland–Swedish culture and society in the region by offering citizen services and activities in Swedish in cooperation with other language and cultural groups (Kulturföreningen Grand r.f., 2017a). In 2016, Kulturföreningen Grand rented its main stage 150 times, as well as the other spaces 781 times (Kulturföreningen Grand r.f., 2017b). It does not have much cultural productions of its own; the cultural fferings at Grand are mostly produced by external actors. The number of external actors renting its spaces has grown in recent years. Kulturföreningen Grand still offers a wide variety of other services, such as ticket sales to performances in Grand and other places. The cultural offerings that take place in Grand are arts exhibitions, movies, a variety of trade shows, and music, theatre and dance performances.

Staff: Kulturföreningen Grand has six employees and an office on the first floor of the building (Kulturföreningen Grand r.f., 2017a). It also employs external technicians and janitors.

Economy: The total revenue of the NGO is about 290,000 euros, of which nearly 58% is derived from ticket sales, rents and other sales (Kulturföreningen Grand r.f., 2017b). The rest are subsidies, mostly from private foundations but also a smaller amount from the state.

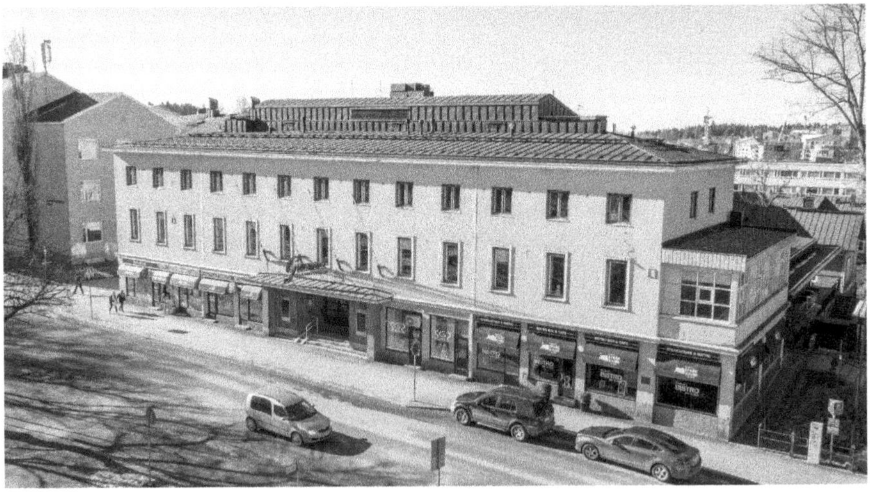

Picture 1.3 The front of cultural center Grand in Porvoo, Finland. A photograph by Niko Laurila.

Kulttuuritehdas Korjaamo

Background: Kulttuuritehdas Korjaamo (Culture Factory Korjaamo) is one of the largest private cultural centers in the Nordic countries (Kulttuuritehdas Korjaamo, 2017). Korjaamo was established in an old tram depot in the Töölö district in Helsinki in 2004. It has three concert or theatre venues and six smaller creative spaces for meetings and seminars.

Organizational structure: The joint-stock company Kulttuuritehdas Korjaamo (Finder.fi, 2018) is part of Korjaamo Group Co., Ltd. (Kulttuuritehdas Korjaamo, 2017), which manages the Jääpuisto (Ice Park) skating ring by the Helsinki railway station and the Helsinki Allas sea pool in the Katajanokka district.

Mission: Korjaamo produces urban culture experiences and events, including music, theatre, visual arts and discussions (Kulttuuritehdas Korjaamo, 2017). It aims to be the broadest and most significant cultural center in the northern region and emphasizes newness, open-mindedness and interactions with its audiences and the global world.

Activities: Korjaamo produces around 400 arts events in music, theatre and the fine arts every year. It furthermore hosts about 300 private events (Kulttuuritehdas Korjaamo, 2017). Korjaamo had around 150,000 visitors in 2016. It annually hosts the Stage Theatre Festival, which showcases a selection of Finnish and international performances. The movie theatre Korjaamo Kino has a varied program, including premieres, opera, ballet, music and documentaries, as well as a movie restaurant. It also has a large lounge and cafe area. Korjaamo is a member of Trans Europe Halles, an European network of cultural centers promoting independent culture and encouraging new initiatives (Kulttuuritehdas Korjaamo, 2017).

Staff: Korjaamo employs approximately 20 professionals in production, sales, marketing, catering and customer service (Kulttuuritehdas Korjaamo, 2017). It also hires a substantial number of freelance professionals as restaurant workers and technicians.

Economy: The turnover of Korjaamo is approximately 4,5 million euros (Kulttuuritehdas Korjaamo, 2017). Ticket sales and rent revenues account for 15% of turnover, subsidies about 17% and cooperation about 4%. Both the turnover and the number of visitors have grown in recent years. The rest of the turnover comes from restaurant sales.

Kulttuuritalo Telakka

Background: Three professional theatres in Tampere, Motelli Skronkle, Moraalia Teatteri and Ryhmä Fagerholm, were looking for a venue and combined to unify their theatres into one, called Teatteri Telakka (Teatteri Telakka, 2017). They found their venue 1996 in a 100-year-old grain magazine. In the rebuilt house, the theatre is on in the third floor, and a restaurant is on the first and second floors.

Mission: Initially founded as a theatre, Telakka today aims to combine different forms of culture, provide a place in the city where many things are possible and serve as a meeting place for a wide variety of cultural forms and people (Anonymous, 2016a).

Organizational structure: Telakka is a union of two NGOs and two joint-stock companies (Anonymous, 2016a). One NGO manages the theatre, and the other one is a support organization for the theatre. The latter owns the house, which makes this cultural center the only one of these cases that does not rent its venues from an external actor. The NGO that owns the house strives to financially support the theatre from the rent revenues. The same NGO also owns all the stocks in both companies. One company maintains the building, while the othermanages the restaurant. The latter also produces all the musical performances taking place in the house, as well as the art gallery.

Activities: Telakka has its own theatre (Teatteri Telakka ry, 2018), art gallery, music stage and cultural event activities (Anonymous, 2016a). Although the house was initially reconstructed as a theatre venue, it has been transformed over the years into a cultural center with versatile cultural offerings.

Staff: Teatteri Telakka has six employees (Teatteri Telakka ry, 2018), while the restaurant employs a producer, a person responsible for the music offerings, four other employees and a number of cooks (Teatteri Telakka ry, 2018).

Economy: The theatre receives up to 90% of its turnover from subsidies from private foundations, the state and the municipality, while the rest comes from ticket sales (Anonymous, 2016a). The turnover is around 150,000 euro. The company with the restaurant Carneval Oy (Ravintola Telakka), has a considerably bigger turnover, but it does not get any subsidies, unlike the associations in this union (Finder.fi, 2019). The annual turnover 2016 was 1,535,000 euro.

Skafferiet Ritz

Background: Ritz was originally built as a movie theatre in Vaasa in the early 1950s (Anonymous, 2016b). It also functioned as a theatre and was empty for a while. Skafferiet Ritz has a stage and venue for artists, musicians, theatres and filmmakers to display their art.

Organizational structure: The NGO Skafferiet was established in 2008 and is the caretaker of Ritz (Skafferiet Ritz, 2017). Skafferiet rents the venue from the owner, a private person.

Mission: Skafferiet r.f. aims to offer a stage and venue for artists, musicians, filmmakers and such to display their art (Skafferiet Ritz, 2017). The goal

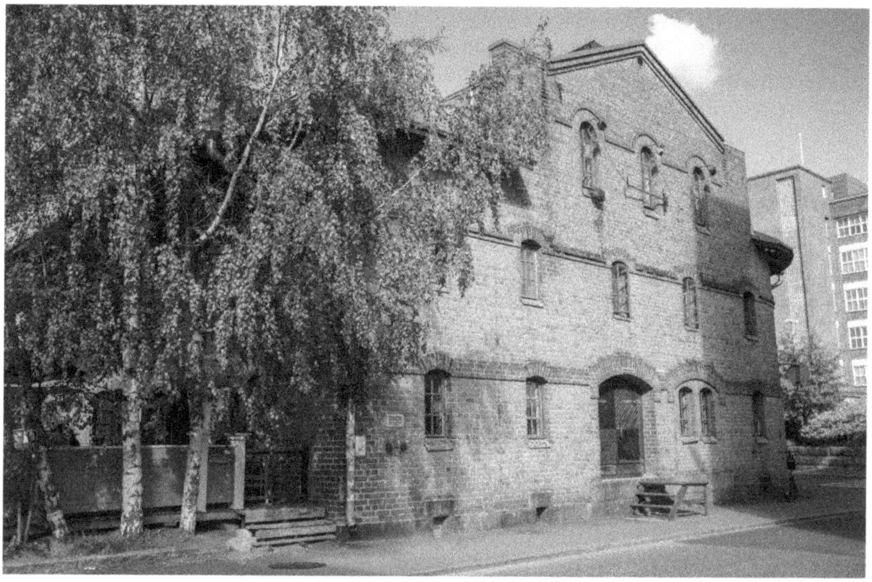

Picture 1.4 The front of cultural center Telakka in Tampere, Finland. A photograph by Petteri Aartolahti.

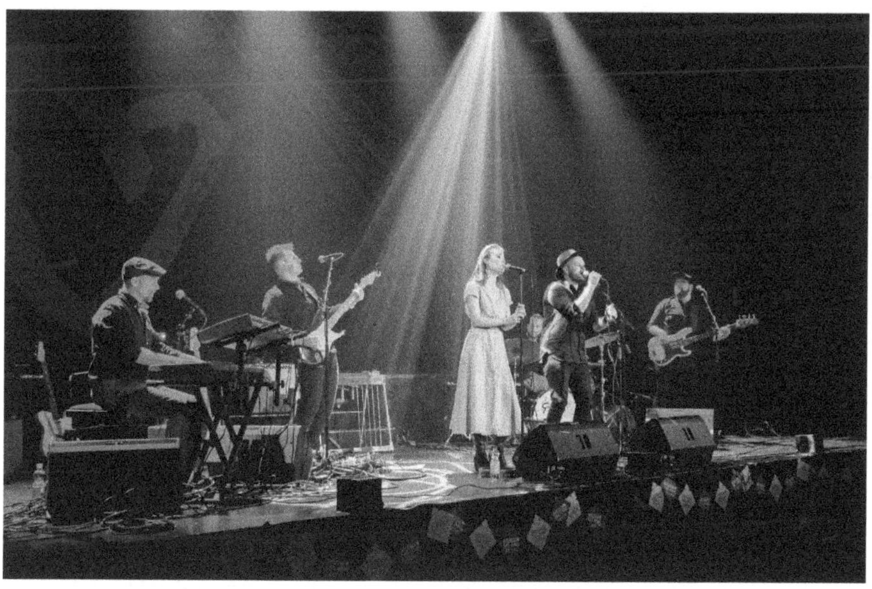

Picture 1.5 The main stage with band at cultural center Ritz in Vaasa, Finland. A photograph by Frida Lönnroos.

is to be a uniting place for all sorts of culture-related ventures and to be a stage for both known and unknown arts.

Activities: Ritz has an average of 20 events in its venue monthly, and a total of 180 per year (Skafferiet rf, 2017). It had an audience of 16,753 in 2016. In 2012, the number was 4811. It has an active board of 18 people who met 19 times in 2016. This board attended every event of Ritz organized. Ritz relies mostly on volunteer workers and had 33 people including the board helping out at events. These active members get discounts on events at Ritz and invitations to member events and parties.

Staff: Ritz has one employee, a director of activities (Skafferiet rf, 2017). This director is not responsible for practicalities during the events, but instead has charge of marketing, booking artists, renting the venues and similar tasks.

Economy: The cultural center has an annual turnover of approximately 220,000 euro, of which 22,7% is subsidies from private foundations and an equal amount from venue rentals. The rest comes from ticket and restaurant sales (Skafferiet rf, 2017).

1.6.2 Quantitative questionnaire

In the second phase of quantitative research, a questionnaire survey was employed to collect data from all the Finnish cultural centers listed by Statistics Finland (2017). This study achieved a 56% response rate as 106 of 189 centers responded to the questionnaire. The questionnaire was sent to both public and private cultural centers.

The sample population was not limited to employees, trustees and such as cultural centers vary greatly. Some have staff, and some do not; some have a director, and some are directly beneath the cultural director of the municipality. This increased the likelihood of responses but may have diminished the participants' knowledge of the details of their institutions' processes. The analysis was done on SPSS.

The scales used and adapted in this research were in two response formats: Likert-scale questions and open-ended questions. For the questionnaire to be clear to all the respondents, the majority of measures in the study used a 5-point Likert scale ranging from 1 (strongly disagree) to 5 (strongly agree). The open-ended questions were later dummy coded.

The quantitative analyses will be presented more thoroughly in those chapters where such analyses are conducted.

1.6.3 Mixed qualitative and quantitative analysis

The intention was to triangulate the data collection by using multiple informants and cross-checking information against the questionnaire data to avoid retrospective bias in the interviews. The qualitative research was performed first to identify different categories of for instance institutional pressures, resource dependencies and strategies for private cultural centers. This analysis enabled testing the ideas with a larger group of cultural centers. This qualitative research enabled generating items for the quantitative research.

The qualitative findings presented an explanation or interpretation of the for instance resource dependence and perceived institutional pressure among private cultural centers. They furthermore contributed statistical validation of both important factors and the variables affecting the perceived institutional pressure. When incorporating and discussing both the qualitative and the quantitative findings in more detail, this study aimed at answering the research questions through an integrated viewpoint. The results from this parallel analysis were compared to allow an explorative theory to emerge. This step involved examining the ways the two groups of research findings were related to each other to get a better understanding of the research problem.

1.7 Summary and conclusions

A cultural center is an organization, generally strongly associated to a building (or other venue), that promotes arts and culture. Cultural centers are usually maintained by private community arts organizations, the municipality or a mixture of both. As we have seen, there are a surprising number of such centers in Europe and all across the world. A cultural center has to be in versatile use, such as concerts, theatre and visual arts. Most of the centers are located in urban areas.

If we go back to the question in the introduction, what is the idea behind connecting citizens with their culture as well as allowing them to learn from each other? Why build stages for multiple use, with restaurants and libraries and other services, all for a usually quite small entrance fee?

Generally, the centers describe their primary mission as to producing (by prioritizing and coordinating) exclusive cultural offerings to the community. They are furthermore often seen as a tool for the municipality's cultural planning and development efforts. Politically, the debate of arts facilities in residential areas was the foundation for starting to build such venues in Finland. The main objective of public cultural centers was the cultural democracy and the highlighting of citizens' activities, needs and understandings of culture. It seems as if the cultural centers are a manifestation of the municipalities quest for fulfilling their cultural program, somewhat of an attempt to kill two birds with one stone. A visible multipurpose center to cater everyone's needs.

The concept of cultural centers was introduced in Finland as a municipal initiative in 1980s, apart from one exception; Kulttuuritalo in Helsinki. In Europe, such centers (called Art labs) were a private initiative in 1960s, followed by a public incentive in 1990s. There are nearly 200 cultural centers in Finland and at least 3000 centers in Europe. According to surveys made in different Nordic countries, there seems to be a general positive attitude towards cultural centers.

There are several studies implicating different turnovers in cultural centers, due to the difficulties in attaining accurate information; as to public centers, the costs may for instance be divided between different budgets in a municipality (culture, buildings, services etc). A mean turnover in Europe seems to be 1,25 M €, fluctuating from 200,000 € to 2 M €. The of subsidies from municipalities vary a lot, covering everything between 0 and 100% of the turnover. The average seems to be 20%. The trend seems to be a decreasing municipal support, with some indications of these centers not being a public service in the future.

Public organizations do not have to tolerate the pressure of competition, at least in the short-term. They do not have to struggle for their existence in the same manner as private organizations, which negatively affects innovation, efficiency and productivity. Furthermore, public organizations, including public cultural centers, have to endure a public scrutiny and demands for insights, transparency and control of information and resources. The respondents emphasized the ability to make quick decision, which may be of paramount importance in a changing society with changing needs. This seems to be a lot more common amongst private cultural centers, than among the public peers.

The results presented in this book draws on 20 semi-structured interviews with 5 interviewees each at 4 cultural centers in Finland, as well as a questionnaire survey sent to all the Finnish cultural centers. It furthermore compares the results with the results from other international studies.

References

Aiken, M., & Alford, R. (1970). Community structure and innovation: The case of public housing. American Political Science Review, 64(3), pp. 843–864.

Ambrecht, J. (2012). *The Value of Cultural Institutions.* Göteborg: Bokförlaget Bas.

Anonymous. (2.6.2016a). Interview with person from Telakka (T. Järvinen, Editor).

Anonymous. (28.5.2016b). Interview with person from Ritz (T. Järvinen, Editor).

Anonymous (2016c). *Interview with a person from Korjaamo* (T. Järvinen, Editor).

Baumol, W. & Bowen, W. (1966). *Performing Arts: The Economic Dilemma*, New York: The Twentieth Century Fund.

Berger, P., & Luckmann, T. (2008). The social construction of reality. Em R. Greenwood, C. Oliver, K. Sahlin, & R. Suddaby (Eds.), *The Sage Handbook of Organizational Institutionalism.* Los Angeles: Sage.

Björklund, M. (2010). *Svenska Gården i Borgå. 75 år i kulturens tjänst* (1 ed.). Helsingfors: Oy Nordprint Ab.

Bogen, P. (2018). *Stronger Arts and Cultural Organisations for a Greater Social Impact. Business Models profiling of Cultural Centres & Performing Arts Organisations.* Sweden: Trans Europe Halles, Creative Lenses.

Bourdieu, P. (1984). *Distinction: A Social Critique of the Judgement of Taste.* Cambridge, MA: Harvard University Press.

Boyne, G. (1 de 2002). Public and private management: What's the difference? Journal of Management Studies, 39, pp. 97–122.

Bozeman, B. (1987). *All Organizations Are Public: Bridging Public and Private Organizational Theories.* San Francisco: Jossey-Bass. MA: Harvard University Press.

Child, J. (1976). *Organization Design and Performance: Contingency Theory and Beyond.* Birmingham: Aston University.

Chong, D. (2008). *Arts Management* (4 ed.). New York: Routledge.

DiMaggio, P., & Powell, W. (1983). The iron cage revisited: Institutional isomorphism and collective rationality in organizational fields. American Sociological Review, 48, pp. 147–160.

DiMaggio, P., & Powell, W. (1991). *Introduction*. Em W. Powell, & P. DiMaggio (Eds.), *The New Institutionalism in Organizational Analysis* (pp. 267–292). Chicago: University of Chicago Press.

Eikenberry, A., & Klover, J. (2004). *The marketization of the nonprofit sector: Civil society at risk?* Public Administration Review, 64(2), pp. 132–140.

Emirbayer, M., & Johnson, V. (2008). *Bourdieu and organizational analysis*. Theory and Society, 37(1), pp. 1–44.

Eriksson, B., Møhring Reestorff, C., & Stage, C. (2018). Forms and potential effects of citizen participation in European cultural centres. Journal of Audience & Receptions Studies, 15(2).

Falleti, T.G. (2005). A sequential theory of decentralization: Latin American cases in comparative perspective. American Political Science Review, 99(3), 327–346.

Finder.fi. (2018). *Kulttuuritehdas Korjaamo*. Acesso em 21 de 4 de 2018, disponível em www.finder.fi/Kulttuuripalveluja/Kulttuuritehdas+Korjaamo/Helsinki/yhteystiedot/1359133

Finder.fi. (2019). *Ravintola Telakka*. Accessed 12.2.2019. Avalaible: www.finder.fi/Ravintola/Ravintola+Telakka/Tampere/yhteystiedot/192550

Finnish Cultural Foundation. (2013). *Suomalaisten näkemykset kulttuurista 2013*. Accessed; 2.2.2014, Available at: www.skr.fi/sites/default/files/Suomalaisten_n%C3%A4kemykset _kulttuurista_2013.pdf

Fitzgerald, S. (2010). *New Times, New Models. Investigating the Internal Governance Models and External Relations of Independent Cultural Centres in Times of Change*. Maribor: Pekarna magdalenske mreže.

Fitzgerald, S. (2014). Independent culture? Revista Antic Teater, 8, pp. 6–7.

Friedland, R., & Alford, R. (1991). *Bringing society back in: symbols, practices, and institutional contradictions*. Em W. Powell, & P. DiMaggio (Eds.), *The New Institutionalism in Organizational Analysis* (pp. 232–263). London: University of Chicago Press.

Froelich, K. (9 de 1999). Diversification of revenue strategies: Evolving resource dependence in nonprofit organizations. Nonprofit and Voluntary sector Quarterly, 28(3), pp. 246–268.

Greenwood, R., Oliver, C., Sahlin, K., & Suddaby, R. (2008). *Introduction*. Em R. Greenwood, C. Oliver, K. Sahlin, & R. Suddaby (Eds.), *The Sage Handbook of Organizational Institutionalism* (pp. 1–46). London: Sage.

Halonen, K. (2011). *Kulttuurituottajat taiteen ja talouden risteyskohdassa*. Jyväskylä: Jyväskylän Yliopisto.

Hall, P. & Taylor, R. (1996). *Political science and the three new institutionalisms*. Political Studies, 44(5): pp. 952–973.

Helsingin kaupunki (2017). *Kulttuurikeskuksen tilinpäätös vuodelta 2016*. Accessed: 14.5.2018, Available at: https://dev.hel.fi/paatokset/asia/hel-2017-001572/kklk-2017- 2/

Henderson, E., Lambert, V., (2018). Negotiating for survival: Balancing mission and money, The British Accounting Review, doi: 10.1016/j.bar.2017.12.001.

Hillman, A. (2005). Politicians on the board: do connections affect the bottom line?. Journal of Management, 31, pp. 464–481.

Hillman, A., Cannella, A., & Paetzold, R. (2000). The resource dependence role of corporate directors: Strategic adaptation of board composition in response to environmental change. Journal of Management Studies, 37(2), pp. 235–255.

Hillman, A., Withers, M., & Collins, B. (2009). Resource dependence theory: A review. Journal of Management, 35, pp. 1404–1427.
Hoffman, A. (1999). Institutional evolution and change: Environmentalism and the U.S. chemical industry. Academy of Management Review, 42(4), pp. 351–371.
Hoffman, A., & Ventresca, M. (2002). *Introduction.* Em A. Hoffman, & M. Ventresca (Eds.), *Organizations, Policy, and the Natural Environment: Institutional and Strategic Perspectives.* Stanford, CA: Stanford University Press.
Jennergren, P. (1981). *Decentralization in organizations.* Em P. Nystrom, & W. Starbuck (Eds.), *The Handbook of Organizational Design.* New York: Oxford University Press.
Kangas, A. (1988). *Kunta ja kulttuuri Kulttuuritoimialanin valossa* (1 ed.). Helsinki: Valtion painatuskeskus.
Kangas, A., & Pirnes, E. (2015). *Kulttuuripolitiikan päätöksenteko, lainsäädäntö, hallinto ja rahoitus.* Em I. Heiskanen, A. Kangas, & R. Mitchell (Eds.), *Taiteen ja kulttuurin kentät. Perusrakenteet, hallinta ja lainsäädäntö* (pp. 23–108). Helsinki: Tietosanoma Oy.
Kangas, A., & Ruokolainen, V. (2012). *Toimintamalli muutoksessa. Tutkimus kuntien kulttuuripalveluista.* Accessed: 3.1.2014, Available at: www.cupore.fi/documents/KuntienKulttuuripalvelut.pdf
Konstsamfundet. (2016). *Beviljade understöd våren 2016.* Accessed: 10.12.2016, Available at: www.konstsamfundet.fi/images/stories/filer/V%C3%A5rens_beviljade_2016.pdf
Kulttuuritehdas Korjaamo. (2017). *Kaupunkikulttuuria, taidetta ja ainutlaatuisia tiloja.* Accessed at: 14.6.2017, Available at: www.korjaamo.fi/fi/tietoa- korjaamosta/esittely
Kulturföreningen Grand r.f. (2017a). *Välkommen till Kulturhuset Grand!* Accessed: 14.6.2017, Available at: http://grand.fi/sv
Kulturföreningen Grand r.f. (2017b). *Grands Annual Report 2016.* Porvoo: Kulturföreningen Grand r.f.
Lambert, P., & Williams, R. (2017). *Ownership and Governance of Urban PACs.* Em P. Lambert, & R. Williams (Eds.), *Performing Arts Center Management* (pp. 120–141). New York: Routledge.
Loeffler, E. (2003). *Die Oekonomisierung des Staates – Versuch einer Beriffserklaerung.* In Harms, J. & Reichard, J. (Eds.), *Die Oekonomisierung des Oeffentlichen Sektors: Instrumente und Trends* (pp. 19–27). Baden Baden, Germany: Nomos Verlagsgesellschaft.
Machado-da-Silva, C., Guarido Filho, E., & Rossoni, L. (2006). Organizational fields and the structuration perspective: analytical possibilities. Revista de Administração Contemporânea, 10, pp. 159–196.
Manninen, M. (2005). *Säätiöt Suomessa.* Accessed 2.5.2015, Available at: www.cupore.fi/documents/saatiot_suomessa.pdf.
Mazza, C., & Strandgaard Pedersen, J. (2004). From press to e-media? The transformation of an organizational field. Organisational Studies, 25(6), pp. 875–896.
Merriam-Webster Dictionary. (2020). *Definition of decentralization.* Archived 29.6.2020-06 at the Wayback Machine. Accessed 3.6.2020, Available at: www.merriam-webster.com/dictionary/decentralization
Metcalfe, L. (1993). Public management: From imitation to innovation. Australian Journal of Public Administration, 52, pp. 292–304.
Meyer, J., & Rowan, B. (1977). Institutionalized organizations: Formal structure as myth and ceremony. The American Journal of Sociology, 83(2), pp. 340–363.
Mulcahey, K. (2000). The government and cultural patronage. Em J. Cherbo, & M. Wyszomirski (Eds.), *The Public Life of the Arts in America.* Newark, NJ: Rutgers University Press.

North, D. (1990). *Institutions, institutional change and economic performance.* Cambridge: Cambridge University Press.

Pfeffer, J., & Salancik, G. (2003). *The External Control of Organizations: A Resource Dependence Perspective.* Stanford, CA: Stanford University Press.

Prahalad, C.K., & Hamel, G. (1990). The core competence of the corporation. Harvard Business Review, 68(3): pp. 79–91.

Rainey, H. (2003). *Understanding and Managing Public Organizations* (3 ed.). San Francisco: Jossey-Bass.

Renko, V., & Ruusuvirta, M. (2018). *Kuntien kulttuuritoiminta lukujen valossa IV: Kulttuuritoiminnan kustannukset 24 kaupungissa vuonna 2016.* Helsinki: Suomen kuntaliitto ja kirjoittajata.

Richmond, V., & McCroskey, J. (2009). *Organizational Communication for Survival: Making Work, Work* (4 ed.). Boston: Allyn & Bacon.

Rushton, M., & Brooks, A. (2007). *Government funding of nonprofit organizations.* Em D. Young (Ed.), *Financing Nonprofits: Putting Theory into Practice.* Lanham, MD: Rowman and Littlefield Publishers.

Ruusuvirta, M., & Saukkonen, P. (2014). *Kuntien kulttuuritoiminta lukujen valossa.* Accessed: 2.1.2014, Available at: www.kunnat.net/fi/Kuntaliitto/media/tiedotteet/2012/01/

Ruuuvirta, M. & Saukkonen, P. (2015). *Taiteen ja kulttuurin kolmas sektori.* In: Heikkinen, I., Kangas, A. & Mitchell, R. (Eds.). *Taiteen ja kulttuurin kentät. Perusrakenteet, hallinta ja lainsäädäntö.* pp. 354–374. Helsinki: Tietosanoma Oy.

Ruusuvirta, M., Saukkonen, P., Ruokolainen, V., & Karttunen, S. (2012). *Kuntien kulttuuritoiminta lukujen valossa. Suomen kuntaliitto.* Accessed: 2.1.2014, Available at: www.kunnat.net/fi/Kuntaliitto/media/tiedotteet/2012/01/ kulttuurilukujenvalossa/ Kuntien%20kulttuuritoiminta%20lukuina.pdf

Schiuma, G., Boge, P. & Lerro, A. (2015). *Creative Business Models: Insights into Business Models of Cultural Centers in Trans Europe Halles.* Lund, Sweden: Framtidens Lund.

Schiuma, G., Bogen, P., & Lerro, A. (2016). *Creative Business Models: Insights into the Business Models of Cultural Centers in Trans Europe Halles.* Lund, Sweden: Trans Europe Halles.

Scott, W. (1994). *Conceptualizing organizational fields: linking organizations and societal systems.* Em H. Derlien, U. Gerhardt, & F. Scharpf (Eds.), *Systemrationalitat und partialinteresse.* Baden Baden: Nomos Verlagsgesellschaft.

Scott, W. (2002). *Organizations: Rational, Natural, and Open Systems* (5 ed.). Upper Saddle River, NJ: Prentice Hall.

Scott, W. (2014). *Institutions and Organizations* (4 ed.). Thousand Oaks, CA: Sage.

Scott, W. R. & Meyer, J. W. (1983). *Organizational Environments: Ritual and Rationality.* Beverly Hills, CA: Sage.

Scott, W., & Meyer, J. (1991). *The organization of societal sectors: Propositions and early evidence.* Em W. Powell, & P. DiMaggio (Eds.), *The New Institutionalism in Organizational Analysis* (pp. 108–140). Chicago: University of Chicago Press.

Scott, W., Ruef, M., Mendel, P., & Caronna, C. (2000). *Institutional change and health care organizations: From professional dominance to managed care.* (C. Mazza, & J. Strandgaard Pedersen, Eds.) *Organization Studies, 25*(6), pp. 875–895.

Sherer, P., & Lee, K. (2002). Institutional change in large law firms: A resource dependency and institutional perspective. Academy of Management Journal, 45(1), pp. 102–110.

Silvanto, T., Linko, M., & Cantell, T. (2008). *From enlightenment to experience: cultural centers in Helsinki neighbourhoods.* International Journal of Cultural Policy, pp. 165–178.

Skafferiet rf. (2017). *Verksamhetsberättelse och bokslut 2016 (annual report).* Vasa: Skafferiet rf.

Skafferiet Ritz. (2017). *About us.* Accessed 14.6.2017, Available at www.kulturskafferiet.com/about/

Statistics Finland. (2017). *Kulttuuritapahtumat ja -keskukset: Suomen kulttuuritaloja ja kulttuurikeskuksia maakunnittain 2017. Tietokantataulukot.* Accessed: 15.3.2017, Available at: www.stat.fi/til/klt/tau.html

Strandgaard Pedersen, J. & Dobbin, F. (2006). In Search of Identity and Legitimation. American Behavioral Scientist, 49, pp. 897–907.

Statistics Finland. (12 de 2017b). *10.5 Kuntien kulttuuritoimen nettokustannukset tehtävittäin 2006–2016.* Accessed: 18.5.2018, Available at: http://pxhopea2.stat.fi/sahkoiset_julkaisut/kulttuuritilasto/html/suom0009.htm

Stenlund, K. (2010). *Effekter av byggandet av Kulturens hus i Luleå.* Luleå: Universitetstryckeriet.

Stigler, G. (2003). *The theory of economic regulation.* Em J. Pfeffer, & G. Salancik (Eds.), *The External Control of Organizations: A Resource Dependence Perspective.* Stanford, CA: Stanford University Press.

Storstad, O. (2010). *Kommunal kultursektor i endring.* Oslo: Norsk kulturrådet.

Streeck, W., & Thelen, K. (2005). *Beyond Continuity: Institutional Change in Advanced Political Economies.* Oxford: Oxford University Press.

Suddaby, R. (2010). Challenges for institutional theory. Journal of Management Inquiry, 19(1), pp. 14–20.

Suddaby, R., & Greenwood, R. (2009). *Methodological issues in researching institutional change.* Em D. Buchanan, & A. Bryman (Eds.), *The Sage Handbook of Organizational Research Methods* (pp. 176–196). London: Sage.

Taalas, S. (2010). *Kohti hybriditalouden haastetta. Keskustelua luavasta taloudesta Suomessa.* Työ- ja elinkeinoministeriön julkaisuja. Helsinki: Työ- ja elinkeinoministeriö.

Teatteri Telakka (2017). Historia. Accessed: 14.6.2017, Available at: www.teatteritelakka.fi/?page_id=819

Teatteri Telakka ry. (2018). *Teatteri Telakka.* Accessed 21.4.2018, Available at www.teatteritelakka.fi/

The Swedish Cultural Foundation in Finland. (2017). *Beviljade understöd.* Accessed: 21.1.2017, Available at: http://beviljade.kulturfonden.fi/

Thornton, P., & Ocasio, W. (2008). *Institutional logics.* Em R. Greenwood, C. Oliver, K. Sahlin, & R. Suddaby (Eds.), *Handbook of Organizational Institutionalism.* California: Sage.

Tolbert, P. (1985). Institutional environments and resource dependence: Sources of administrative structure in institutions of higher education. Administrative Science Quarterly, 30, pp. 1–13.

Torch, C. (2010). *Why independence?* Em S. Fitzgerald (Ed.), *New Times, New Models. Investigating the Internal Governance Models and External Relations of Independent Cultural Centres in Times of Change.* Maribor: Pekarna magdalenske mreže.

Townley, B., Beech, N., & McKinlay, A. (2009). Managing in the creative industries: Managing the motley crew. Human Relations, 62(7), pp. 939–1112.

Turun VPK. (2018). *Palokunnantalo.* Accessed 30.5.2018, Available at: www.turunvpk.fi/palokunnantalo

Vickers, J., & Yarrow, G. (1991). Theory construction as disciplined imagination. The Academy of Management Review, 14(4), pp. 516–531.

Webb, D. (2017). *Trends in the development and operation of PACs*. Em P. Lambert, & R. Williams (Eds.), *Performing Arts Center Management* (pp. 45–62). New York: Routledge.

Wolff, S.A. (2017). *The evolution of the performing arts center: What does success look like?* (pp. 20–44). In: Lambert, P., & Williams, R. (Eds.), *Performing Arts Center Management*. New York: Routledge.

Zucker, L. (1977). *The role of institutionalization in cultural persistence*. American Sociological Review, (42), pp. 726–743.

2 Research on cultural center management

As the field of cultural centers is very underresearched, the aim of this chapter is to provide a brief overview of the most important research contributions on the field. I fear calling them *the most important* is in this case equivalent to *only*. This book may have overlooked a study or two, but that does not change the fact that futile attempts have been made to map the field of cultural centers throughout the world. Lambert and Williams (2017) put this interestingly:

> *It seems to be taken for granted that these complex, multi-million-dollar institutions will be built and maintained by communities and be responsibly managed by whatever organization is working behind the scenes to support a vibrant and dynamic local art scene.*
>
> (p. xi)

Although there has been very little research on cultural centers, related international research has shown that culture has positive impacts on cities (Lorentzen & Van Heur, 2013; Rehn et al., 2013). This book, therefore, also aims at presenting useful information and tools for the administration of these centers. There are, however, many difficulties in managing these complex organizations, and the field of cultural centers are divided into many different actors and center types. On top of this, there are of course quite a few angles one could use to study these institutions; organizational change, marketing, the social impact of arts, citizen participation and so forth. Would we have more studies, the obvious way to present these would be to divide them according to the research angle of the authors. As this is not the case, the scarce number of researches will simply be presented in a somewhat chronological manner.

2.1 Earlier studies on cultural centers

Apart from some masters and PhD theses not presented here, there are also some studies older than 2005 that were dismissed. The oldest one introduced in this chapter is the article *Why Are Non-profit Performing Arts Organisations Successful in Mid-sized US Cities?* by Poon and Lai (2008). As the title implies, the authors examine the success on nonprofit performing arts (cultural centers) organizations

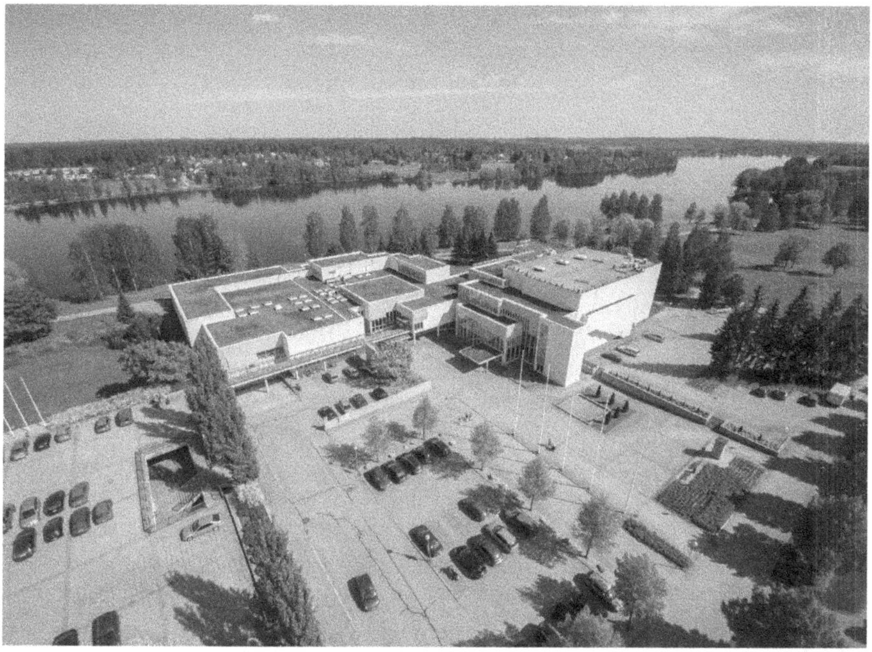

Picture 2.1 The front of cultural center Virta in Imatra, Finland.

in USA. The six cities in focus do not apparently manage well on the Florida's creativity index, but still position within top 30 of 400 North American cultural cities. The authors have grounded their conclusions on interviews with 63 performing arts directors and have found out that cities where urbanization economy factors are ranked low can be a good breeding ground for the performing arts centers with their nonprofit nature. The centers rely on private donations (as there generally are no big companies in such small towns), their social networks (for expertise and social capital) and availability of local talents (the cities where the centers are located in serve as vital urban hatchery for the growth of local performing artists). Other advantages performing arts centers may have in mid-sized cities highlighted in the article was localization economies, affordable facilities and production, access to localized professional networks, and lastly, the possibility to establish better local community links (Poon & Lai, 2008).

Among the older studies on cultural centers is also the article *From Enlightenment to Experience: Cultural Centres in Helsinki Neighbourhoods* by Silvanto, Linko and Cantell (2008), where the authors explore how cultural policy objectives have been negotiated and executed in the urban cultural centers of three different districts in the city of Helsinki in Finland. Based on interviews and a survey, they analyze how cultural centers shape the belief of the users and thus influence the cultural policy. The authors proclaim that cultural centers, although being founded in the 1970s, still stay on the wave crest and provide experiences to people and mirror the latest issues of society. Even though people are not knowingly searching for enlightenment or empowerment – rather merely for experiences (which has become ever more important lately) – they still come in contact with it at the cultural centers (Silvanto et al., 2008).

Bishop, Kavanagh and Palit (2010) published the article *The Role of Performing Arts Centers: A Case for the City University of New York* in 2010. The assumption of their research was that there is a cultural shift happening on university campuses, as the universities are starting to understand the importance of an active creative arts environment to appeal to and hold on to the best students and to make these ready to do well in today's economy. The City University of New York has got 16 performing arts centers spread across the town, and the focus of the paper was to analyze how the performing arts centers leaders consider the idea of the university reconstructing itself as a creative campus and how to go about to spread this idea across the country. The authors seem to have reached the conclusion that both increasing the interest towards the university as a creative campus as well as spreading this idea all over the country is possible. However, the University appears to look upon the matter slightly differently than the leaders of the performing arts centers, which presents a smaller obstacle for this process to advance. The different parties still see this development as mutually beneficial (Bishop et al., 2010).

In 2015, Jureniene and Stonyte published the article *Recreational Activities in Cultural Centres: A Theoretical Approach*, where the main objective was to analyze the role of cultural centers in the framework of recreation. The authors examined this through a case study on cultural centers in Lithuania by interviewing consumers, managers of cultural centers as well as experts. It seems as if the concept of recreation was not clearly perceived by the respondents, and therefore the conclusion was somewhat ambiguous; the consumers could not connect recreation with the cultural center, as they saw the cultural center as a location rather than an institution. However, the experts as well as the managers did see a connection between recreation and cultural centers (Jureniene & Stonyte, 2015). The problem with the article, as it seems, is that the question really should have been whether arts and recreation go together. Therefore, the role of the cultural center became somewhat obsolete in this study, and no plausible conclusions could be made.

Jureniene also published the article *Possibilities for Intercultural Cooperation Development in Cultural Centres* in 2015, based on a both quantitative and qualitative research conducted in eight cultural centers located in the border areas of Lithuania. The aim was to study intercultural cooperation and communication among these cultural centers on a macro-, meso- and micro level. This study revealed, hardly surprising, a cooperation between the community and cultural centers. The intercultural cooperation seems to take place primarily on micro- and meso levels, whereas macro is manifested by bilateral agreements (Jureniene, 2015). As with the earlier article by the same author, the conclusion was left on a fairly unexploited level.

There are some reports made on cultural centers by Trans Europe Halles, a Sweden-based cultural network with 127 members in 36 different countries (Trans Europe Halles, 2020), such as *Creative Business Models: Insights into the Business Models of Cultural Centers in Trans Europe Halles*, which is an explorative European survey involving 27 Countries and 45 centers as well as a case study on 5 centers by Schiuma, Bogen and Lerro in 2016. The aim with this specific report was to analyze the perception of creative business models in cultural organizations, and hereafter to build an understanding for the model contribute to the adoption of such models by the cultural centers in Europe (Schiuma et al., 2016). It appears as if none of the centers in the case study had an agreed, long-term plan or strategy, and a few even lacked a short-term plan. This seemed to have been the case even with the survey results. According to the report, there is a need for outside consultancy in order for the cultural centers to be able to start developing their business model and financial sustainability.

Edited by Lambert and Williams (2017), the book *Performing Arts Center Management* focuses on presenting both theory and best practice of leadership of performing arts centers in the United States. This is by far the most extensive collection of scientific and practical information on cultural centers yet. Containing altogether 13 articles, this book aims attention institutions and practices, as well as cultural planning, urban revitalization and economic development. This book undoubtedly expands our perception of the management of performing arts centers (or cultural centers as they are mainly called in Europe). Amongst other things, it presents important conceptual frameworks, cites recent literature and introduces many cases of diverging cultural venues, and mostly due to the inevitable fact that this field is under researched; it presents a resource for both students and leaders in arts organizations and sets the stage for further research on cultural centers. To highlight a few articles in the book; *Executive Leadership for Performing Arts Centers* by Williams, Harris and Lambert (2017), a plunge into the difficulties of managing a center. A visionary and strategic leadership is needed, and the authors go about to emphasize the necessities to achieve these features. Webb (2017) in turn analyzes the change in the management and operation of these centers and explains how present leaders undertake the difficult task of outward focusing in the search for a mission and a long-term viability, in his chapter *Trends in the Development and Operation of Performing Arts Centers*. Tony Micocci (2017) engages in the dichotomy between arts and business, in his paper *Programming the Performing Arts: Balancing Mission and Solvency.* He explores the available programming alternatives for the leadership of performing arts centers, and the significance of these alternatives. He concludes that private centers with sole responsibility for upholding expensive infrastructure without the support from for instance the municipality, are the most exposed. He still sees new trends amongst new center leaders, and a shift towards new technological solutions and a larger openness towards all sorts of different target audience. He sees the future of the performing arts centers more of urban connective nodes that should not be afraid of expanding their range of their programming options (Micocci, 2017). The articles in the book explain how the public value of the centers are actually growing

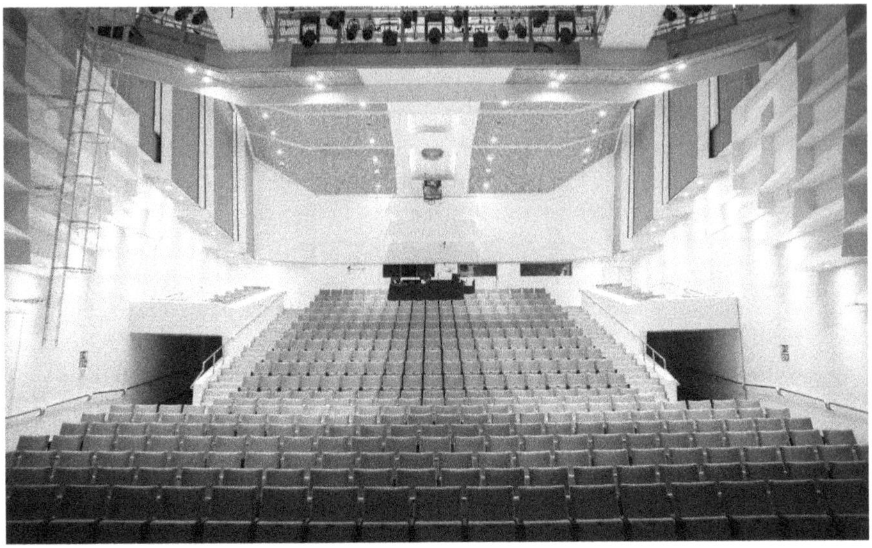

Picture 2.2 The stand at the main stage at cultural center Martinus in Vantaa, Finland. A photograph by Cata Portin.

in importance, centers that serve all needs of all community members. Albeit turbulent change and shifting expectations, the performing arts centers prevail and evolve.

In 2017, Järvinen (2017) published the chapter *From one mission statement to two organizational fields: The effects of reverse isomorphism in private cultural centres*, in the book with the title *Making Sense of Arts Management* (Johansson & Luonila, 2017). The focus of this study was to analyze how isomorphic pressure may lead to a field-level change in the context of cultural centers. The change happening among the aforementioned centers was thought to happen between private and public cultural centers in Finland. The aim was to investigate the impact of triggers for change upon a field and what role isomorphic pressure has in an organizational change on a field level. The study suggest that a field-level change is happening, as the private cultural centers are striving to reshape and reinvent an organizational field of their own, simultaneously indicating that isomorphism also works in reverse (Järvinen, 2017).

There are a few reports on cultural centers and arts organizations within the frames of the project called Creative Lenses, a project co-funded by the Creative Europe program of the European Union (Creative Lenses, 2020). The project, which was carried out from 2015 to 2019, examined the matter of obtaining sustainability in cultural centers without endangering their missions and values. For instance, Kimbell (2018) published the working paper *Modelling shared value and mediating values: Describing business models in performing arts organizations and cultural venues* for Creative Lenses in 2018. This paper reviews articles examining business models, reporting both outside academia and studies published in research of management and organization. The main assumption of the working paper is that the business model construct is pertinent and interchangeable to the arts and cultural sector (Kimbell, 2018). The paper highlights the potential of using business models in arts and cultural organizations.

Other reports that can be found on the same matter, is the one University of the Arts London initiated BOP Consulting to commence in 2017, as a part of the Creative Lenses project (BOP Consulting, 2018). This was an online survey of cultural centers and performing arts organizations across Europe and was designed to make arts and cultural organizations more viable and sustainable by developing their business models as well as improving their long-term strategic and innovation competence. The results of the survey implicate a change happening amongst the centers across Europe, mostly due to a technological shift as well as a change in funding. The latter seem to point in two directions, partly supporting a growth in innovative solutions, and partly in hindering such (BOP Consulting, 2018).

Eriksson, Møhring Reestorff and Carsten Stage (2018) analyzed citizen participation in European cultural centers as a part of the program *RECcORD: Rethinking Cultural Centres in a European Dimension* carried out in Denmark 2015–2017. The citizen participation was researched as a method and an object, and the article presents six forms of citizen participation in the centers: (1) attention, (2) education, (3) co-creation, (4) co-habitation, (5) publics and (6) co-decision (Eriksson et al., 2018). The first form, attention, is about both attending and paying attention to cultural activities with others. The second form, education, refers to participating in learning activities. The third, co-creation, relates to the producing of events or objects as a group. The fourth, co-habitation, is about being around other citizens in the same space. The fifth, publics, is interconnecting verbally and collectively, and the sixth, co-decision, is about committing to equal and shared decision-making (Eriksson et al., 2018).

As participation is imperative for cultural centers, this study underlines that the examined centers perceive themselves as significant places for citizen participation. The authors furthermore stress that participation is presumed and practiced in a more broad and comprehensive way than what is seen in most theories. In fact, the cultural center enables diverse effects and forms for participation (Eriksson et al., 2018).

In 2018, Paul Bogen published his report *Stronger Arts and Cultural Organisations for a Greater Social Impact. Business Models profiling of Cultural Centres & Performing Arts Organisations*, as a part of the aforementioned Creative Lenses project (Bogen, 2018). The aim was to define dimensions, features and challenges regarding the business model innovation as well as management approaches and strategies for audience development within cultural centers and performing arts organizations. In addition to presenting descriptive information about the cultural centers in Europe and some business models identified among the respondents, the report quite clearly states that people involved in cultural centers know what benefit the center offers their artists, audiences, users and funders, they still do not grasp the elements of their business model. More of this in the following chapter.

Rex, Kaszynska and Kimbell (2019) published the project report *Business models for arts and cultural organizations: Research findings from Creative Lenses*. Much as the earlier Creative Lenses working paper by Kimball alone, this report too focuses on why business models are beneficial and important to the values-orientated and creative arts and cultural organizations. The authors still conclude that the adoption of business models by arts and cultural organizations is not unproblematic. The cultural centers all have business models, even if their terminology would not reveal this. By putting the tools and terminologies associated with this process into action, the organization conducts something called business modeling. The authors recommend arts and cultural organizations to do so, in order of '*identifying new opportunities for co-creating and capturing value as appropriate to their context and mission, whether it be underpinned by social, aesthetic or a combination of goals*' (Rex et al., 2019, p. 82).

2.2 Summary and conclusions

These publications above have forwarded understanding and raised awareness of the concept of cultural centers as well as arts and culture organizations. They still have not made any significant developments to management research within the field of cultural centers, mostly due to small number of studies. Adding the number of studies on arts organizations in general, or organizational studies for that matter, will of course broaden the insight on how to administrate a cultural center. But as became clear in Chapter 1, cultural centers cannot be paralleled with museums any more than theatres can be compared to music halls; they simply function under different logics. Therefore, the field of cultural centers need more research on every angle of its existence, from marketing to production, from organizational structure to business model. There is a need for academic studies of different ways to interpret the diverse logics within organizations resulting from interplay with the systems they are part of.

If something were to be deducted from earlier research, this could be the common red threads that can be perceived throughout these papers; there is a vast number of centers all over the world, and the significance of these in their local community is ample and yet growing. The interest towards these often quite complex institutions is rapidly increasing, as is the awareness of them amongst citizens. Furthermore, if they ever have been inadequately managed, there is a trend and a will to correct this development. It would appear as if cultural centers are in the vanguard of transposing the image of arts organizations as poorly managed economical disasters to swiftly changing forerunners of versatile service production hubs.

References

Bishop, S., Kavanagh, K., & Palit, M. (2010). The role of performing arts centers: A case for the City University of New York. International Journal of Learning, 17 (8), pp. 473–484.

Bogen, P. (2018). *Stronger Arts and Cultural Organisations for a Greater Social Impact. Business Models profiling of Cultural Centres & Performing Arts Organisations.* Sweden: Trans Europe Halles, Creative Lenses.

Bop Consulting (2018). *Business Model Innovation in Cultural Centres and Performing Arts Organisations.* Prepared for the Creative Lenses project, Trans Europé Halles.

Creative Lenses (2020). About Creative Lenses. Accessed: 1.8.2020. Available at: https://creativelenses.eu/about-us/

Eriksson, B., Møhring Reestorff, C., & Stage, C. (2018). Forms and potential effects of citizen participation in European cultural centres. Journal of Audience & Reception Studies, 15(2), pp. 205–228.

Järvinen, T. (2017). *From one mission statement to two organizational fields: the effects of reverse isomorphism in private cultural centers.* Em T. Johansson, & M. Luonila (Eds.), *Making Sense of Arts Management: Research, Cases and Practices* (Vol. 1, pp. 128–132). Helsinki: Unigrafia, University of Arts Helsinki.

Johansson, T. & Luonila, M. (2017). *Making Sense of Arts Management: Research, Cases and Practices.* Helsinki: Unigrafia, University of Arts Helsinki.

Jureniene, V. (2015). Possibilities for intercultural cooperation development in cultural centres. Cross-Cultural Communication, 11(2), pp. 5–16.

Jureniene, V., & Stonyte, A.A. (2015). Recreational activities in cultural centres: A theoretical approach. International Journal on Global Business Management and Research, 4(1), pp. 83–93.

Kimbell, L. (2018). *Modelling shared value and mediating values: Describing business models in performing arts organizations and cultural venues.* Creative Lenses Working Paper No. 3.

Lambert, P., & Williams, R. (2017). *Preface.* Em P. Lambert, & R. Williams (Eds.), *Performing Arts Center Management* (1 ed., pp. xi–xii). New York: Routledge.

Lorentzen, A., & Van Heur, B. (2013). *Cultural Political Economy of Small Cities.* Abingdon: Routledge.

Micocci, T. (2017). *Programming the performing arts: Balancing mission and solvency.* Em P. Lambert, & R. Williams (Eds.), *Performing Arts Center Management* (pp. 63–83). New York: Routledge.

Poon, P.P.H. & Lai, C.A. (2008). Why are non-profit performing arts organisations successful in mid-sized US cities? Urban Studies, 45(11), pp. 2273–2289.

Rehn, A., Kivinen, N., Huopalainen, A., Tailas, J. & Mård, M. (2013). *Great expectations: Turku as the European capital of culture 2011.* In: Lindberg, L. & Lindkvist, L. (Eds). *The value of arts and culture for regional development.* Abingdon: Routledge.

Rex, B., Kaszynska, P., & Kimbell, L. (2019). *Business Models for Arts and Cultural Organizations: Research Findings from Creative Lenses.* Project Report. Trans Europe Halles, Lund, Sweden.

Schiuma, G., Bogen, P., & Lerro, A. (2016). *Creative Business Models: Insights into the Business Models of Cultural Centers in Trans Europe Halles.* Lund, Sweden: Trans Europe Halles.

Silvanto, T., Linko, M., & Cantell, T. (2008). From Enlightenment to Experience: Cultural Centers in Helsinki Neighbourhoods. International Journal of Cultural Policy, 14(2), pp. 165–178.

Trans Europe Halles (2020). *About us*. Accessed at: 5.8.2020. Available at: https://teh.net/about-us/

Webb, D. (2017). *Trends in the development and operation of PACs*. Em P. Lambert, & R. Williams (Eds.), *Performing Arts Center Management* (pp. 45–62). New York: Routledge.

Williams, R., Harris, K., & Lambert, P.D. (2017). *Executive leadership for performing arts centers*. Em P. Lambert, & R. Williams (Eds.), *Performing Arts Center Management* (pp. 238–259). New York: Routledge.

3 Cultural center business models

There has been an increased attention aimed at the role and relevance of both the business model and business model innovation recently (Chesbrough, 2011). The main ambition has been to support and drive the development of organizational performance. Still, the focus has been mainly on big multinational corporations or ICT companies. Small and medium enterprises, especially those within the field of culture, have been somewhat neglected. Business model innovation is still seen as essential to creative and cultural organizations' success (Hume et al., 2006; MunozSeca, 2011). A successful business model needs to be both viable and sustainable (Boons et al., 2013). Value is at its core, so any organization with the capability to create, offer and capture value, also has a business model (Amit & Zott, 2001). In the cultural sector with its large portion of subsidies, there is also an accountability to the funders (Schiuma et al., 2016). A business model will help managing these sorts of tasks.

As will be apparent in this chapter, it seems as if cultural centers in most cases do not have a clearly articulated business model. That does not mean that there is none. The probability is that it has been unconsciously copied from other organizations in the same field. Therefore, this chapter will strive to focus on the development of business models within the field of cultural centers. For centers to develop more viable strategies for audience development, financial sustainability and resource administration, it is imperative to reassess as well as to search for new methods for cultural centers to create value and to improve and reconstruct the organizational appearance and management.

So, why do cultural centers exist and in which way do they bring value to the customer? How do they make money on their activities? It is important to strive to answer the question about how to do what you do most efficiently while also making an earning in the process. Let us first take a dive into the concept of business model, and thereafter position it in relation to the cultural centers, before analyzing how the centers themselves perceive their situation.

3.1 What exactly is a business model?

Well, as with many concepts within science, there is not one clear definition of a business model. However, the concept of business models became common in the wake of the rising of the internet in the mid-1990s (Chesbrough, 2011; Lindman 2011; Zott et al., 2011). That is not to say that business models did not exist before that, they only became acknowledged by internet after having been essential to trading and economic behavior on a lesser scale since preclassical times (Teece, 2010). The business model concept was in fact introduced by Peter Drucker already in 1954 (Drucker, 1954). A dive into the existing literature reveals that there are quite a few definitions of the concept, as it has been applied to address an extensive range of research questions in differing contexts as well as management areas. Chesbrough (2011), for instance, aims attention on the connection between business and innovation. Hedman and Kalling (2003) in turn point out that the business model concept has achieved a footing within the field of information systems. Afuah (2004) describes business models as structures of connected activities, for instance value chains, business systems and vertical linkages.

The development of new business models has consistently been paramount in the diffusion of innovations (Teece, 2010). The business model an organization chooses is increasingly used for evaluating their strategies to address sustainability challenges (Boons et al., 2013). Although there are some points of reference for characterizing business models in earlier studies, the term remains debated; both as to the organizational components that are described (Osterwalder et al., 2005), as well as to the system boundaries of individual organizations or networks of organizations (Upward and Jones, 2015; Zott et al., 2011). Conceivably the most generally used definition (Boons and Lüdeke-Freund, 2013) is from Osterwalder & Pignuer (2010) who singled out four basic components. These are:

1) The value proposition.
2) The supply chain.
3) The customer interface.
4) The financial model.

This characterization contributes with a 'meta-model' of features that are universal to all business models and can therefore be applied in multiple contexts (Osterwalder et al., 2005). You could thus summarize, that business models incorporate the very essence of the value brought to customers, the undertaking involved in bringing that value, as well as the means of collecting earnings from these activities, in economic, social, cultural or other contexts (Boons et al., 2013). Georg and Bock (2011) define business models neatly as the architecture of organizational structures to act out on a commercial opportunity. Lastly, Amit and Zott (2001, p. 216) characterize a business model as '*the content, structure, and governance of transactions designed so as to create value through the exploitation of business opportunities.*' That is, a business model is shortly how an organization delivers value to the customer.

Drucker, who invented the concept of business models, introduced five questions for nonprofit or profit organizations to consider as a strategic framework

(Drucker, 2008). In order to discover a path and to start exploring it, the organization has to answer these questions;

1) What is our mission?
2) Who is our customer?
3) What does the customer/user value?
4) What are our results?
5) What is our plan?

As you can see, there are quite a few suggestions for the basic components of a business model (see Amit & Zott, 2001; Casadesus-Masanell & Ricart, 2010; Osterwalder & Pignuer, 2010). In this chapter, we will be focusing on three main features; the value proposition, value creation and delivery, as well as value capture. The first feature, value proposition, provides measurable social value in agreement with economic value (Boons & Lüdeke-Freund, 2013). The second feature, value creation and delivery, is kind of the essence of any organization; the aim at developing value by capturing new business opportunities, new revenue streams and new markets (Teece, 2010). The third feature, value capture, is about how to earn those revenues from supplying the goods, information or services to customers.

Business models are far from static, they need to be calibrated over time to stay dynamic, especially in changing environmental conditions and pressures (see Chapter 5) (Amit & Zott, 2012; Bucherer et al., 2012). As expected, not all business models change, they rather disappear or simply become irrelevant. A change may be set-off by internal or external conditions as well as due to the current business model (Demil et al., 2015; DaSilva & Trkman, 2014). Furthermore, business model dynamics are proactive or reactive. Proactive changes are initiated and introduced by the focal organization, whereas reactive changes emerge as a response to the rise of new circumstances affecting the effectiveness of the focal organizations business model (Vives & Svejenova, 2011). Ecosystems that change swiftly can press organizations to conform to new circumstances, and thus change their business models to better profit from new market opportunities (Casadesus-Masanell & Zhu, 2013; Teece, 2010). Organizations are not isolated, and business models are not executed nor planned in a void, wherefore the business model is a tool for competition (Amit & Zott, 2014; Casadesus-Masanell & Ricart, 2010). Lastly, business models are not everlasting. The point is to be able to adapt to transformations in the ecosystem to keep pace with changing needs and threats and not to become irrelevant and perish (Linder & Cantrell, 2000).

Earlier, the organizations were anticipated to have a vision, a strategy as well as a business plan (Casadesus-Masanell and Ricart, 2011). As of now, the organizations advance and share their business models. In response to criticism about business models being a too loose model of how an organization makes money (Alt & Zimmermann 2001), some scholar created – or rather noticed the existing of – a connection between strategies and business models (Anderson & Markides, 2007; Lehmann-Ortega & Schoettl, 2005). This connection is that an organizations business model is an element of its overall business strategy: it is the fundamentals behind how the organization intends to obtain its goals, one of them being making a profit (Amid & Zott, 2014).

A business model may be different from a strategy, but these two concepts are still complementary – even if they need to be distinguished; a business model focuses on the 'how' when offering customers products and services (Yip, 2004). It addresses not only the nature of the offerings that the organization provides the customer, but also the way it distributes resources, as well as the activities the organization carries out to hand over those offerings (Chesbrough & Rosenbloom, 2002; Magretta, 2002; Zott & Amit, 2010). Although the traditional strategy interconnects such branches as the industry structure view (Brandenburger & Nalebuff, 1996) and the resource-based view (Barney, 1991; Wernerfelt, 1984) with a focus on the competitive advantage of organizations, and therefore also value allocation, the business model is a complementary approach with its concern on total value creation. Value creation in turn is essential to the strategic management field, as it is a necessity for value appropriation (Brandenburger & Stuart, 1996; Porter, 1985). The business model transfers the logic behind the organizations value creation and value appropriation (Amit & Zott, 2001; Casadesus-Masanell & Ricart, 2010; Casadesus-Masanell & Zhu, 2013). Putting it bluntly: where strategy generally concentrate on competitors, business models focuses on value creation and financial aspects in organizations (Magretta, 2002).

A business model is neither an organizational structure nor a product–market positioning strategy (Zott & Amit, 2010), even if it is, as stated above, a part of the organization's strategy. The business model specifies how the focal organizations is embedded in its business ecosystem (Adner & Kapoor, 2010), the ecosystem being the multiple networks of organizations, customers and different stakeholders in the near surrounding. An organization can detect feasible partners as well as competitors with a business model. Consequently, the business model is a crucial strategic choice that an organization has to make (Amit & Zott, 2014). Creating a new model calls for partners or networks, either new or existing (Kimbell, 2018). These may necessitate new activities and changes in leadership, as well as availability to a variety of resources.

3.2 Positioning cultural centers in the landscape of business models

There has been very little research or discussion on the matter of business models in cultural organizations (Coblence and Sabatier 2012; Searle 2017). Therefore, classification of business models such organizations is hardly surprising quite futile (Fielt, 2014). The thing is, that the concepts by which different types of models should be classified, have not been improved sufficiently. Thus, the current classifications are merely lists not grounded theoretically or empirically.

According to a survey in 2017 (BOP Consulting, 2018), the search for business model innovation amongst cultural centers and performing arts organizations is quite widespread, and almost 80% of the respondents said they pursued a change in their business model during the last 5 years. The background for this seemingly wild chase for a change are many, but the most common reasons are the need for a shared vision and a strong leadership, as well as sudden changes in type of funding. A limiting factor is the lack of funding or the funding with restricted purposes, which hinders organizations from innovating. Another slowing down factor is the absence of long-term strategic plans amongst arts organizations, albeit there are signs of them making changes to their business routines as well as a growing amount of collaborations, new income generation approaches and audience development (BOP Consulting, 2018).

However, there seems to be doubts about whether the cultural centers really have grasped the notion of a business model (Bogen, 2018). This is mainly due to a lack of a clear mission and vision, as well as a long-term strategy and relatively stable finances. When asked during interviews about the status of centers in Europe, no respondent was able to explain their business model. It appears as if the theory and practice of business models, business model innovation as well as value propositions are obscure and unfamiliar to most working in the cultural sector (Bogen, 2018). The inconsistency in this claim of the respondents in this study, as well as the one mentioned above (Bogen, 2018), is that nearly all cultural centers are nonetheless constantly working on developing their business model, simply out of necessity (Bogen, 2018). How can they work with something they do not fully comprehend? This is of course is no paradox, there is a rather simple reason for this – they simply do not know the right terms for what it is they are working with.

It would appear as if the strategical attempts of the cultural centers are rather shortsighted, according to Bogen (2018). Other studies give the same impression; there seem to be no long-term plans amongst the cultural centers, not amongst the centers in this specific study, nor amongst the centers of the study done by Trans Europe Halles with a population of the 45 private cultural centers located in 27 European countries, a study on the notion of creative business models in cultural organizations (Schiuma et al., 2016).

Still, if the cultural centers do not identify their business models, or have the right tools and techniques, that does not mean there is not a model or that one could not be identified, adopted or managed (Schiuma et al., 2016). It is of no necessity that these business models of the cultural centers should be governed exactly by the language or the concepts of the commercial sector. As with the diversity within any field, the fields themselves may be differing at a level that implies a need of dissimilar rules; cultural organizations have specific characteristics, and as such, the traditional business rules will not work with same benefits (Schiuma et al., 2016).

As the business landscape changes, the economic systems anticipate a development of a constellation of value impacts to a greater extent, which in turn provides cultural organizations with a more proactive role (Schiuma et al., 2016). If ecosystems are the networks that organizations surround themselves with, these

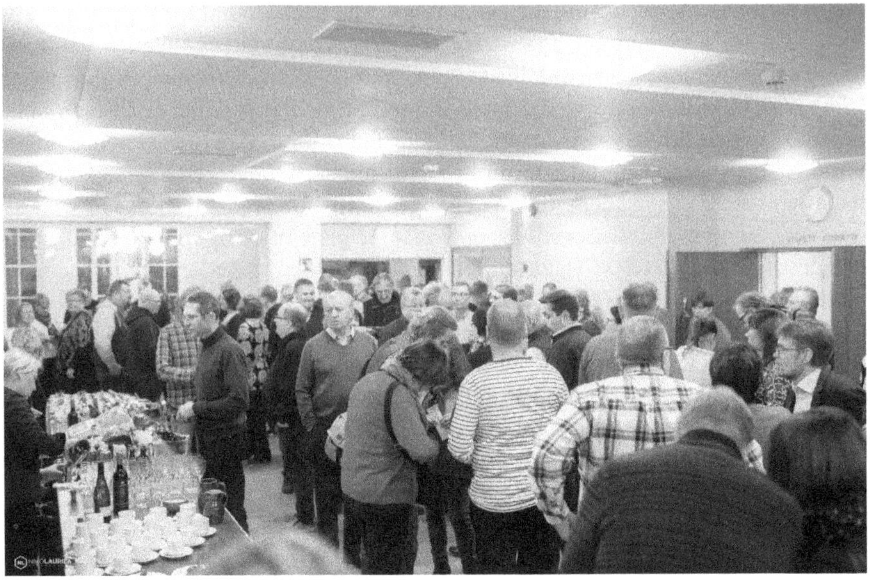

Picture 3.1 The lobby restaurant and bar of Grand in Porvoo, Finland. A photograph by Niko Laurila.

changes allow cultural organizations to position themselves in the system not merely as the entity offering cultural activities, but can extend their role as

> *actors for social innovation and development as providers of cultural and creative services and catalysts for change and performance improvements of organizations operating in other traditional sectors.*
>
> (Schiuma et al., 2016, p. 12)

There seems to be two reasons for the centers to develop their business plan, first, the need to obtain economic viability without endangering their mission, secondly not only for growth but also the opportunity to act for social innovation and development while providing cultural and creative services, and to be a contributor for change (Schiuma et al., 2016).

As presented in Chapter 1, there is a vast diversity of cultural centers around the world. The centers vary in size, operating markets, main activities, value chains and last but not least, the application of new business models (Dümcke, 2015). Therefore, there is not one single business model valid for the whole sector, which makes the task of dividing them into clear business models anything but easy. It is not possible to extract an umbrella business model for all sorts of centers without losing the uniqueness of every single one of them (Rex et al., 2019). However, according to Rex, Kaszynska and Kimbell (2019), there are enough of

Table 3.1 Common business model types in arts and cultural organizations

Business model variants	*Examples of activities and assets*	*Underlying business model activities & assets*
The performer model	The activities of the organization include initiating a show or taking part in a show. Assets in turn involve creative and production competence. Revenues can come from artist fees or ticket sales.	This model where the creator and the audience are present during the performance, is considered a solutions model.
The product model	The activities of this model include for instance writing a play or creating a physical artwork. Assets in turn involve creative and production competence. Revenues can come from artist fees, licensing intellectual property or product sales.	This model in which the creator produces an artwork (but not directly entangled in the audience experience), is called a product model.
The commissioner model	The activities of the organization involve commissioning an event, cultural programming and connecting with audiences. Assets in turn involve both expertise, relationships as well as data. The commissioner usually pays a fee for the commissioning of the event, and thereafter receives revenues from funders and/or ticket sales.	This model, where the organization is a type of mediator producing a program or a show by creators and engages or finds audiences and other partners, can be seen as a matchmaking model.
The landlord model	The activities involve renting out for instance office, studio or co-working space. Assets in turn involve availability to a venue and competence in facilities management. Incomes are renting and/or non-financial income.	A venue where tenants and other users of the space are involved, is called a solutions model.

(*continued*)

Table 3.1 Cont.

Business model variants	*Examples of activities and assets*	*Underlying business model activities & assets*
The hub model	The activities include running a venue, festival or platform with numerous intersecting activities. Assets in turn involve competence in cultural programming, staff expertise, audience development and data. The organization that applies the hub model gets income from funders, ticket sales and such on top of providing access to some without payment.	A venue that brings together more than two participants in creating value (not all of them pay), is called a multi-sided model.
The service model	The activities involve bringing an event for customers; managing workshops or courses; upholding a café or bar; supplying services to tenants. Assets in turn involve competence in training, teaching or offering catering or bar services. The revenues for such activities include income from delivering services.	When the provider and the customer are present during the service, it is referred to as a solutions model.

Adapted from Kimbell (2018, p. 14).

equivalent features to make an approximation of archetypes. These archetypes will not explain in detail that much, as they are simplifications, but they can give a clearer overall picture of the field.

Kimbell (2018) has, by drawing on Baden-Fuller et al. (2017), classified business models of arts and cultural organizations and suggests six distinct variations that connects both internal and external actors and assets to produce value. The author furthermore points out that an organization may have several models running simultaneously. These differing models may even support one another; for instance, the restaurant surplus that covers the deficit of the theatre (Rex et al., 2019). The co-existence of many models may work well at some centers and less so at others. The question is if the financial side is overemphasized in business models and other indicators for success are called for (e.g., Chapter 8).

As with the study of Rex, Kaszynska and Kimbell (2019), this research also shows that cultural centers most commonly employ the multisided hub model, typically complemented by the landlord model. In Finland, the service model is also quite common. As stated earlier, these models are simplifications. They still give a general idea of what is happening in the field. This idea seems to point to institutional pressures pushing the centers closer each other. We will look closer on these institutional pressures in Chapter 5.

3.3 Business model innovation among private cultural centers

Generally speaking, the respondents of this study seem to grasp what their specific cultural center is about. Partly because of the self-explanatory concept of a cultural center, but they also have embraced the core mission of their center. The centers all have had occasional strategical sessions where the mission and vision has been polished, but as with the European studies mentioned above (Bogen, 2018), there are mostly no clear business models to be identified among the Finnish cultural centers. What seems to be somewhat of a reason for this reluctancy for – or simply unawareness of – business models, is the very same reason for not having long-term strategies – the cultural centers feel they need to be able to make radical and fast decisions mostly every year, in order to stay ahead of the game. As one respondent put it:

> *if I have an idea, something I want to carry out, I only present that idea and the budget, and if he [CEO] believes in it, you get the chance to do it. Even if it goes beyond what we have actually agreed that I should do.*
>
> Respondent E

This in turn supports the view of Schiuma et al. (2016) that cultural centers are actors for social innovation and function as catalysts for change. But instead of adding it as a feature to their business model, they repel the model altogether. One center nevertheless had a respondent stating clear thoughts about their business model, even if the rest of the respondents from the same center could not explain this as easily.

> *we build urban oases in urban centers that act as oases in an urban environment. An oasis means a place that is not quite a home, not a school, not an office, not a business space, not a shop, not a hospital, but something else. And the rest is, uh, meant for the kind of services and experiences that people in cities are increasingly looking for. People are looking for more and more intangible things in their lives, and the whole economy is turning from products to services and experiences, so we are a part of it. If you look at it from an economic perspective, then the economy is becoming more intangible. If we look at it from a cultural point of view, then we are producing content experiences of urban culture, services for the citizens. If you still look at it from an urban perspective, then we are making cities more*

> *comfortable places where more and more people would like to move or enjoy themselves.*
>
> Respondent C

He goes on to explain how this mission supports profitability by stating the importance of: *'finding the right balance between finding a business model that is business-sound enough, and functional and content-minded enough, and should I say, different'* (Respondent C).

But how do the majority of the respondents perceive their business model? As earlier suggested, the concept does not seem to be clear for most of them. This does not mean that the cultural centers would not have a business model, quite the opposite, as Bogen (2018) pointed out. There is simply a need to extract the business models from the respondent's descriptions.

Most respondents clearly present more of an idealistic view when asked about the mission of their center; bringing culture to the people, serving as a gathering place or even a more organizational perspective – a platform for different groups to work for arts, and so forth. As soon as it comes to the economical side, they refer to different grants or the restaurant. A few mention the primary mission being renting the venue to be able to provide unlucrative cultural offering. The same applies to the mission of the restaurant, which in turn suggest the landlord model of the six business models classified by Kimbell (2018).

All of the centers arrange events for customers to some extent, three of them quite extensively and regularly. It may concern workshops or courses, and all of them have a bar. These all function as important revenue sources. This in turn suggests the service model of the six business models.

Three of the centers at hand furthermore have multiple intersecting activities when running both a venue, a platform and festivals. They plan all their programs themselves and educate their staff – both their personnel and their voluntary staff. The incomes are generated from funders and ticket sales. This suggests the hub model of the business models.

All of the centers do commission shows to some extent, some of them more, some less. This is a part of the strategy to cut down costs and still be able to offer the same shows as before, by collaborating with other organization in the same field. One respondent describes their view on collaboration:

> *We are moving in the same direction as society, that when people change, and values change, and the way you do things change in a certain way: more and more to a kind of off-substance and more towards sharing. Not everyone needs to own everything, and we pitch things to each other, and [...] we can work together.*
>
> (Respondent A)

This would imply a commissioner model of the business models.

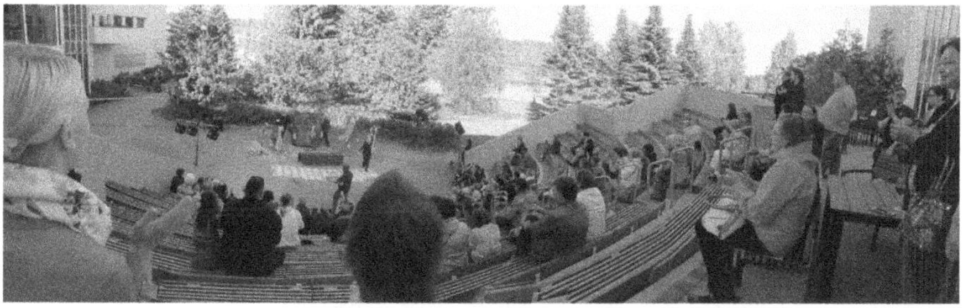

Picture 3.2 The outside auditorium at cultural center Virta in Imatra, Finland. A photograph by Tuuli Parikka.

The product model, that is where the activities include that the personnel of the centers write music or for instance create a physical artwork, can only be found in one center, where they have two employed actors in their theatre. It seems as if the general rule is to not have any artistic personnel, but exceptions occur.

The last of the six business models for cultural centers classified by Kimbell (2018) is the performer model. This model is about creating a show or performing in a show. Both creative and production expertise can be found among the staff in the centers, and all of the centers create different shows. None of them however perform in a show, except for the abovementioned actors. This however suggest that even the performer model is at play among the centers. All of this is done in economic terms to raise tickets sales.

As we can see, the centers do work with different business plans, although they do not acknowledge or articulate which plan they follow. The personnel however appear to have some kind of understanding what is expected from them, which suggests that at least the mission of the centers is communicated.

The centers in this case study seem to have adopted very differing organizational structures. One center is solely an association, with all volunteers, except for one employee, who arrange most of the events themselves. The board and other volunteers handle all the practical issues during events. The second case is also an association, but it hardly does no event production at all. The employees, all three of them, handle every practical issue; the board merely makes decisions. The third case has a variety of organizations in its mix: two associations and two joint-stock companies. One association arranges everything related to theatre in the cultural center. The other association is an endorsement association that owns the building and the two joint-stock companies and supports the theatre financially. One of the companies is the center's restaurant, while the other company takes care of potential renovations of the house. The fourth case is a joint-stock company within a corporate group that aims to establish different cultural oases, such as the cultural center, all over the city.

The respondents clearly reflect on their organizational structure. According to themselves, they adapt structures in agreement with their analyses of the best

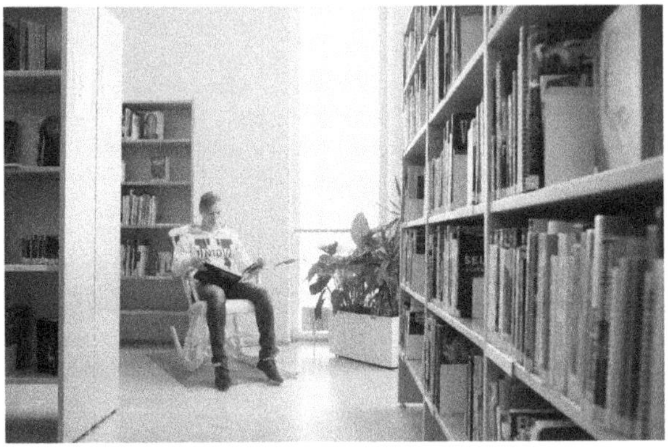

Picture 3.3 The library at cultural center Virta in Imatra, Finland.

environmental fit and consider indicators such as ownership, development opportunities and activity characteristics a front seat while designing the structure. Furthermore, two centers do not have a specific leader—or a clear hierarchy, for that matter—and the two with leaders stress the importance of employees having independence in their work. This too affects the implementation of a business model.

Although an organizational model naturally is not the same as a business model, these things affect each other as to what can be done. Furthermore, and as can be seen in Chapter 6, the resource scarcity is another fact that affects and to some extent changes the business model at hand over time.

3.4 Summary and Conclusions

The aim with this chapter was to highlight both the theoretical and the practical side of business models among cultural centers. Business models have become common among any larger organization after the 1990s. This applies to arts organizations as well. There are quite a few definitions of the concept, as it has been applied to address an extensive range of research questions in differing contexts as well as management areas. As you can see, there are quite a few unconnected features to business models and recommendations to what works best for whom. It still seems as if business models more easily accepted as narrative schemes and stories than as a specific plan (Magretta, 2002). The niche of a business plan is the ability to emerge discussions on how the organization can create, produce and accomplish value and single out business opportunities; it connects resources and activities in a greater scale.

A business model is neither an organizational structure nor a product–market positioning strategy. Business models incorporate the very essence of the value brought to customers, the undertaking involved in bringing that value, as well as the means of collecting earnings from these activities, in economic, social, cultural or other contexts. Four basic components to business models are: (1) the value proposition, (2) the supply chain, (3) the customer interface and (4) the financial model. Where strategy generally concentrate on competitors, business models focuses on value creation and financial aspects in organizations Business models do change, due to internal or external reasons, and may also become obsolete.

If we return to the questions posed in the introduction of this chapter, we could focus on why the cultural centers exist according to themselves and in which way do they bring value to the customer? And how do they make money on their activities?

The concept of business models seems to be acknowledged among the respondents, but in practice omitted. This is mainly due to a lack of a clear mission and vision, as well as a long-term strategy and relatively stable finances. However, although the centers do not entirely seem to grasp the concept of business models, there is still always one at play. It is rather a question of having the right terminology.

As the centers vary for instance in size, operating markets, main activities and value chains, there is naturally not one single business model valid for the whole sector. There are still enough of equivalent features to make an approximation of archetypes, that is, simplifications. The six archetypes are: (1) the performer model, (2) the product model, (3) the commissioner model, (4) the landlord model, (5) the hub model and (6) the service model. The most typical models employed by cultural centers are the hub model complemented by the landlord and service model, but all models are at play among the respondents. In other words, the cultural centers seem to have clear models to profit on their activities and how to bring value to the customers. The mission, or why they exist, also seem to be clear for most of the respondents. The mission often appears to have an ideological nuance, as in bringing cultural value to the customer. However, when digging deeper, there can also be found a quite elaborated view on what purpose the center has, balancing on profitability, functionality, content focused and different than what usually is offered to the customer.

It still seems quite clear that an art organization such as the cultural centers would benefit on having a straightforward and articulated business model. As a multipurpose venue, the fear is that the center will start to spread too thin instead of focusing on the core purpose of the mission. The point is not to continue with one or two activities, such is not the character of a multipurpose venue, but to be aware of the inner connection between the varieties of activities, as well as the connection between the existing activities and revenue streams.

A question which the current situation with quite a few empirical studies on business models amongst arts organization cannot answer yet, is that does the business model really help the cultural center? Will it balance the focus between culture and economy or arts and business? Or will it unnecessarily change the focus too much against making money? On the other hand, this may be a question that cannot be answered from an umbrella perspective but should rather be something for the single center to contemplate over; how does a business model fit a specific organization with a specific mission at a specific location? You cannot adapt a preexisting business model and expect it to work. There has to be an active approach and a modelling to your specific organization and situation, which thereafter can give priority to your opportunities and your limitations. Lastly, as the resource scarcity seem to be a reality for most of the cultural centers, a clearly defined and articulated business plan could be exactly what is needed.

References

Adner, R. & Kapoor, R. (2010). Value creation in innovation ecosystems: How the structure of technological interdependence affects firm performance in new technology generations. Strategic Management Journal, 31(3), pp. 306–333.

Afuah, A. (2004). *Business Models: A Strategic Management Approach.* New York: McGraw-Hill.

Alt, R., & Zimmermann, H. D. (2001). Introduction to special section on business models. Electron Markets, 11(1), pp. 3–9.

Amit, R., Zott, C. (2001). Value creation in e-business. Strategic Management Journal, 22, pp. 493–520.

Amit, R. & Zott, C. (2012). New business models – creating value through business model innovation. MIT Sloan Management Review, 53(3) pp. 41–49.

Amit, R. & Zott, C. (2014). *Business model design: A dynamic capability perspective.* Working Paper Wharton Business School.

Anderson, J. & Markides, C. (2007). Strategic innovation at the base of the pyramid. Sloan Management Review, 49(1), pp. 82–88.

Baden-Fuller, C., Giudici, A., & Morgan, M. (2017). Business models and value. Academy of Management Proceedings, 1 Accessed: 4.8.2020. Available at: https://doi.org/10.5465/AMBPP.2017.90

Barney, J.B. (1991). Firm resources and sustained competitive advantage. Journal of Management, 17(1), pp. 99–120.

Bogen, P. (2018). *Stronger arts and cultural organisations for a greater social impact. Business Models profiling of Cultural Centres & Performing Arts Organisations.* Sweden: Trans Europe Halles, Creative Lenses.

Boons, F., & Lüdeke-Freund, F. (2013). Business models for sustainable innovation: state-of- the-art and steps towards a research agenda. Journal of Cleaner Production, 45, pp. 9–19. https://doi.org/10.1016/j.jclepro.2012.07.007.

Boons, F., Montalvo, C., Quist, J., & Wagner, M., (2013). Sustainable innovation, business models and economic performance: An overview. Journal of Cleaner Production, 45, pp. 1–8. https://doi.org/10.1016/j.jclepro.2012.08.013

Bop Consulting (2018). *Business model innovation in cultural centres and performing arts organisations.* Prepared for the Creative Lenses project, Trans Europé Halles.

Brandenburger, A.M. & Nalebuff, B.J. (1996). *Co-opetition.* New York: Doubleday Currency.

Brandenburger, A.M. & Stuart, H. (1996). Value-based business strategy. Journal of Economics and Management Strategy, 5 pp. 5–25.

Bucherer, E., Eisert, U., & Gassmann, O. (2012). Towards systematic business model innovation: Lessons from product innovation management. Creativity and Innovation Management, 21(2), pp. 183–198.

Casadesus-Masanell, R., & Ricart, J.E. (2010). From strategy to business models and onto tactics. Long Range Planning, 43(2–3), pp. 195–215.

Casadesus-Masanell, R. & Ricart, J. E. (2011). How to design a winning business model. Harvard Business Review, 89, pp. 100–107.

Casadesus-Masanell, R. & Zhu, F. (2013). Business model innovation and competitive imitation. Strategic Management Journal, 34(4), pp. 464–482.

Chesbrough, H. (2011). *Open Services Innovation.* San Francisco: JosseyBass.

Chesbrough, H., & Rosenbloom, R.S. (2002). The role of the business model in capturing value from innovation: Evidence from Xerox corporation's technology spin-off companies. Industrial and Corporate Change, 11(3), pp. 529–555.

Coblence, E., & Sabatier, V. (2012). Articulating growth and cultural innovation in art museums. International Studies of Management & Organisation, 44 (4), pp. 9–25.

DaSilva, C.M., & Trkman, P. (2014). Business model: What it is and what it is not. Long Range Planning, 47(6), pp. 379–389.

Demil, B., Lecocq, X., Ricart, J.E., & Zott, C. (2015). Introduction to the SEJ special issue on business models: Business models within the domain of strategic entrepreneurship. Strategic Entrepreneurship Journal, 9(1), pp. 1–11.

DiMaggio, P., & Powell, W. (1983). The iron cage revisited: Institutional isomorphism and collective rationality in organizational fields. American Sociological Review, 48, pp. 147–160.

Drucker, P. (1954). *The Practice of Management.* New York: Harper & Row.

Drucker, P. (2008). *The Five Most Important Questions You Will Ever Ask About Your Organisation.* San Francisco, CA: Jossey-Bass.

Dümcke, C., (2015). *New Business Models in the Cultural and Creative Sectors (CCSs).* European Expert Network on Culture ENCC. Accessed: 28.7.2020. Available at: www.interarts.net/descargas/interarts2540.pdf

Fielt, E. (2014). Conceptualising business models: Definitions, frameworks and classifications. Journal of Business, 1(1), pp. 85–105.

George, G., & Bock, AJ. (2011). The business model in practice and its implications for entrepreneurship research. Entrepreneurship Theory and Practice, 35(1), pp. 83–111.

Hedman, J., & Kalling, T. (2003). The business model concept: Theoretical underpinnings and empirical illustrations. European Journal of Information Systems, 12(1), p. 49.

Hume, M., Sullivan Mort, G., Liesch, P., & Winzar, H. (2006). Understanding service experience in non-profit performing arts: Implications for operations and service management. Journal of Operations Management, 24(4), pp. 16–42.

Kimbell, L. (2018). *Modelling shared value and mediating values: Describing business models in performing arts organizations and cultural venues.* Creative Lenses Working Paper No. 3.

Lehmann-Ortega, L. & Schoettl, J. (2005). *From Buzzword to Managerial Tool: The Role of Business Models in Strategic Innovation.* CLADEA. Santiago de Chile: 14.

Linder, J.C. & Cantrell, S. (2000). *Changing Business Models: Surveying the Landscape.* Outlook Point of View, Institute for Strategic Change, Accenture

Lindman, J. (2011). *Not Accidental Revolutionaries: Essays on Open Source Software Production and Organizational Change.* Helsinki: Aalto University.

Magretta, J. (2002). Why business models matter. Harvard Business Review, 80(5), pp. 86–92.

Meyer, J., & Rowan, B. (1977). Institutionalized organizations: Formal structure as myth and ceremony. The American Journal of Sociology, 83(2), pp. 340–363.

Munoz-Seca, B. (2011). *A business model for cultural services. A joint design and production of a customer experience*. Working Paper 941, University of Navarra.

North, D. (1990). *Institutions, Institutional Change and Economic Performance*. Cambridge: Cambridge University Press.

Osterwalder, A., & Pigneur, Y. (2010). *Business Model Generation: A Handbook for Visionaries, Game Changers, and Challengers*. https://doi.org/10.1523/JNEUROSCI.0307-10.2010.

Osterwalder, A., Pigneur, Y., & Tucci, C.L., (2005). Clarifying business models: Origins, present, and future of the concept. Communications of the Association for Information Systems, 16, pp. 1–25. https://doi.org/10.1.1.83.7452

Pfeffer, J. (2003). Introduction to the classic edition. Em J. Pfeffer, & G. Salancik (Eds.), *The External Control of Organizations: A Resource Dependence Perspective*. Stanford: Stanford University Press.

Porter, M.E. (1985). *Competitive Advantage*. New York: Free Press.

Rex, B., Kaszynska, P., Kimbell, L. (2019). *Business Models for Arts and Cultural Organizations: Research Findings from Creative Lenses*. Project Report. Lund, Sweden: Trans Europe Halles.

Schiuma, G., Bogen, P., Lerro, A. (2016). *Creative Business Models: Insights into the Business Models of Cultural Centers in Trans Europe Halles*. Lund, Sweden: Trans Europe Halles.

Searle, N. (2017). *Business Models, Intellectual Property and the Creative Industries: A Meta-analysis*. CREATe Working Paper Series DOI:10.5281/zenodo.808267.

Streeck, W., & Thelen, K. (2005). *Beyond Continuity: Institutional Change in Advanced Political Economies*. Oxford: Oxford University Press.

Suddaby, R. (2010). Challenges for institutional theory. *Journal of Management Inquiry*, 19(1), pp. 14–20.

Teece, D.J., (2010). Business models, business strategy and innovation. Long Range Planning. 43(30), pp. 172–194. https://doi.org/10.1016/j.lrp.2009.07.003

Upward, A., & Jones, P. (2015). An ontology for strongly sustainable business models: Defining an enterprise framework compatible with natural and social science. Organization & Environment, 1–27. https://doi.org/10.1177 /1086026615592933.

Vives, L. & Svejenova, S. (2011). To, from and beyond the margins: Business models: Towards an integrative framework. Management Research: The Journal of the Iberoamerican Academy of Management, 9(3), pp. 230–242.

Wernerfelt, B. (1984). A resource-based view of the firm. Strategic Management Journal, 5(2), pp. 171–180.

Yip, G. (2004). Using strategy to change your business model. Business Strategy Review, 15(2), pp. 17–24.

Zott, C. & Amit, R. (2010). Business model design: An activity system perspective. Long Range Planning, 43(2–3), pp. 216–226.

Zott, C., Amit, R., & Massa, L. (2011). The business model: Recent developments and future research. Journal of Management, 37(4), pp. 1019–1042. https://doi.org/10.1177 /0149206311406265.

4 The business of art or the art of business?

Andy Warhol supposedly once said that '*being good in business is the most fascinating kind of art. Making money is art, working is art, and good business is the best art*'. Whether he is right or not is up for debate, but his remark did challenge the traditional view on arts and business. Creativity is not something exclusive for art, and neither is business exclusive for nonart. It's all about the balance between these two contrasting worlds, especially when it comes to arts organizations. Paradoxically, while doing business, organizations tend to forget the creative work in the short run, but in the long run, they still depend on creativity for their survival. This is often due to the blind focus on efficiency, doing things as quickly as possible, while aiming ample attention on questions such as how and why only ever so often.

This chapter takes a closer look at cultural centers and whether they are active in the field of making business or in the field of making arts, or as likely, in both. Unlike Chapter 8, with seemingly the same focus, this chapter aims attention on describing the settings of the arts field and the dichotomy of the business and arts, whereas Chapter 8 focuses less on the aspect of dichotomy and more on quality instead of merely art. Furthermore, the somewhat playful title of this chapter is not all about a dichotomy. This chapter will, as a matter of fact, also be looking into both aspects of the title, where one side is the profitability of arts and the other is the aim for efficiency in doing business. Rephrasing the aim in a question would result in the following; should cultural centers focus on arts or business, or both – and why? The cultural centers are as many other arts organizations in between these opposite ends and need to know how to navigate in both worlds.

4.1 Business and arts

During the past decades both scientists and strategists have highlighted creativity as the very source for development within companies (Basadur, 2004; Ford, 2002; Reiter-Palmon & Illies, 2004). This is very much in contrast with the historic paradigm where creativity was merely seen as something irrational and conflicting with good management (Lataif et al., 1992; Mintzberg & Sacks, 2004; Pech, 2001). Art has however been given an increasing amount of attention during the recent years, especially how it could contribute to business organization, as well as marketing

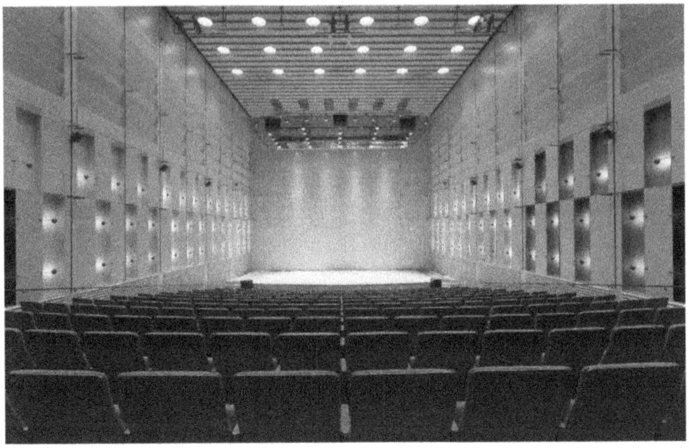

Picture 4.1 The hall of cultural center Korundi in Rovaniemi, Finland.

and strategy. The implications seem to be among other that exposure to art positively effects profitability and marketing skills, both internal and external company relationships and the development of organizational culture and leadership (Berthoin Antal & Strauß, 2013; Eriksson, 2009; Katz-Buonincontro, 2008). Nonetheless, ever so often it seems as if the pursuit is to separate arts from creativity and sort of cherry-pick the side that does not seem too 'anti-business'. This book would like to claim that business depends utterly on art. Change is the constant (see Chapter 5), and without creative breakthroughs, companies deteriorate.

Scott Adams (1996, p. 324) said that '*Creativity is allowing yourself to make mistakes. Art is knowing which ones to keep*'. Creativity and art are separate yet interconnected; creativity within business has been defined as the production of innovative and appropriate solutions to organizational problems (Amabile, 1997; Gryskiewicz & Taylor, 2003). As organizations increasingly have recognized the benefits of creativity, quite a few art programs have been engaged in workplaces as a new method to generate innovation (Berthoin Antal & Strauß, 2013). The literature on approaches like these are however limited and neither is it the focus of this book. Nevertheless, what is of interest is the connection between arts, creativity and business. A large number of studies have anyhow found a correlation between engagement in artistic activities and the capacity for divergent and imaginative thinking (Chamorro-Premuzic et al., 2009; Feist & Brady, 2004; Furnham & Avison, 1997; Rawlings et al., 2000). These findings contribute with a theoretical support for the assumption of a positive relationship between arts and business.

What about the apparent paradox between the artistic and business-related needs? Eikhof and Haunschild (2007) stated that arts and business have to be combined even though the danger of contradictory elements that might damage one another. The demand of making money might weaken the position of the art, which in turn could be diminished to a product of repetition with no connection to creative behavior. Still, the same applies the other way around, where the business side, which includes not only profitability per se but also the creation of new workplaces, could be impossible if the artistic goals become the sole commitment (Hirsch, 1972). This is of course hardly surprising. But is the dichotomy between art and business more of a false dichotomy? Making money alongside anything else, say raising a family, would arguably present the same friction as making money and arts. Still, you do not have to convince anybody about the necessity in making enough money in order to pay your bills while raising your family. Neither will you solely let the money-making dictate the fostering of your children. It is an interchange, as with everything else. Oversimplifications like these often overshadow the complicated relationship between multiple different types of practices at play in a process such as one where the prizing of artistic creativity takes place. As a result, we will not focus on any form of dichotomy between arts and business, having settled for a frame of reference where both sides are equally important.

Even if many cultural centers do not acknowledge a friction between commercial and noncommercial activities, and for those that do sense a friction, managing competing priorities especially for space use is of importance (BOP Consulting 2018). The thing with cultural centers is that they are mainly situated in the field of arts (Silvanto et al., 2008). The creative economy is in turn not consistently recognized as a market economy but as a quid-pro-quo economy (Taalas, 2010). This is a Latin phrase meaning an exchange of goods or services, 'a favor for a favor' (Investopedia, 2020). This complicates entrepreneurship, business activities and the development of organizational forms in the field (Taalas, 2010). Then again, in the creative hybrid economy – not to be confused with the hybrid model cultural center presented above – actors tend to lean against both the quid-pro-quo and the market economy. Here, both economies work in synergy, adopting the best features from both, challenging the institutional boundaries of the field. The creative hybrid economy questions the prior views on ownership, revenue logic and the common practice of organizing, for instance, co-creations and peer networking. This chapter argues that this quid-pro-quo and market economy synergy can be seen among cultural centers in Finland. Due to resource scarcity (see Chapter 6), private centers may be moving towards the creative hybrid economy and thus diverging from current institutional forces (see Chapter 5) within the field of cultural centers. This movement is commonly the result of population changes and the role and status of the public sector, as well as continuous technical development and the internal dynamics of the cultural field.

Within the creative industries, where cultural centers are positioned, the work carried out is symbolic and produces experiential goods of nonutilitarian value (Townley et al., 2009). Arts organizations work with '*expressive or aesthetic tastes rather than utilitarian needs; their meaning and significance determined by the consumer's coding and decoding of value*' (Townley et al., 2009, p. 942). Creative cultural offerings are used and consumed differently than traditional goods, so there is uncertainty about their response to a presumed market. In fact, according to Chong (2008, p. 14), an arts organization should '*be in the business of helping to shape taste, which suggests leading rather than merely reacting*'. Furthermore, arts organizations do not consider economic equity to be as important as cultural equity, whereas institutions in the business of mass production have an opposite view on the matter (Halonen, 2011). As Baumol and Bowen pointed out in 1966, the creation of artwork is not correlated with productivity gains, the costs always grow over time, and revenue increases are limited by market forces, so the arts organization are likely to fall behind (Webb, 2017). Nevertheless, arts organizations need to be cost-effective and aim to diversify their funding sources and achieve efficiency in management structures in order to ensure financial stability without being guided by money (Chong, 2008). Quality and profitability, however, are not mutually exclusive (see Chapter 8). Cultural economics gained the status of a discipline in the 1960s with the works of William Baumol and William Bowen (1966) and their extensive analysis of cost structure in the arts. Regardless of the half century that has gone by since this study, many still argue that economics continues to overlook the creative industries (Throsby and Throsby, 2001). Which is astonishing, when you think that 3% of consumption expenditure by European Union households in the year of 2015 was used on culture-related goods and services (Eurostat, 2020).

4.2 Business of art: dealing with the profitability aspect

Whilst the art of business is becoming more colloquial, how is with the business of art? Well, income-producing possibilities for artists have grown considerably (Caplin, 1998). Simultaneously, both the tax laws and the art marketplace have changed, which makes it imperative that artists or those working in the field of arts grasp the business side of art – since there is no manna from heaven. Albeit some resistance amongst artists, there is clearly a change happening within the field of arts and business, a movement towards the business-minded artist (Hirvi-Ijäs et al., 2020). The same applies to arts organizations; social, economic and technological trends that continuously change influence how audiences participate in culture and the arts, as well as how the industry both presents and produces creative work (Townley et al., 2009). The call for collaboration with networks and stakeholders and for setting joint objectives will increase.

According to Paul Bogen (2018), there is what he likes to call a '*funding dependent culture*' amongst those private cultural centers that are members to Trans Europe Halls. Still, the centers only have 20% contributed income of their total income, and the rest is earned. Yet, as the finances are limited, only a small reduction in their earned (or contributed) income could be a survival question. With no or little reserves and uncertain income, many innovations might be too risky to make.

It seems as if there is awareness among the interview respondents of different ends of the spectrum interplaying in the everyday activities. Most respondents stress the importance of diversified, meaningful cultural offerings. Nevertheless, there is an underlying economy present in the actions of the centers.

> *Sometimes you simply cannot give a Saturday night to an event that would be of big interest to you, but knowing that the economic structure of the whole house is in principle strict, it will cost a lot and you know that it will not bear its own weight. [...] This we cannot do when we work within our framework.*
>
> (Respondent O)

Although a handful of the respondents representing all the centers seems to be aware of an economic reality that dictates some choices concerning cultural offerings, they equally emphasize the possibility to choose cultural content that supports the whole. Instead of choosing merely artists who sell tickets or perhaps are more artistically interesting but most likely will not sell many tickets, the centers aim to build a palette of artists with both qualities.

> *You need to select the right artist at the right time. It's definitely a really important thing, that you have a little knowledge about what kind of entertainment there is at the moment and complement it, I would say. Then you have the opportunity to ... the more successful events you have, the more events you have when you have a full house.*
>
> (Respondent T)

Several respondents believe that artists should be able to decide the content themselves, with no interference by the cultural center. One respondent even mentions that if the center has its own productions, he always tells the artists the budget in advance to create goodwill and understanding towards the imminent project. Another respondent state that he has different kinds of deals with the artists he books. Some get fully paid in advance; some gets a percentage of their normal fee and then share the ticket revenue. Others come solely on ticket risk. The point seems to be that these are deals made based on common agreement. The artists have the opportunity to decline, and if they come, they are aware of the deal. Cultural centers want to present a broad variety of artists, but given the economic reality of scarce resources, the centers handle situations with different deals. Additionally, all the centers rent their venues to external actors, thereby getting rent without risk and letting artists do whatever they want at the same time. Most of the centers still want to influence what they display and when.

Private cultural centers need to be involved in the region's networks connected to culture. Not only culture is stressed but also business as the centers aim to get earnings through business. Even though self-sufficiency and business earnings are emphasized repeatedly, the importance of businesses not being too market-driven is also highlighted. Private cultural centers must have their own vision about things.

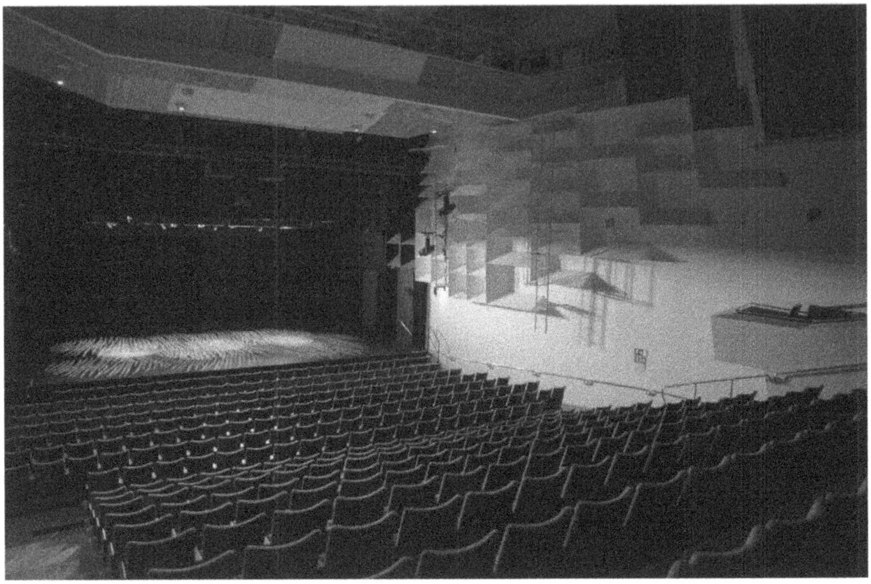

Picture 4.2 The main stage of cultural center Martinus in Vantaa, Finland. A photograph by Cata Portin.

There is also agreement on the idea of balancing cultural activities with business. Cultural activities are seldom a golden goose for the centers, so they need to balance their economy with their commercial operations, especially if public subsidies are low. The content of the cultural activities is repeatedly emphasized, even over the number of working hours the center can put into projects. Wages usually are the biggest expenses, so this is also one place to make savings. Private cultural centers usually work with modest resources, so some respondents highlight the need for the employees to have an ideological rather than a monetary approach to their work. This is also supported in the idea of reinforcing a culture of new ideas and a readiness to experiment, as even if an experiment is not economically efficient, it might be mentally or socially efficient.

4.3 Art of business: a pioneer mindset

In the interviews, clear activities of the private cultural centers emerge; weighing how to use the economic resources at hand and finding more interesting and more efficient ways of doing things. Furthermore, there is a notable critical attitude towards the municipality's approach to cultural offerings, which is not considered to be the most efficient way of producing cultural activities. The municipality should instead, according to some respondents, facilitate activities at the grass-roots level and ensure their continuity. The idea here is to have a distinct distance between the cultural offerings and the municipal organization and budget. This way, the money goes to the activities themselves, not merely to maintaining the public organization. In addition, the lack of sufficient time resources compels private center managers to choose the most efficient way of doing things as there is not time to do them insufficiently. Still, an openness among the respondents to new and exciting activities is highlighted:

> *You should not get stuck stirring the same soup. You need to constantly track how the field changes. In that way, if something new and interesting comes along, you should get involved.*
>
> (Respondent O)

The four walls of the center are not considered to be a necessity; the constant focus on networks and joint productions emphasize the outgoing, expansive sphere of the private cultural center. Nonconformity is highlighted as a niche to be versatile and offer what the municipality does not offer. The word *pioneer* is used frequently, emphasizing a need for private initiatives to offer cultural services missing in the municipal palette.

> *The word meaningful distinguishes this from entertainment in my point of view. I see that entertainment is really a different thing, and I myself enjoy entertainment, but it does not maybe generate significance in that sense or create new and renew stuff, but it is more of a replay. And that's why I use that word* meaningful. *And then with* impressive, *I mean that at best, some stuff becomes a phenomenon that grows in significance so much that a surface impact is created. It was what we were aiming at back then. [...] I think that we were in some sort of pioneer role back then and then piloted in good and in bad a new type of operating model.*
>
> (Respondent C)

When asked what the reaction would be if the respondents' centers would cease to exist, there was surprising agreement in the responses. The recurrent answer was that one's center itself probably would not leave such a drastic hole in society as some new group of private initiatives would take over its service. The need for culture among citizens is not questioned but, rather, the municipality's capability to satisfy this need. This is not to say that the respondents feel their centers do not have impacts on the society. Rather, instead of focusing on a specific center, the attention is simply aimed at the cultural services in society as a whole.

According to several respondents, one of the biggest challenges for cultural centers is competition with local public cultural centers, which have municipal security and support. Then again, this competition is not solely viewed as a negative thing:

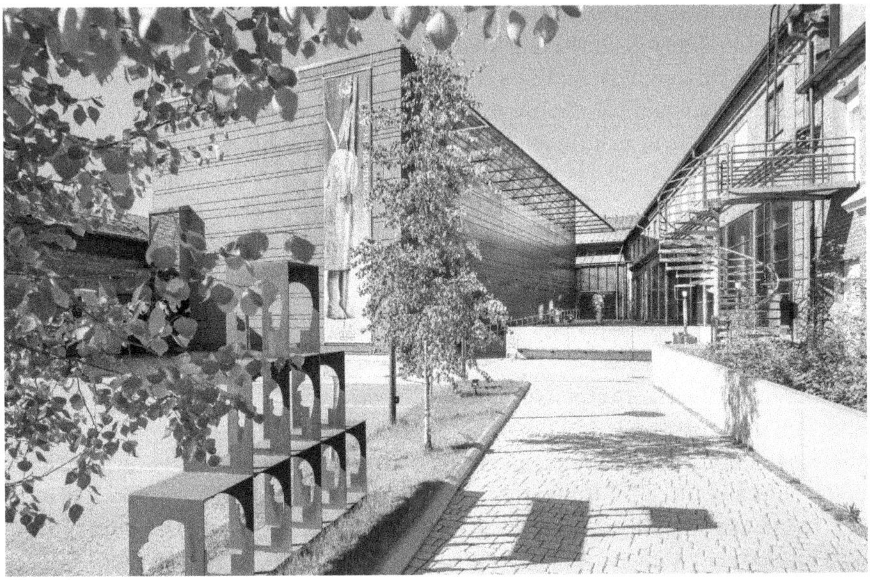

Picture 4.3 The front of cultural center Korundi in Rovaniemi, Finland.

> *It challenges to work harder, and to be a little more innovative when looking for new customers and to try to find ones true and own niche. So, despite being challenging, it's a positive challenge.*
>
> (Respondent H)

In other words, the respondents display a distinct pioneer mindset. Beyond being true to the mission, which is continually confirmed as producing versatile cultural and arts offerings to local inhabitants, the respondents aim to invent the way to do this. Their objective is to be part of a larger network and thus take advantage of what is happening in the field, but moreover, they seek to influence the field. As one respondent puts it, '*in that way, we have been involved and influenced and participated in that stream in what direction it goes*'. (Respondent E). The main issue is reinventing not art or culture but how to display it. The respondents repeatedly mention their ideas about changing the way to offer culture, even though they seem to be somewhat secretive about the outcomes:

> *We have one project that will be explored for next year, and maybe it will happen if there is one event and a coffee shop elsewhere [...]. And then I would be interested in this, like [an] event platform and the development of a production house model.*
>
> (Respondent C)

The interplay between business and arts is constantly underscored.

4.4 Summary and conclusions

Creativity has become what many believe to be the very source for development within companies, in contrast with the view where creativity was merely seen as something irrational and conflicting with good management. Creativity within business has however lately been defined as the production of innovative and appropriate solutions to organizational problems. In fact, a large number of studies have anyhow found a correlation between engagement in artistic activities and the capacity for divergent and imaginative thinking.

What comes to the paradox between the artistic and business-related needs? Well, the demand of making money might weaken the position of the art, which in turn could be diminished to a product of repetition with no connection to creative behavior. Still, the same applies the other way around, where the business side, which includes not only profitability per se but also the creation of new workplaces, could be impossible if the artistic goals become the sole commitment. The dichotomy between arts and business should rather be seen as a balance, as with everything else; both are needed for success. Arts organizations simply need to be cost-effective and aim to diversify their funding sources and achieve efficiency in management structures in order to ensure financial stability without being guided by money.

As with making money on arts, that is the business of arts, it seems as if many European centers have a good variety of revenues and only a 20% share of contributed income of their total income – the rest is earned. Respondents of the interviews for this book also emphasize that their cultural centers mission is not to make money from the cultural content but to display art that makes a difference within the community. Some even state that what they do would not be possible to do if the goal was to make profits. Nevertheless, there are also notions of having to conform to the rules of business to maintain their centers, having to comply with certain rules of business to have any chance of earning revenue.

Even more interesting than the possible aim for making money on the cultural content is the fact that most of the centers seem to have dodged the problem of being to business-oriented by creating purely business-oriented side-businesses supporting the main mission of producing arts. As one respondent summarized this: '*Alongside the restaurant business, we produce cheap cultural experiences*' (Respondent C). The idea of balancing cultural activities with business is obvious even if the respondents feel the need to highlight the arts.

In addition, the respondents do not think municipalities should produce cultural activities, rather facilitate such at grass-root level and ensure their continuity. This way the public resources would go to the activities, not to maintain expensive public institutions. Private organizations are simply more effective.

Lastly, we will intend to answer the question whether cultural centers should focus on arts or business, or both – and why? As it would appear, the dichotomy between arts and business is somewhat of the false sort, and the aim should be on maintaining a healthy approach to both. The business side needs a content to sell, and the arts need money to sustain and evolve. All in all, it seems as if there is a quite good balance between arts and business, being true to the mission while still displaying a distinct pioneer mindset. It would appear as if the cultural centers rather creatively organize their way of functioning in order to uphold as high standard as possible and a balance between the versatile offering of arts, culture and services, and maintaining a business approach to certain chosen aspects of the organizational activities, such as the restaurant.

References

Adams, S. (1996). *The Dilbert Principle*. New York: Harper.

Amabile, T.M. (1997). Entrepreneurial creativity through motivational synergy. Journal of Creative Behaviour, 31(1), pp. 18–26.

Basadur, M. (2004). Leading others to think innovatively together: Creative leadership. Leadership Quarterly, 15(1), p. 103.

Baumol, W.J., & W.G. Bowen (1966), *Performing Arts: The Economic Dilemma*. New York: The Twentieth Century Fund.

Berthoin Antal, A. & Strauß, A. (2013). Artistic interventions in organizations: Finding evidence of value-added. Creative Clash Report. Berlin: WZB.

Bogen, P. (2018). *Stronger Arts and Cultural Organisations for a Greater Social Impact. Business Models profiling of Cultural Centres & Performing Arts Organisations*. Sweden: Trans Europe Halles, Creative Lenses.

Bop Consulting (2018). *Business Model Innovation in Cultural Centres and Performing Arts Organisations*. Prepared for the Creative Lenses project, Trans Europé Halles

Caplin, L. (1998). *The Business of Art*. Englewood Cliffs, NJ: Prentice-Hall.

Casciaro, T., & Piskorski, M. (2005). Power imbalance, mutual dependence, and constraint, absorption: A close look at resource dependence theory. Administrative Science Quarterly, 50, pp. 167–199.

Chamorro-Premuzic, T., Reimers, S., Hsu, A., & Ahmetoglu, G. (2009). Who are thou? Personality predictors of artistic preferences in a large UK sample: The importance of openness. British Journal of Psychology, 100, pp. 501–516.

Chong, D. (2008). *Arts Management* (4 ed.). New York: Routledge.

DiMaggio, P., & Powell, W. (1983). The iron cage revisited: Institutional isomorphism and collective rationality in organizational fields. American Sociological Review, 48, pp. 147–160.

Eikhof, D.R., & Haunschild, A. (2007). For art's sake! Artistic and economic logics in creative production. Journal of Organizational Behavior, 28, pp. 523–538.

Eriksson, M. (2009). *Expanding Your Comfort Zone. The Effects of Artistic and Cultural Intervention on the Workplace. A study of AIRIS 2005–2008*. Göteborg: Institute for Management of Innovation and Technology.

Eurostat (2020). *Culture Statistics*. Online Eurostat publication. Accessed: 24.7.2020. Updated: 1.4.2020. Address: https://ec.europa.eu/eurostat/statistics- explained/index.php?title=Culture_statistics.

Feist, G.J., & Brody, T.R. (2004). Openness to experience, non-conformity, and the preference for abstract art. Empirical Studies of Arts. 22(1), pp. 77–89.

Ford, C.M., (2002). The futurity of decisions as a facilitator of organizational creativity and change. Journal of Organizational Change Management, 15(6), p. 635.

Froelich, K. (1999). Diversification of revenue strategies: Evolving resource dependence in Nonprofit organizations. Nonprofit and Voluntary sector Quarterly, 28(3), pp. 246–268.

Furnham, A., & Avison, M. (1997). Personality and preference for surreal paintings. Personality and Individual Differences, 23(6), pp. 923–935.

Gryskiewicz, S., & Taylor, S. (2003). Making creativity practical: Innovation that gets results for the practicing manager. *An Ideas into Action Guidebook*. Center for Creative Leadership, Greensborough.

Halonen, K. (2011). *Kulttuurituottajat taiteen ja talouden risteyskohdassa*. Jyväskylä: Jyväskylän Yliopisto.

Hirsch, P.M. (1972). *Processing fads and fashions: An organization-set analysis of cultural industry systems*. American Journal of Sociology, 77, pp. 639–659.

Hirvi-Ijäs, M., Kautio, T., Kurlin, A., Rensujeff, K., & Sokka, S. (2020). *Taiteen ja kulttuurin barometri 2019. Taiteilijoiden työ ja toimeentulon muodot*. Kulttuuripolitiikan tutkimuskeskus Cupore, Taiteen edistämiskeskus. Cuporen verkkojulkaisuja 57.

Investopedia (2020). *Quid Pro Quo*. Accessed: 25.9.2020). Available at: www.investopedia.com/terms/q/quidproquo.asp

Katz-Buonincontro, J. (2008). Using the Arts to promote creativity in leaders. Journal of Research on Leadership Education, 3(1), pp. 1–27.

Lataif, L.E., Mintzberg, H., Leonard, E.W., Saka, B., Steele, L.,& Haruyama, A., (1992). MBA: Is the traditional model doomed? Harvard Business Review, 70, p. 128.

Leblebici, H., Salancik, G., Copay, A., & King, T. (1991). Institutional change and the transformation of interorganizational fields: An organizational history of the U.S. radio broadcasting industry. Administrative Science Quarterly, 36, pp. 333–363.

Mintzberg, H. & D. Sacks 2004. The MBA menace. Fast Company, 83, pp. 31–32.

Oliver, C. (16 de 1991). Strategic responses to institutional processes. Academy of Management Review, 16(1), pp. 145–179.

Pech, R.J. (2001). Reflections: Termites, group behaviour, and the loss of innovation: Conformity rules! Journal of Managerial Psychology, 16(7/8), p. 559.

Pfeffer, J., & Salancik, G. (2003). *The External Control of Organizations: A Resource Dependence Perspective*. Stanford, CA: Stanford University Press.

Rawlings, D., Barrantes, I., Vidal, N. & Furnham, A. (2000). Personality and aesthetic preference in Spain and England: Two studies relating sensation seeking and openness to experience to liking for paintings and music. European Journal of Personality, 14(6), pp. 553–576.

Reiter-Palmon, R., & Illies, J. J. (2004). Leadership and creativity: Understanding leadership from a creative problem-solving perspective. Leadership Quarterly, 15, p. 55.

Silvanto, T., Linko, M., & Cantell, T. (14 de 2 de 2008). From enlightenment to experience; cultural centers in Helsinki neighbourhoods. International Journal of Cultural Policy, 14(2), pp. 165–178.

Taalas, S. (2010). *Kohti hybriditalouden haastetta. Keskustelua luavasta taloudesta Suomessa*. Työ- ja elinkeinoministeriön julkaisuja. Helsinki: Työ- ja elinkeinoministeriö.

Throsby, D., & Throsby, C. (2001). *Economics and Culture*. Cambridge: Cambridge University Press.

Townley, B., Beech, N., & McKinlay, A. (2009). Managing in the creative industries: Managing the motley crew. Human Relations, 62(7), pp. 939–1112.

Webb, D. (2017). Trends in the development and operation of PACs. Em P. Lambert, & R. Williams (Eds.), *Performing Arts Center Management* (pp. 45–62). New York: Routledge.

5 Institutional pressures and cultural center management

According to the Institutional Theory (IT), institutions work as forces upon individuals and organizations (DiMaggio & Powell, 1983). In practice, this happens by creating social pressures and restrictions, as well as setting boundaries for what is accepted and what is not.

Organizations along with institutions impact one another through their interplay within an organizational field. DiMaggio and Powell (1983) asked the question why organizations are so similar. Their answer was institutional pressures. In order to survive, the organizations assume similar processes and practices. The growing similarity of the organizations gives rise to an organizational field, distinct to isomorphism.

At the same time, there are indications of isomorphism working in reverse, which logically should be possible. Where do we find the different types of cultural centers in relation to isomorphism? Which institutional pressures do the centers suffer most from? Are there any ways of coping with these pressures?

This chapter will also study whether cultural centers are exposed to institutional pressures, and if the results differ depending on center type. The hypotheses for this quantitative part are:

H1: Public cultural centers experience more institutional pressure than private centers.

H01: Public cultural centers do not experience more institutional pressure than private centers.

But let us leave the question of institutional pressures aside for a moment and define some basic subjects first. In order to grasp the institutional pressures, it is important to understand how institutional theory and isomorphism works. Let us begin with these, then we dive into the pressures. Lastly, we will look upon how to deal with these pressures as an organization.

5.1 A glimpse into institutional theory

Organizations and institutions sharing the same goals generally have similar actions (Scott, 2014). IT suggests that change is triggered primarily by exogenous shocks that disrupt the current situation in a field and lead to periods of innovation. Institutional theory provides valuable guidelines for analyzing organizations, with an emphasis on expectations, norms, social rules and values as sources of pressure on organizations (Scott, 2014).

IT is a strand of organizational research in which researchers have employed an open systems perspective to understand organizations (Scott, 2014). In practice, the theory focuses on how the organization's environment both affects and interacts with the organization. IT traditionally is divided into old and new IT. In what has become a seminal work on old IT, an article entitled 'Foundations of the theory of organization', Selznick (1948) perceived organizations as organisms that adapt to environmental threats. He saw tension between the formal and informal structures inside organizations. These tensions were also in tension with the institutional environment, which can repeatedly undermine the legitimacy of the managers in an organization. The managers, in turn, may choose to co-opt the undermining environmental force to maintain legitimacy and survive. The consequence of this action is that the organization has to adapt to its environment (Selznick, 1948).

Both old and new IT focuses on how organizations adapt to forces in their institutional environment, especially in the action of maintaining legitimacy (DiMaggio & Powell, 1983). New IT supplements rather than contradicts old IT. A difference nonetheless can be detected. In the old perspective, conflict is a political process, and constraints are imposed by compromises with vested interests. In the new perspective, both the political process and constraints arise from legitimacy and present common understandings (Scott, 2008). Another difference is that the old theory views the concept of environment as loose and local, with multiples ties and treaties. The new theory, in contrast, sees the environment at the field level as nonlocal (Scott, 2014).

New IT created new paradigms to grasp how institutional pressures form organizations and stimulate organizational change (Meyer & Rowan, 1977). In what has become the fundamental work in new IT, the article 'Institutionalized organizations; formal structure as myth and ceremony', Meyer and Rowan (1977) argued that a formal structure emerges in organizations as they conform to institutional norms and beliefs in their organizational environment. When an organization conforms, it becomes restrained by rules and practices. These rules may not be efficient or the best organizational practices, but are a necessity for obtaining resources and surviving. The rules are simply a result of institutional pressures to appear legitimate.

DiMaggio and Powell (1983) expanded new IT by focusing on field-level institutional forces that increases organizational similarity over time. Organizations may adopt specific elements to seem normative within a field. This can also be done as a strategy to cope with uncertainty, for instance, by imitating those seen as the most successful in their specific fields. This is called institutional isomorphism. We will look upon isomorphism more closely in the following subchapter.

IT focuses on deeper aspects of social structure (Scott, 2014) and examines the mechanisms that establish structures (e.g. schemes, rules, norms and routines) as valid codes for social behavior. IT suggests that society consists of various institutions that give sense to and enforce conformity in social behavior, thereby influencing and limiting organizations' actions (Pache & Santos, 2010). As Suddaby (2010) put it:

> *The empirical reality is that organizations often behave in ways that defy economic logic or norms of rational behavior. And IT offers a paradigm devoted to understanding that.*
>
> (p. 15)

IT is considered to be a preeminent perspective within macroorganization theory (Greenwood et al., 2008). An organization is affected by institutions that draw from its external environment and from within the organization itself (Zucker, 1987; Scott, 2008). Along with social and cultural pressures, economic pressures that emerge from organizations' interactions in their institutional environments affect organizations (Meyer & Rowan, 1977).

There are many different approaches to IT (DiMaggio & Powell, 1991). Although there have been suggestions of a single paradigm for organizational studies, such umbrella-type institutionalism has also been criticized as the variety and complexity of the knowledge derived from organizational studies does not support it (Suddaby, 2010). Theories are developed for a diverse set of circumstances, and their premises and conclusions, as expected, echo these variations (Kingston & Caballero, 2009). For example, DiMaggio and Powell (1983) focused on organizations and the organizational field as units of analysis, whereas Schmidt (2010) focused on '*culturally specific practices*' or 'institutions' as the unit of analysis, with institutions made of the '*norms, cognitive frames, scripts, and meaning systems that guide human action*' (p. 10).

5.2 Why is institutional isomorphism still relevant?

Institutional isomorphism was presented by Powell and DiMaggio in their 1983 article 'The iron cage revisited' (DiMaggio & Powell, 1983). Institutional change was described as organizations and institutions becoming increasingly similar, also known as the process of isomorphism. This dominant perspective within IT seeks to explain how and why isomorphism happens.

In the beginning of the organization's lifecycle, it causes changes in the field in comparison to existing organizations, but it eventually finishes in institutional isomorphism to gain field stability (DiMaggio & Powell, 1983; Scott, 2014). '*Once an organizational field becomes well established, ... there is an inexorable push toward homogenization*' (DiMaggio & Powell, 1983, p. 148). The idea is that organizations adjust to *rationalized myths* of proper organizations in society (Meyer & Rowan, 1977; Boxenbaum & Jonsson, 2008). These myths are thought to be answers to problems on a wider scale, which become rationalized as they are perceived as appropriate solutions. The very same notion that organizations in the same environment become increasingly alike was introduced by Weber in 1916, who proposed that organizations are forced into similarity by the *iron cage of rationality* and the competitive forces in society (Greenwood et al., 2008). Isomorphism is an important alternative to efficiency-based explanations of organizational change in organization theory (Scott, 1987; Zucker, 1987).

DiMaggio and Powell (1983) defined the process of institutionalization by identifying three distinct mechanisms through which institutional isomorphism is achieved: (1) *coercive isomorphism*; (2) *mimetic processes*; and (3) *normative pressures*. They are treated as mechanisms for isomorphism rather than types or forms of isomorphism (Mizruchi & Fein, 1999). DiMaggio and Powell (1983) acknowledged that these analytically distinct mechanisms are empirically hard to separate. Furthermore, two or more might operate at the same time.

5.2.1 Coercive isomorphism

When an organization experiences institutionalized pressure to behave in a certain way from an organization on which it is dependent, this is called coercive isomorphism (DiMaggio & Powell, 1983). These pressures are considered by organizations to be forces for action, a sort of invitation to join collusion (DiMaggio & Powell, 1983), but also as threats of sanctions if not complied with (Boxenbaum & Jonsson, 2008). Coercive pressures can be a consequence of resource dependence, where the organization, for instance, has to adopt certain practices to be eligible for state grants (DiMaggio & Powell, 1983). Coercive pressures that can lead to organizational isomorphism include, for example, government mandates, the budget cycle, financial reporting requirements and regulatory agencies.

5.2.2 Mimetic processes

Organizations have a tendency to imitate others that appear to be successful and legitimate within their environment (DiMaggio & Powell, 1983). This isomorphic propensity is a result of mimetic pressures and often uncertain environments and unclear organizational objectives. Thus, when organizations perceive the correct course of action as unclear, they may mimic the actions of other organizations that appear to be legitimate (Mizruchi & Fein, 1999). This mimicking can go unnoticed by the organization mimicked and provides appropriate actions that a copying organization can make use of (DiMaggio & Powell, 1983). Mimicking has a favorable low cost in human capital. It provides a viable, low-cost solution to a problem due to an ambiguous environment. Of these three mechanisms, mimetic processes have received the most attention in research (Mizruchi & Fein, 1999).

5.2.3 Normative pressures

DiMaggio and Powell (1983) defined normative pressures as the result of professionalism within particular organizational fields, characterized as

> *the collective struggle of members of an occupation to define the conditions and methods of their work, to control the 'production of producers', and to establish a cognitive base and legitimation for their occupational autonomy.*
>
> (p. 70)

In other words, the operations of organizations can be influenced by employees' experiences in other organizations and education structures. One mode of legitimization thus is the interorganizational networks that span organizations. Meyer and Rowan (1977) and Zucker (1987) expressed the viewpoint that social processes assume a rule-like status in thought and deed (Scott, 1987). Social processes become the shared definition of social reality and evoke conformity with common understanding defining rational, appropriate behaviors. Similarly, Meyer and Rowan (1977), Zucker (1987) and DiMaggio and Powell (1983) discussed the development of institutional templates as a catalyst of isomorphism, leading to a high level of structural homogeneity among organizations. Although the concept of isomorphism suggests no real opportunity for the organization to differ from existing organizations within an organizational field, at least not in the long term, there is an articulated escape plan coined as *institutional entrepreneurs*, those who introduce change (DiMaggio, 1988).

Boxenbaum and Jonsson (2008) raised the question of what makes organizations more or less similar to each other. They challenged the notion of environment, asking: which is the relevant environment to which the organization reacts in isomorphism? In what ways are organizations presumed to become similar? Some answers may be found from Ostrom (2005), who presumes that due to the uncertainty surrounding founding of new institutions, most people are not willing to experiment with profound institutional changes. This argument is again in stark contrast to DiMaggio and Powell (1983) and Scott (2014), who argued that it is in the beginning of the lifecycle that organizations implement changes before ending up in institutional isomorphism. Furthermore, Hambrick, Finkelstein, Cho and Jackson (2005) questioned the current focus on observing isomorphism, in many cases, among organizations selected for their internal similarity.

DiMaggio and Powell (1983) emphasized coercive, mimetic and normative pressures as most essential sources of isomorphism. Here, both individuals and organizations are involved in a comparatively passive process of accepting institutionalized models in response to institutional pressures and thus become isomorphic to achieve external legitimacy. Friedland and Alford (1991), though, argued that institutional change is brought about by potential for individuals and organizations to not only reproduce institutional orders but also actively change them:

> *When institutions are in conflict, people may mobilize to defend the symbols and practices of one institution from the implications of changes in others. Or they may attempt to export the symbols and practices of one institution*

> *in order to transform another. [...] Thus the sources of change and resistance within institutions are just as likely to be found in the contradictions between them.*
>
> (p. 255)

DiMaggio and Powell (1983) indicated that if organizations expand their transactions with the state or, in this study, the municipality, this will increase isomorphism due to the rules, formality and standards of government agencies that enforce conformity. According to Hambrick, Finkelstein, Cho and Jackson (2005), expanding DiMaggio and Powell's (1983) argument could just as easily lead to greater differentiation among organizations if governmental influence diminished for some reason. Whereas early new institutionalist theory viewed the institutional process as somewhat a one-way effect on organizations, it is instead a dual-direction process as organizations are not consistently passive or powerless (Oliver, 1991; Powell, 1991; Scott, 2014). Facing institutional pressures, organizations can act in numerous ways, for example, by passively accepting or actively resisting pressures to adjust. This is very much what Oliver (1991) recognized in her five types of strategic responses: acquiescence, compromise, avoidance, defiance and manipulation.

Although the iron cage hypothesis has gained support over the years, there has been a shift towards recognition of heterogeneity within the institutional environment (Boxenbaum & Jonsson, 2008; Scott, 2014). Powell (1991) addressed this later but merely as a sort of error variance (Czarniawska, 2008). Hambrick, Finkelstein, Cho and Jackson (2005), Thornton and Ocasio (2008) and Dunn and Jones (2010) presented arguments that organizations become more heterogeneous, not more homogeneous, as DiMaggio and Powell (1983) stated. The isomorphism in reverse that Hambrick, Finkelstein, Cho and Jackson (2005) presented shows an alternative or an expansion of the isomorphic viewpoint of DiMaggio and Powell (1983), in which macrocultural forces actually diminishes isomorphic pressure on organizations. The iron cage hypothesis, which focuses on how contextual forces affect the extent of homogeneity within an organizational field, highlights how increasing contextual forces lead to increased homogeneity. However, this hypothesis neglects the compatible logic that decreasing contextual forces lead to decreased homogeneity – in other words, heterogeneity within an organizational field.

Furthermore, how is transmission of such new practices even possible in an isomorphic institutional field? This question is partly explained by the concept of power (DiMaggio & Powell, 1983): only institutions that have adequate resources are capable of introducing institutional change. However, DiMaggio and Powell (1983) stated that it is usually new organizations that introduce changes, which does not explain how power could be a sole explanation to the problem at hand. Boxenbaum and Jonsson (2008) argued that there is very little evidence on institutional isomorphism: The '*extant evidence is simply not conclusive*' (Boxenbaum & Jonsson, 2008, p. 79).

5.3 How do the institutional pressures work?

This section introduces the external forces, or institutional pressures, laid upon organizations in a specific field. Institutions act as forces upon individuals and organizations, developing social pressures and constraints and setting limits for all things accepted and not accepted (DiMaggio & Powell, 1983). These influences can be in the shape of normative, coercive and mimetic pressures (Davidsson et al., 2006; DiMaggio & Powell, 1983), as discussed earlier in Subchapter 5.3. Oliver (1991) constructed a typology of responses to institutional pressure based on the following questions: why are pressures applied? Who is applying them? What kinds of pressures are they? How are they applied? Where do they occur? All these questions are related to the predictive factors influencing the choice of strategy (i.e. acquiescence, compromise, avoidance, defiance and manipulation). This typology indicates a new institutional perspective as it highlights the deliberate capacity of organizations as they strategically counter the demands of their environment. Oliver (1991) noted that there has been very little research on the flexibility of organizational responses to institutional pressures. She proposed that researchers should critically examine early institutional frameworks, which, in turn, has emphasized the passive role of organizations within institutional environments. Oliver (1991) thus challenged the hypothesis of early institutionalists by simplifying the ways that organizations can (and usually even do) take action to change, influence and resist institutional pressures. She did this by presenting five distinct types of organizational strategic responses to institutional processes while focusing on managing the institutional context.

5.3.1 Acquiescence

This response consists of complete compliance with taken-for-granted norms, accepting and obeying rules of the field and mimicking models promoted and endorsed by the field (Oliver, 1991). This may happen through habit, compliance or imitation. Habit is unconscious adherence to accepted norms and values. Compliance is conscious obedience to institutional requirements, norms or values. Imitation is organizations' mimicking of successful organizations within their environment.

5.3.2 Compromise

This response is adopted by organizations when they face conflicting institutional demands or inconsistencies between institutional and organizational goals and demands (Oliver, 1991). Compromise is a sign of partial compliance. This response in intended to balance, bargain or pacify institutional demands through negotiation with institutional stakeholders. When balancing, the organization plays institutional actors against each other. Bargaining is accommodating some institutional elements and discussing compromises with institutional actors at the same time. To pacify is to partially conform to one or more constituents to pacify any threats.

5.3.3 Avoidance

This strategy incorporates activities that to some extent disguise or absorb organizational disagreement with institutional norms (Oliver, 1991). If organizations use such an approach, they may aim to alleviate their institutional attachments in order to modify the goals or activities the institutional context forces upon them. Avoidance may be done through concealing, buffering or escaping. Concealing is symbolic compliance to institutional norms or procedures. Buffering involves reducing institutional inspections from outsiders. The organization can also escape conformity by changing its goals, activities or physical location (DiMaggio & Powell, 1983).

5.3.4 Defiance

In this response, organizations take actions directly challenge or attempt to shape institutional requirements. Oliver (1991) presented three methods of defiance: dismissal, challenge and attack. The organization may altogether ignore institutional pressures when, for instance, these norms differ dramatically from organizational values. They also challenge the rules, norms and expectations of the institutional environment to enforce their own vision, especially if these rules are not broadly shared. To attack is to actively resist. The organization can try to change institutional values by denouncing or belittling them.

5.3.5 Manipulation

Manipulation is the most active strategy and encompasses organizational recognition and understanding of institutional rules and their value to organizational sustainability (Oliver, 1991). This response requires that the organization has a dominant position within the institutional context. The methods of manipulation are influence and control. In influencing, the organization may try to change the acceptable practices by, for instance, lobbying the government. In controlling, the organization may try to establish dominance and power over the source of institutional pressures, forcing it to change (Pfeffer & Salancik, 2003).

The five distinct organizational responses presented in Figure 5.1 are also in focus while analyzing the empirical material in this book. In contrast to the framework for organizational strategic responses presented by Oliver (1991) stands the already-presented view of isomorphism, in which organizations have much less room to influence their development and position within their organizational field.

Oliver's (1991) model introduces some problems, according to Reale and Seeber (2010). For example, the predicting factors can foretell conflicting responses but cannot determine which one is accurate as there is no ranking of the responses (Reale & Seeber, 2010). In other words, there is no possibility of full acquiescence as it is not possible for both responses to work alongside each other. Oliver's (1991) typology is grounded on the assumption that organizations

Passive Conformity	◄	———————	►	**Active Resistance**
Acquiescence	**Compromise**	**Avoidance**	**Defiance**	**Manipulation**
Imitation	Bargain	Buffer	Attack	Control
Habits	Balance	Conceal	Dismiss	Co-opt
Comply	Pacify	Escape	Challenge	Influence

Figure 5.1 Responses to institutional pressures.
Adapted from: Jamali (2010).

do not change their habits. If they have nothing to gain, organization will not participate in processes. This assumption is overturned occasionally as organizations may have something to lose if they do not change, according to Reale and Seeber (2010). Furthermore, pressures need to be clearly defined in order for the typology to fully work, as would be hard to do, for example, if analyzing organizational reactions to funding cuts.

5.4 Institutional change

Every strand of IT has its own specific features (Amenta & Ramsay, 2010), but all still try to explain from different perspectives the causal relationship between distinct effects in society and higher-order conditions. This chapter highlights sociological theory, which, according to Hodgson (2006), sees institutions as '*systems of established and prevalent social rules that structure social interactions*' (p. 2). Researchers have long debated the concepts of change and transformation (Mazza & Strandgaard Pedersen, 2004).

Institutions are somewhat stable social arrangements and practices through which collective actions are taken (Suddaby & Greenwood, 2009). A social arrangement is institutionalized when it is practiced extensively, resistant to change and undisputed. When a set of institutional arrangements is exchanged with another or reshaped substantially, institutional change occurs. This can occur for both external and internal reasons (Scott, 2008). External reasons for change, which can be political, social or economic, are interruptions in neighboring systems that undermine current rules and perceptions. Among internal reasons for change are gaps and discrepancies between macrosystems and microactivities in reactions to local situations, expectations not met by persistent poor performance levels, and conflicts between institutional elements and competing frameworks.

Institutional change, however, usually is incremental, not abrupt (North, 1990). New practices emerge when creative organizations collect the benefits of new methods (Meyer & Rowan, 1977; Mahoney & Thelen, 2009). At the same time, organizations are said to be affected by institutions through regulations. Organizations endure by adjusting to the institutional norms (Meyer, et al., 1983) and social expectations of the environment (DiMaggio & Powell, 1983; Meyer

& Rowan, 1977). Even institutions that endure a long time are not immune to change. However, if actors, through their actions, actively create social structures that are themselves socially constructed, and if these actors also have the ability to both change and create new institutions, this poses a paradox to resolve: *'How can actors change institutions if their actions, intentions, and rationality are all conditioned by the very institution they wish to change?'* (Holm, 1995, p. 398). As Scott (2014) put it:

> *Change poses a problem for institutional theorists, most of whom view institutions as the source of stability and order. If the nature of actors and their modes of acting are constituted and constrained by institutions, how can these actors change the very institutions in which they are embedded?*
>
> (p. 181)

Institutional change was conceptualized as a six-stage process by Greenwood, Suddaby and Hinings (2002), a process presented in Table 5.1. In stage 1, the institution likely undergoes jolts that destabilize norms and established practices. In stage 2, a process of deinstitutionalization commences and interferes with the socially constructed consensus. Stage 3 is the preinstitutionalization level, where innovations that may come to replace the previous norms and practices are introduced. In stage 4, also called the theorization period, the institution develops the pragmatic and moral legitimate arguments for the new norms and practices. Next, in stage 5, the new norms are spread among other organizations in the field. Finally, stage 6 is the reinstitutionalization phase when the new norms and practices gain cognitive acceptance and become taken for granted (Greenwood et al., 2002).

Scott (2014) highlighted that IT as a whole is built on the notion that organizations are open to their social and cultural environment. In fact, much of the literature considers institutional change to be an evolutionary Darwinian process of variation, selection and inheritance (Kingston & Caballero, 2009). Still, the cultural contexts in which organizations are active are often viewed as permanent, which suggests that actors do not always recognize or reflect upon the cultural contexts (Suddaby & Greenwood, 2009). This assumption, in turn, supports Veblen's theory from 1889, the old institutionalism, which holds that institutional change is driven by changes in population and technology, so institutions never completely adapt to the demands of the present and are subject to constant change (Veblen, 2009). Continuous change is also supported (Dacin et al., 2002). Nevertheless, Czarniawska (2008) emphasized that continuous change is a feature of old institutionalism, whereas stability is the norm according to new institutionalists, who have not adequately explained the issue of change. Consequently, the persistence of institutions is identified by many as the very thing that makes institutions meaningful (North, 1990; Scott, 2008). This persistence, though, also prevents attempts at institutional change, at least theoretically, and makes all changes profoundly gradual.

Table 5.1 Stages of institutional change

Stages	*Characteristics*
1. Precipitating jolts	Regulatory, social or technological events that destabilize practices
2. Deinstitutionalization	Rise of new actors Dominance of players Institutional entrepreneurship
3. Preinstitutionalization	Technical viability predominant Independent innovation
4. Theorization	Specification of accepted organizational shortcoming Justification of conceptual possible solution Moral and/or pragmatic solution
5. Diffusion	Growing objectification Pragmatic legitimacy
6. Re-institutionalization	Cognitive legitimacy

Source: Greenwood et al. (2002).

The theory of institutional change has been criticized for its lack of understanding contemporary changes (Greenwood et al., 2008; Streeck & Thelen, 2005). Earlier, institutions were often seen as immutable entities (Dacin et al., 2002; Greenwood et al., 2008) in the midst of homogenization (Dacin et al., 2002). However, a growing number of studies today have pointed towards institutions as dynamic and somewhat political processes (Greenwood et al., 2008; Streeck & Thelen, 2005). According to Czarniawska (2008), the common institutional view has become that change takes place within boundaries made up by institutional thought structures. However, a vast number of changes still occur, and among the unforeseeable changes are radical ones. This implies that other factors are at play in addition to the institutional pressures of an organizational field.

To illustrate the interdependence between organizations in a specific domain, the idea of an organizational field has been presented (Scott, 1994). Organizations become more homogeneous over time as they strive to gain legitimacy within their environment, according to IT (DiMaggio & Powell, 1983). In a process known as isomorphism, the institutional context offers organizations a *template for organizing* (DiMaggio & Powell, 1991, p. 27). Organizational fields nevertheless may vary in both the structure and the strength of the institutional pressure exercised within them (Tolbert, 1985; Battilana et al., 2012). Organizations, however, are to an increasing extent seen as active agencies (Oliver, 1991) that may respond to institutional pressures in a variety of ways. Oliver's (1991) ideas correlate to field-level dynamics.

Leblebici, Salancik, Copay and King (1991) drew the conclusion that the organization of a field is not perpetual but is conditional to institutionalized definitions of the things that are transacted. Rather than looking at fields as stable, they are viewed as in a state of constant change (Thornton & Ocasio, 2008). Thus, institutional complexity is accepted and regarded as the instrument for institutional change rather than enduring institutional stability. According to Suddaby (2010), contemporary organization theorists nevertheless focus merely on change as the favored outcome and overlook the aspects of institutionalization that maintain institutions and create stability.

Meyer and Rowan (1977) discussed that any attempt to change institutional environments can advance in two dimensions. The first dimension is where powerful organizations compel their networks to adjust to their practices, much like DiMaggio's (1988) concept of power. The second dimension also includes powerful organizations, especially those associated with the state, that seek to impose their goals and practices onto society as institutional rules. Here, we can draw a parallel with the public cultural centers. If we put aside the unilateral view of powerful organizations as the only possible game-changers, Leblebici et al. (1991) raised a second theoretical problem:

> *Why do those who occupy the positions of power in the existing institutions willingly change its practices? Their self-interests are isomorphic with the prevailing practices, and they would have the most to lose.*
>
> (p. 377)

Leblebici et al. (1991), in a sense, thus, paved the way for the *embedded paradox* (Holm, 1995): how actors can change institutions if their actions, intentions and rationality are all conditioned by the very institution they wish to change?

DiMaggio (1988) tried to give an answer to this question by explaining that the

> *success of an institutionalization process creates new ... legitimated actors who... pursuing distinct interests, tend to delegitimize and deinstitutionalize aspects of the institutional forms to which they owe their autonomy and legitimacy.*
>
> (p. 13)

This leads to an uneven distribution of resources, and a number of actors has to look for other alternatives (Leblebici et al., 1991). DiMaggio (1988) also referred to this scenario, acknowledging that standards might not be consistently applied as they might not appeal to every organization.

What, though, if the constant change is not a change other than in comparison to the boundaries of the original organizational field? Where do we draw the outer limits for an organizational field? When is change merely a shift in paradigms within an organizational field, and when is it a split into two organizational fields? Private cultural centers appear to have presented an alternative method for the field, with contrasting funding and content. With a different structure, they have also introduced a different set of dependencies into the original field of cultural centers in Finland.

5.5 Managing a cultural center through the minefield of institutional pressures

As the prior chapters has presented, institutional theorists claim that the organizations' needs to conform to external pressures are directly related to their pursue for legitimacy. Resources are crucial for organizations, something we will discuss further in Chapter 6, and external actors may hence allocate resources to organizations while thinking that these organizations are legitimate, needed or appropriate (Deephouse and Suchman, 2008). Accordingly, organizations will conform with coercive, mimetic and normative pressures by adjusting their internal organizational practices and structures to become consistent with external norms and buffer criticism (Meyer and Rowan, 1977). By doing so, organizations become isomorphic with similar organizations in their field (DiMaggio and Powell, 1983).

Nonetheless, isomorphism contributes to homogeneity and makes it more difficult for organizations to emphasize their characteristics features (DiMaggio and Powell, 1983). Institutional pressures to change, if they are adopted, may negatively affect the internal routines that bring about organizational efficiency. It is therefore probable that some organizations adopt visible structures of compliance, structures that do not change ongoing practices, merely to move the spotlight away from allegations of illegitimacy (Elsbach and Sutton, 1992). There are many such cases of ceremonial practices in the literature (e.g. Boxenbaum and Jonsson, 2008; Orton and Weick, 1990).

If the management of an organizations decides to decouple from external pressures of change, it is a sign of its endeavor to maintain its current identity and isolate the values asserted by the external pressure (Kraatz and Block, 2008). The institutional pressures to change may not always be in line with the core values of the organization, wherefore the conflict between the organizational and institutional identity can motivate both the organization as well as its members to dismiss the values of the latter (Sauder and Espeland, 2009).

Organizational responsiveness to institutional pressures will in other words be contingent only on the extent of how the organization agrees with such goals (Oliver, 1991). Therefore, when an organization expects that conformity will add to its social legitimacy, that is, its social responsibility or accountability, acquiescence to institutional prospects will be the most feasible response (Oliver, 1991).

Thus, research indicates that the organization itself is the judge of what is to come. Whether the decision is to comply or to resist, it has to be a decision founded in the core values of the organization, otherwise you will find yourself pushing daisies in no time. Therefore, the cleverest thing to do is to listen to what the field of the cultural centers has to offer.

According to nearly every interview respondent, the private cultural centers mostly struggle with issues concerning money, product pricing, subsidies and lack of sufficient audiences. Those cultural centers that have their own restaurants seem to be very focused on how that business is succeeding as it is a cornerstone of their economy. Thus, current legislation is considered to be an influencing factor:

> *Legislation per se, a framework like time, how long is your event allowed to continue, and how to handle the serving of alcohol and perhaps such general decrees.*
>
> (Respondent D)

The private cultural centers have sole liability for their economy, so a central issue among factors exerting pressure on the centers are ticket sales to their own productions. Even if the private cultural centers have considerable private or municipal funding, their offerings of cultural activities still rest to a significant degree on ticket sales. The centers, therefore, have to constantly rely on conscious risk-taking to attract audiences and aim to balance the cultural offerings between less risky and pioneering offerings.

> *Overall, in Finland, they [ticket sales] have declined. For five years, maybe. Often, during the recession, people focused even more consumption than culture as it was inexpensive and produced good spirits. [...] I believe that the future can be found in interesting cultural content. But perhaps so that this interest is weighed more and more every day, every night, every performance.*
>
> (Respondent C)

The strategic response of private cultural centers seems to be straightforward defiance, according to the respondents. As they detect a problem, they consider the best solution, whereupon the decision is made. It is of upmost importance for the centers to be able to make own decisions rapidly. There still seems to be a somewhat unspoken discontent about the public centers receiving such a large share of subsidies for doing the same work the private centers do. And when the private centers do get grants, they come with restrictions as to what is to be done with that money. The private centers consider the public centers existing in a different reality than theirs, with a lot more restrictions than them

One of the centers, with a quite substantial palette of activities, notices that many of its activities have to compete with every other private actor in the city. Although its activities are in line with its mission as a cultural center, there are specialized private actors with much broader offerings of specific services, such as office rentals. The center tried to rent offices to cultural actors, but as the offices of other private actors did not differ in any way, the rental prices were the decisive factor. The center then decided not to rent any office space and rather go in for cinema activity, thus compromising and directing attention elsewhere.

A respondent concludes that private centers have to consider the flow of customers, which influences the decisions it makes. Even if there is a possibility to react beyond the frames of an accepted mission statement, it, however, is not a decision to be made based only on the preferences of the board or employees; the surrounding environment must also be considered. Private centers have no

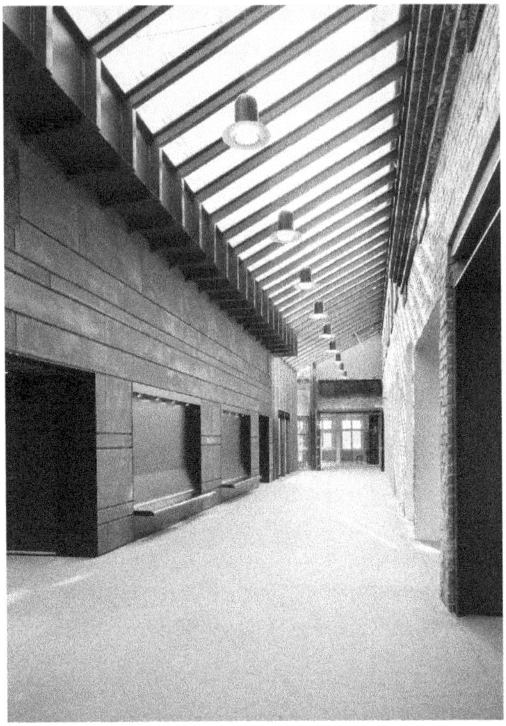

Picture 5.1 The foyer of cultural center Korundi in Rovaniemi, Finland.

municipal safety nets, so they cannot face too many economic setbacks. The same respondents repeatedly mention the need to monitor every activity to prevent economic catastrophe. This seems to be said in awareness that most private entrepreneurs need to do so, but with an implication of differences with private centers, where the repertoire is constantly undergoing significant changes. None of the respondents subscribes to a unilateral view of cultural offerings, which increases economic risk and decreases the possibility for steady revenue. It, though, appears that many respondents view the scarce resources among private centers as a stimulus for better decision-making.

> *I feel it's an advantage, not having as good basic resources [...] as the public sector. [...] We have a better chance of doing things that are considered necessary for the development of this area. [...] At the end of the day, the question is about people's expertise, and we have the chance to use a freelancer network quite widely, which may not be so easy in the public sector.*
>
> (Respondent A)

This economic pressure on private cultural centers, however, generates a need to be as effective as possible and to find a novel area for business. As a few respondents mention, they simply cannot afford not to do what they do efficiently. It, though, is not exclusively about doing things in a less expensive way. It is also about justifying the work they do in economic terms and finding their own niche in the market of cultural offerings. They even stress the importance of not being as insufficient as municipal service.

> *To find the right balance [...] of a business model that is commercially sound enough, functional and sufficiently interesting, and would you say, divergent. [...] We would want to depart from the traditional entertainment providers, in which can be counted, for instance, typical gig venues or even cinemas. Or even amusement parks, the producers of traditional municipal cultural services, [...] including city libraries, city theatres, city cultural centers, city museums, city art museums and city orchestras. So, from our point of view, there is an interesting area between these two worlds, that has something of each of these worlds but builds its own entity.*
>
> (Respondent C)

One respondent emphasizes that from the very beginning, the center's mission has been not to copy or adapt existing activities but to be a pioneer in everything. It reacts quickly and alters its plans if it, for instance, gets a hint of a new production

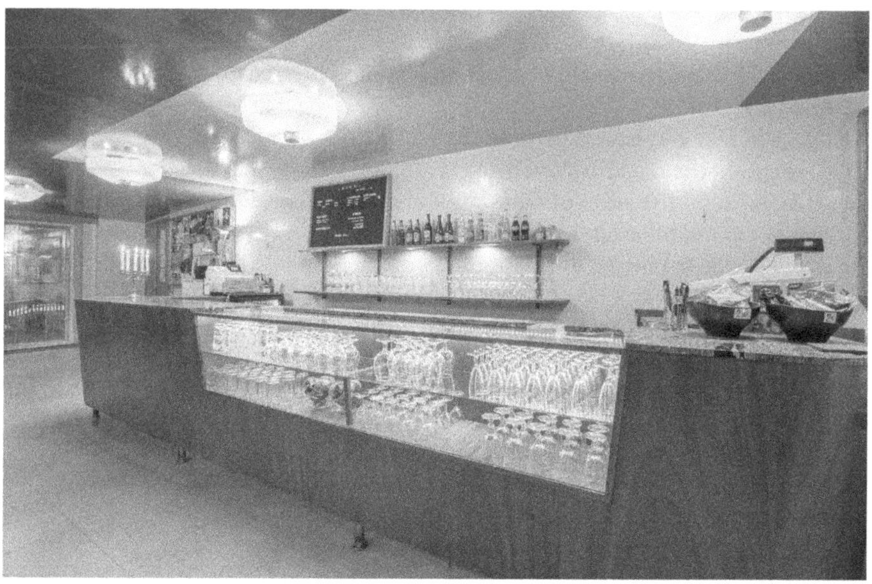

Picture 5.2 The bar counter at cultural center Ritz in Vaasa, Finland. A photograph by Valter Lidsle.

abroad. This seems to be a general mission of all the private centers and can be understood as a prime agenda in most interviews. The main point is not only to have diverse cultural and arts offerings nor to alter the audiences' perception of arts but also to find a new way to do so and fill gaps in the current offerings of leisure-time cultural activities.

5.6 Institutional pressures according to center type

In this subchapter, the aim is to study whether cultural centers are exposed to institutional pressures, and if the results differ depending on center type. In the theoretical part of this chapter (Subchapter 5.1), institutional pressures are considered to take place as institutions exert forces upon individuals and organizations, developing social pressures and constraints and setting limits for acceptability.

The hypotheses are:

H1: Public cultural centers experience more institutional pressure than private centers.

H01: Public cultural centers do not experience more institutional pressure than private centers.

The variables used in this construct are:

1) *Environmental pressure to change*
(Do you experience that society places any pressures on your centre to change?)
2) *Changed expectations local inhabitants*
(Have the expectations of the local inhabitants changed during the last years?)
3) *Need for change*
(Do you feel you have a need to change?)
4) *Changes in the administration*
(Has the administration of your cultural center changed in recent years?)
5) *Effect/local inhabitants*
(How do the following entities affect your activities: local inhabitants?)
6) *Effect/state*
(How do the following entities affect your activities: the state?)
7) *Effect/municipality*
(How do the following entities affect your activities: Municipality?)
8) *Economic effect/taxes*
(How much do the following things affect your activities: taxes?)
9) *Effect/funders*
(How do the following entities affect your activities: funders?)
10) *Contest private/public*
(In your opinion, do you have to compete with municipal cultural services?)

All the variables were based on a 5-point Likert scale. Cronbach's alpha was used to establish the internal consistency and reliability of all the items. The reliability coefficient values are .707 for these 10 items.

5.6.1 Mann–Whitney U*-test*

The results were analyzed with Mann–Whitney *U* test as the data were partly skewed and not normally distributed according to Shapiro–Wilk test. Statistical significance is acceptable, at the 95% level. This study compared the medians of the Likert test survey, revealing the perceived view on institutional pressure between private and public centers.

The p-value is the estimated probability of rejecting the null hypothesis of a research question when that null hypothesis is false. For this thesis, the null hypothesis is that there is no difference in how private and public cultural centers identify institutional pressures. The null hypothesis is rejected if the p-value is smaller than $\alpha = 0.05$. Smaller p-values suggest that the null hypothesis is less likely to be true; in other words, there are differences in the perceived institutional pressure.

Mann–Whitney *U* test (Table 5.2) shows a significant difference in the perceived institutional pressure between the two cultural centers groups in the following four items (those with significant values).

Descriptive statistics show that public cultural centers (median = 3.50; M rank = 44.23) score higher on environmental pressure to change than private centers (median = 3.00; M rank = 34.11). Mann–Whitney *U* value is found to be statistically significant (U = 564.500 (Z =-2.009); $p < 0.045$), and the difference between the public and private centers is small (Z/sqrt N = R = .226). Furthermore, public cultural centers (median = 4.00; M rank = 45.75) score higher on affect/municipality than private centers (median = 3.00; M rank = 28.14). The Mann–Whitney *U* value is found to be statistically significant (U = 367.500 (Z = -3.608);

Table 5.2 Mann–Whitney *U* test on institutional pressures

Quantitative statistically significant results by center type (Mann–Whitney U test)

	Center type	*Median*	*Mean rank*	*U*	*Z*	*p*	*R*
Environmental pressure to change	**Private**	3,00	34,11	564,500	-2,009	0,045	,226
	Public	3,50	44,23				
Effect / Municipality	**Private**	3,00	28,14	367,500	-3,608	0,000	,417
	Public	4,00	45,75				
Need for change	**Private**	3,00	33,45	543,000	-2,261	0,024	,254
	Public	3,50	44,70				
Economic effects / taxes	**Private**	3,00	46,39	416,000	-3,071	0,002	,355
	Public	2,00	31,40				

$p < 0.001$), and the difference between public and private centers is considerable ($R = .417$). Public cultural centers (median = 3.50; M rank = 44.70) also score higher on need for change than private centers (median = 3.00; M rank = 33.45). The Mann–Whitney *U* value is found to be statistically significant ($U = 543.000$ ($Z = -2.261$); $p < 0.024$), and the difference between public and private centers is small ($R = .254$). Private cultural centers (median = 3.00; M rank = 46.39) score higher on economic affects/taxes than public centers (median = 2.00; M rank = 31.40). The Mann–Whitney *U* value is found to be statistically significant ($U = 416.000$ ($Z = -3.071$); $p < 0.002$), and the difference between public and private centers is notable ($R = .355$). All the Z score are negative because the ordering of the groups is not taken into account by this test in SPSS (IBM, 2016).

These results suggest that there are slight differences between private and public centers. Public centers seem to have more institutional pressure from their environment and from their owner, the municipality, whereas private centers experience bureaucratic pressures. Thus, the results suggest rejecting the null hypothesis for these four items.

The size of the subgroups hybrid and governmental organization is too small to test the significance of the M/median differences. The descriptive statistics still reveal some characteristics in hybrid centers that seem to be similar to private centers, whereas governmental organizations lean towards public centers. These claims are based on the differences in the Ms and SDs of the variable economical affect/taxes for private centers (M: 2.88, SD: 1.474) compared to hybrid centers (M: 3.17, SD: 1.329) and for public centers (M: 1.83, SD: .853) compared to governmental organizations (M: 1.58, SD: .900) and the differences in the Ms and SDs of the variable need for change for private centers (M: 3.06, SD: 1.088) compared to hybrid centers (M: 3.00, SD: 1.118) and for public centers (M: 3.59, SD: .884) compared to governmental organizations (M: 3.58, SD: 1.084).

5.7 Summary and conclusions

As we have learned in this chapter, organizations along with institutions impact one another through their interplay within an organizational field. According to isomorphism, organizations tend to end up quite similar due to institutional pressures. There are three distinct mechanisms through which institutional isomorphism is achieved: (1) *coercive isomorphism*; (2) *mimetic processes*; and (3) *normative pressures*. Institutional theory is a strand of organizational research which offers a perspective to understand organizations.

External forces, or institutional pressures, are laid upon organizations in a specific field. In practice, it is the institutions that act as forces upon individuals and organizations, developing social pressures and constraints and setting limits for all things accepted and not accepted. Organizations thereafter strategically counter the demands of their environment, by taking action to change, influencing and resisting institutional pressures. This happens through five possible responses to institutional pressures: acquiescence, compromise, avoidance, defiance and manipulation.

Organizational change is essential to institutional theory, as organizations are open to their social and cultural environment. Institutions themselves are somewhat table social arrangements and practices through which collective actions are taken. Change can still happen for both external and internal reasons. The change is usually incremental, not abrupt, and no organizations are immune to change. According to IT, organizations become more homogeneous over time as they strive to gain legitimacy within their environment.

This chapter brought forward three questions; where do we find the different types of cultural centers in relation to isomorphism? Which institutional pressures do the centers suffer most of? Are there any ways of coping with these pressures? Furthermore, this chapter also focused on the following hypotheses:

The hypotheses are:

H1: Public cultural centers experience more institutional pressure than private centers.

H01: Public cultural centers do not experience more institutional pressure than private centers.

Let us try to give some answers. Current theoretical perspectives and theories, as those presented in this chapter, express constructs that help explain trends towards either isomorphism or isomorphism in reverse within an organizational field. The qualitative results do not imply any isomorphism among the private

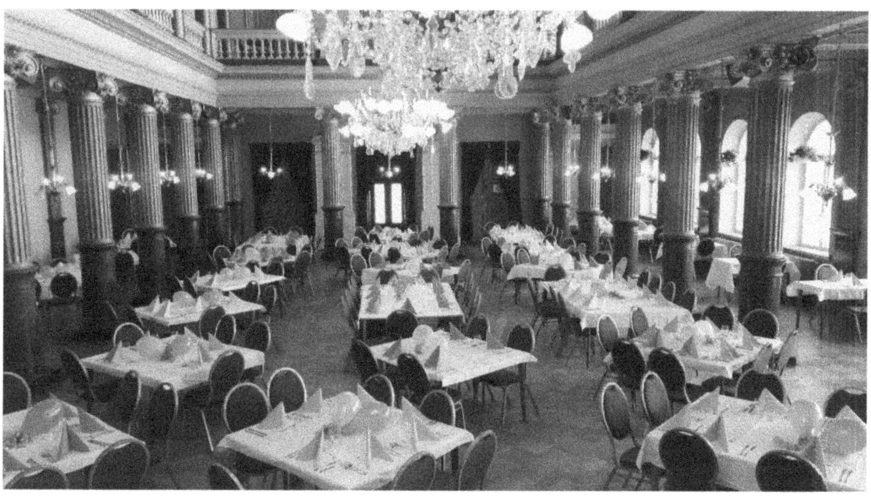

Picture 5.3 The hall of Turun VPK in Turku, Finland.

cultural centers. On the contrary, the private centers repeatedly emphasize being able to make their own decisions quickly and to react to matters as they choose. The findings furthermore show that all the private cases are internally vastly different in cultural content, structure and economy. In the case of the economy, a hint of restriction surfaces as some respondents say the grants they receive may come with certain restrictions. Especially, the municipalities seem to want to influence some issues related to public funding, as Meyer and Rowan (1977) emphasized. Nevertheless, the centers do not collaborate with the municipalities in any wider sense, which implies that the level of these restrictions is quite low.

Private centers experience vast differences between them and public centers. They see public centers as much more restricted to municipal government, much more passive in reacting to situations and less likely to make changes of any sort. This is in line with the findings of Silvanto, Linko and Cantell (2008), which highlighted the political and common interests in the administration of the public centers result in restraining rules and practices, leading, as Meyer and Rowan (1977) described, to conformity. Based on the qualitative data, this chapter interprets public centers as more likely to advance towards isomorphism. As stated in Subchapter 5.5, the quantitative study variables suggest that there is more institutional pressure among the public centers. However, the qualitative data collected on this issue do not include any respondents from public cultural centers, so interpretations on public centers must be made with caution.

Private cultural centers, on the other hand, show no signs of conformity. The constant theme of piloting and pioneering during the interviews does not support isomorphism but rather isomorphism in reverse (Hambrick et al., 2005). The question arises whether private cultural centers were ever really institutionalized (see Leblebici et al., 1991). As field norms and conventions become less restricting for private cultural centers, management seems to rely more on their own understanding of the situations the organization encounters, resulting in actions derived from managerial decisions. This finding is in line with the concept of strategic option, in which the manager reduces resource dependence by managing dependencies (Davis & Cobb, 2010; Malatesta & Smith, 2014; Pfeffer & Salancik, 2003). As Oliver (1991) put it, organizations are active agents and may respond to institutional pressures in a variety of ways. Private centers are clearly applying the resistant strategy within the dimension of consistency in the institutional factor of content. They seem to experience that the exerted pressures are not consistent with organizational goals.

Although private centers have no safety net in the municipality, they seem to be more willing to take risks and find new activities. This finding agrees with the assumption that organizations such as private cultural centers may use the avoidance strategy by hiding their nonconformity, shielding themselves from institutional pressures, and conversely by avoiding institutional rules or expectations (Oliver, 1991). The findings of this study (Järvinen, 2017) furthermore imply that even if private and public cultural centers share a common purpose and, to a certain extent, a same set of activities, they may still exist in two separate fields.

Alternatively, they have evolved into such different organizational types that they are in the process of creating new fields, a possibility also noted in earlier studies (Järvinen, 2017).

References

Amenta, E., & Ramsey, K. (2010). Institutional theory. Em K. Leicht, & J. Jenkins (Eds.), *Handbook of Politics: State and Society in Global Perspective* (pp. 15–39). New York: Springer.

Barley, S.R., & Tolbert, P.S. (1997). Institutionalization and structuration: Studying the links between action and institution. Organization Studies, 18, pp. 93–117.

Battilana, J., Lee, M., Walker, J., & Dorsey, C. (2012). In search of the hybrid ideal. Stanford Social Innovation Review, 10, pp. 51–55.

Boxenbaum, E., & Jonsson, S. (2008*)*. Isomorphism, diffusion and decoupling. Em R. Greenwood, C. Oliver, K. Sahlin, & R. Suddaby (Eds.), *The SAGE Handbook of Organizational Institutionalism* (pp. 78–98). London: Sage.

Czarniawska, B. (2008). How to misuse institutions and get away with it: Some reflections on institutional theory(ies). Em R. Greenwood, C. Oliver, K. Sahlin, & R. Suddaby (Eds.), *The SAGE Handbook of Organizational Institutionalism* (pp. 768–782). London: Sage.

Dacin, T., Goodstein, J., & Scott, W. (2002). Institutional theory and institutional change: Introduction to the special research forum. Academy of Management Journal, 45(1), pp. 45–56.

Davis, G., & Cobb, J. (2010). Chapter 2 Resource dependence theory: Past and future. Em Stanford's Organization Theory Renaissance, 1970–2000. Online: Stanford.

Davidsson, P., Hunter, E., & Klofsten, M. (2006). Institutional forces: The invisible hand that shapes venture ideas? International Small Business Journal, 24(2), pp. 115–131.

Deephouse, D.L., & Suchman, M.C. 2008. Legitimacy in organizational institutionalism. In R. Greenwood, C. Oliver, K. Sahlin & R. Suddaby (Eds.), *The SAGE Handbook of Organizational Institutionalism* (pp. 49–77). London: SAGE.

DiMaggio, P. (1988). Interest and agency in institutional theory. Em L. Zucker (Ed.), *Institutional Patterns and Organizations: Culture and Environments* (pp. 3–21). Cambridge, MA: Ballinger Publishing Company.

DiMaggio, P., & Powell, W. (1983). The iron cage revisited: Institutional isomorphism and collective rationality in organizational fields. American Sociological Review, 48, pp. 147–160.

DiMaggio, P., & Powell, W. (1991). Introduction. Em W. Powell, & P. DiMaggio (Eds.), *The New Institutionalism in Organizational Analysis* (pp. 267–292). Chicago: University of Chicago Press.

Dunn, M., & Jones, C. (2010). Institutional logics and institutional pluralism: The contestation of care and science logics in medical education, 1967–2005. Administrative Science Quarterly, 55, pp. 114–149.

Elsbach, K.D., & Sutton, R.I. 1992. Acquiring organizational legitimacy through illegitimate actions: A marriage of institutional and impression management theories. Academy of Management Journal, 35, pp. 699–738.

Friedland, R., & Alford, R. (1991). Bringing society back in: symbols, practices, and institutional contradictions. Em W. Powell, & P. DiMaggio (Eds.), The New Institutionalism in Organizational Analysis (pp. 232–263). London: University of Chicago Press.

Em R. Greenwood, C. Oliver, K. & Tolbert, P. (1985). Institutional environments and resource dependence: Sources of administrative structure in institutions of higher education. Administrative Science Quarterly, 30, pp. 1–13.

Greenwood, R., Suddaby, R., & Hinings, C. (2002). Theorizing change: The role of professional associations in the transformation of institutionalized fields. Academy of Management Journal, 45(1), pp. 58–80.

Greenwood, R., Oliver, C., Sahlin, K., & Suddaby, R. (2008). Introduction. Em R. Greenwood, C. Oliver, K. Sahlin, & R. Suddaby (Eds.), *The Sage Handbook of Organizational Institutionalism* (pp. 1–46). London: Sage.

Hambrick, D., Finkelstein, S., Cho, T., & Jackson, E. (2005). Isomorphism in reverse: Institutional theory as an explanation for recent increases in intraindustry heterogeneity and managerial discretion. Em B. Staw, & R. Kramer (Eds.), *Research in Organizational Behavior* (Vol. 26, pp. 307–350). Greenwich, CT: JAI Press.

Hodgson, G. (2006). What are institutions? Journal of Economic Issues, 40(1), pp. 1–25.

Holm, P. (1995). The dynamics of institutionalization: Transformation processes in Norwegian fisheries. Administrative Science Quarterly, 40, pp. 398–422.

IBM. (2016). *IBM Support.* Accessed 31.7.2018, Available at www-01.ibm.com/support/docview.wss?uid=swg21479010

Jamali, D. (2010). MNCs and international accountability standards through an institutional lens: Evidence of symbolic conformity or decoupling. Journal of Business Ethics, 95(4), pp. 617–640.

Järvinen, T. (2017). From one mission statement to two organizational fields: The effects of reverse isomorphism in private cultural centers. Em T. Johansson, & M. Luonila (Eds.), *Making Sense of Arts Management: Research, Cases and Practices* (Vol. 1, pp. 128–132). Helsinki: Unigrafia: University of Arts Helsinki.

Kingston, C., & Caballero, G. (2009). Comparing theories of institutional change. Journal of Institutional Economics, 5(2), pp. 151–180.

Kraatz, M., & Block, E. 2008. Organizational implications of institutional pluralism. In R. Greenwood, C. Oliver, R. Suddaby,K. Sahlin-Andersson (Ed.), *Handbook of Organizational Institutionalism*: 243–275. London: Sage Publication.

Leblebici, H., Salancik, G., Copay, A., & King, T. (1991). Institutional change and the transformation of interorganizational fields: An organizational history of the U.S. radio broadcasting industry. Administrative Science Quarterly, 36, pp. 333–363.

Mahoney, J., & Thelen, K. (2009). *Explaining Institutional Change: Ambiguity, Agency, and Power.* Cambridge: Cambridge University Press.

Malatesta, D., & Smith, C. (2014). Lessons from Resource Dependence Theory for Contemporary Public and Nonprofit Management. Public Administration Review, 74(1), pp. 14–25.

Mazza, C., & Strandgaard Pedersen, J. (2004). From press to e-media? The transformation of an organizational field. Organisational Studies, 25(6), pp. 875–896.

Meyer, J., & Rowan, B. (1977). Institutionalized organizations: Formal structure as myth and ceremony. The American Journal of Sociology, 83(2), pp. 340–363.

Meyer, J., Scott, W., & Deal, T. (1983). Institutional and technical sources of organizational structure: Explaining the structure of educational organizations. Em J. Meyer, & W. Scott (Eds.), *Organizational Environments: Ritual and Rationality* (pp. 45–67). Beverly Hills, CA: Sage.

Mizruchi, M., & Fein, L. (1999). The social construction of organizational knowledge: A study of the uses of coercive, mimetic, and normative isomorphism. Administrative Science Quarterly, 44(4), pp. 653–683.

North, D. (1990). *Institutions, Institutional Change and Economic Performance.* Cambridge: Cambridge University Press

Oliver, C. (1991). Strategic responses to institutional processes. Academy of Management Review, pp. 145–179.

Orton, J.D., & Weick, K.E. (1990). Loosely coupled systems: A reconceptualization. Academy of Management Review, 15(2), 203–223. doi:10.5465/amr.1990.4308154

Ostrom, E. (2005). *Understanding Institutional Diversity*. Princeton, NJ: Princeton University Press.

Pache, A., & Santos, F. (2010). When world collide: The international dynamics of organizational responses to conflicting institutional demands. Academy of Management Review, 35(3), pp. 455–476.

Pfeffer, J., & Salancik, G. (2003). The External Control of Organizations: A Resource Dependence Perspective. Stanford, California: Stanford University Press.

Powell, W. (1991). Expanding the scope of institutional analysis. Em W. Powell, & P. DiMaggio (Eds.), *The Institutionalism in Organizational Analysis* (pp. 183–203). Chicago: The University of Chicago Press.

Reale, E., & Seeber, M. (2010). Organisation response to institutional pressures in Higher Education: The important role of the disciplines. Higher Education, 61(1), pp. 1–22.

Sahlin, & R. Suddaby (Eds.), *Handbook of Organizational Institutionalism*. California: Sage.

Sauder, M., & Espeland, W.N. (2009). The discipline of rankings: Tight coupling and organizational change. American Sociological Review, 74, pp. 63–82.

Schmidt, V. (2010). Taking ideas and discourse seriously: Explaining change through discursive institutionalism as the fourth 'new institutionalism'. European Political Science Review, 2(1), pp. 1–25.

Scott, W. (1987). The adolescence of institutional theory. Administrative Science Quarterly, 32, pp. 493–511.

Scott, W. (1994). Conceptualizing organizational fields: Linking organizations and societal systems. Em H. Derlien, U. Gerhardt, & F. Scharpf (Eds.), *Systemrationalitat und partialinteresse*. Baden Baden: Nomos Verlagsgesellschaft.

Scott, W. (2008). Approaching adulthood: The maturing of institutional theory. Theory and Society 37, pp. 427–442.

Scott, W. (2014). *Institutions and Organizations* (4 ed.). Thousand Oaks, CA: Sage.

Selznick, P. (1948). Foundations of the theory of organization. American Sociological Review, 13(1), pp. 25–35.

Silvanto, T., Linko, M., & Cantell, T. (14 de 2 de 2008). From enlightenment to experience: cultural centers in Helsinki neighbourhoods. International Journal of Cultural Policy, pp. 165–178.

Streeck, W., & Thelen, K. (2005). *Beyond Continuity: Institutional Change in Advanced Political Economies*. Oxford: Oxford University Press.

Suddaby, R. (2010). Challenges for institutional theory. Journal of Management Inquiry, 19(1), pp. 14–20.

Suddaby, R., & Greenwood, R. (2009). Methodological issues in researching institutional change. Em D. Buchanan, & A. Bryman (Eds.), *The Sage Handbook of Organizational Research Methods* (pp. 176–196). London: Sage.

Thornton, P., & Ocasio, W. (2008). Institutional Logics. Em R. Greenwood, C. Oliver, K. Sahlin, & R. Suddaby (Eds.), Handbook of Organizational Institutionalism. California: Sage.

Veblen, T. (2009). *The theory of the leisure class: An economic study of institutions*. (C. Kingston, & G. Caballero, Eds.) *Journal of Institutional Economics*. 5(2), pp. 111–132.

Zucker, L. (1987). Institutional theories of organization. Annual Review of Sociology, 13, pp. 443–464.

6 Resource dependence and strategic cultural center management

Resource dependence theory (RDT) is the study of how the dependence on external resources of organizations influence the behavior of the organization. As the heading of this chapter perhaps already suggests, this will be a more theoretical section with a contrasting view on why some organizational decision are made and how they fall in line with contemporary theoretical views. Beside the theoretical approach, this chapter also aims to explore the resource access strategies adopted by cultural centers operating in challenging business environments.

The following chapter (Chapter 7) will focus on mission drift, which is the situation where the activities of organizations drift away from its initial mission due to the aim of earning money. This chapter will have a slightly related focus, as it among other things deals with the concept of receiving revenues without letting these steers the organization too much.

This chapter aims to point out that the dependence on diverse revenue sources among private cultural centers, unlike their public counter peers, can lead to heterogeneity. To examine the need of diversified funding, we will examine the following hypotheses together with the qualitative data. The hypotheses are:

H2: The type of perceived resource interdependence leads to a higher degree of resource diversification in private cultural centers.
H02: The type of perceived resource interdependence does not lead to a higher degree of resource diversification in private cultural centers.

To examine how the cultural centers perceive their interdependencies, this chapter focuses on the following hypotheses.

The hypotheses are:

H4: Cultural centers in general have a manageable environmental interdependence.
H04: Cultural centers in general do not have a manageable environmental interdependence.

The qualitative questions this chapter aims to focus on are how cultural centers perceive the concept of resource dependence, and how they manage this dependency in practice. Before examining these viewpoints, this chapter will shortly present the fundamentals of RDT.

6.1 Basics of resource dependence theory

RDT suggests that organizations cannot internally generate all the resources required to sustain their activities and, therefore, must conduct transactions with elements in the environment to secure a stable flow of resources (Pfeffer & Salancik, 2003).

Pfeffer and Salancik (2003) first proposed the RDT in 1978 in their book *The external control of organizations*, but it has its roots in Emerson's (1962) power-dependence relations. RDT has become highly influential mostly because it is empirically accurate and appropriate for the social environment of research (Davis & Cobb, 2010). RDT is connected to organizational theories, and its aim is to explain the behavior and performance of organizations (Nienhuser, 2008). Pfeffer and Salancik (2003) initially proposed that organizations are not self-sufficient and in complete control of their destiny, so they need to identify their external environment as a source for being controlled and affected by others (Casciaro & Piskorski, 2005).

> *Organizations must transact with other elements in their environment to acquire needed resources, and this is true whether we are talking about public organizations, private organizations, small or large organizations, or organizations which are bureaucratic or organic.*
>
> (Burns & Stalker, 1961, p. 62)

This is very much what Pfeffer and Salancik (2003) highlighted in 1978: the organization's environment '*encompasses every event in the world that may potentially have an effect on the organization's activities*' (Pfeffer & Salancik, 2003, p. 3). Hatch (2013) further developed this definition by emphasizing that an organization's dependence on its environment is a reaction of '*its need for resources such as raw materials, labor, capital, equipment, and outlets for its products and services*' (Hatch, 2013, p. 70). Hence, the environment can influence organizations through elements as '*competitive process, desirable products and services, and efficient organizational structures and processes*' (Hatch, 2013, p. 70).

The range of the organization's dependence on specific exchanges needed for its activities determines its vulnerability to extraorganizational influence (Pfeffer & Salancik, 2003). The two somewhat interrelated dimensions of the significance of a resource exchange are the relative magnitude of the exchange and the urgency of the resource. There must be either a concentration of resource control or a few (or only one) significant organizations doing all the input or output transactions for one organization to depend on another. In other words, the critical point is whether the organization has access to the same resources from other sources. The mere quantity of resource suppliers (or purchasers, for that matter) is not as important

(Pfeffer & Salancik, 2003). Dependence on the environment for successes and tribulations per se is not a challenge (Pfeffer & Salancik, 2003; Hillman et al., 2009). Rather, it is the undependability of the environment. There might be changes, new competition or perhaps a decrease in the supply of resources. A change in the environment thus can lead to either to ruin or modifications of organizational activities.

Before mid-twentieth century, the dominant view on organizations were prescriptive, as if one ideal structure fit all without a regard for organizational differences (Tausky, 1978). These theories were debunked by many researchers, who showed that the structures of organizations are connected to a variety of factors (Burns & Stalker, 1961; Lawrence & Lorsch, 1976). Features of the environment, the size of the organization and other factors influence both the structures and the activities of organizations.

RDT is by no means the only or even the first theory to stress the significance of the environment. Environmental dimensions emerged in Williamson's (1975) transaction cost economics theory, Meyer and Rowan's (1977) IT and Hannan and Freeman's (1975) population ecology. Nevertheless, these theories are not the same; transaction cost economics emphasizes uncertainties (demand, behavioral, technological and supplier uncertainty) that add to the cost of exchanges (Williamson, 1979). The environment is said to directly form the organization in population ecology (Hannan & Freeman, 1975) and in IT (DiMaggio & Powell, 1983). In contrast, RDT emphasizes the possibility of managerial action to both shape and react to the environment (Pfeffer & Salancik, 2003).

Whereas one might agree that the initial study by Pfeffer and Salacik (2003) accorded well with the empirical world of its time, some have pointed out that it has become a child of its time (Casciaro & Piskorski, 2005). As Casciaro and Piskorski (2005) highlighted, the need for modification is apparent, especially in tactics, such as diversifying, which very well might do more harm than good among industry corporations. Although Pfeffer and Salancik's (2003) book is frequently quoted, few studies have contributed empirical validation of the theory's predictions.

> *RDT has acquired the status of a powerful general metaphor, but it was marginalized as an engine for theoretical advancement and a basis for testable empirical research.*
>
> (Carsciaro & Piskorski, 2005, p. 167)

Despite the theory's period of inactivity, it seems to have seen a revival of interest, among authors such as Amy Hillman (2005), Westphal et al. (2006) and Katila et al. (2008). The latter claimed that RDT has neglected the competitive side of tie formation and called recent efforts to update it a '*recent renaissance of resource dependence theory*' (Katila et al., 2008, p. 321).

6.2 Interdependency, strategic options and power

RDT has three main themes crucial to understanding how organizational decision making is constrained by the environment: (1) *interdependency*; (2) *strategic options*; and (3) *power* (Pfeffer & Salancik, 2003).

Interdependency. Organizations are embedded in networks of both interdependencies and social relations. Organizations use resources acquired from external relations as inputs to ensure their survival (Pfeffer & Salancik, 2003; Casciaro & Piskorski, 2005). Dependencies are generally mutual and occasionally indirect. If organizations could generate all the resources they need to survive, there would be no need to establish relations with the external environment (Pfeffer & Salancik, 2003). However, organizations need to interact with other organizations to obtain a continuous and sufficient flow of resources in order to satisfy their stakeholders. Resource availability depends on the dynamism, complexity and generosity of the environment. Thus, organizations interact with the environment to guarantee the availability of the resources on which they depend (Pfeffer & Salancik, 2003).

> *Virtually all organizational outcomes are based on interdependent causes or agents. Interdependence characterizes the relationship between the creating an outcome, not the outcome itself.*
>
> (Pfeffer & Salancik, 2003, p. 40)

RDT adds a new perspective to the debate of interorganizational relations by adding a detailed register of organizational responses to interdependence. The resources on which organizations traditionally dependent are financial, informational and physical (Davis & Cobb, 2010; Frooman & Murrel, 2005; Pfeffer & Salancik, 2003).

Strategic option. RDT emphasizes managers' role in reducing resource dependence by managing the dependencies (Davis & Cobb, 2010; Malatesta & Smith, 2014; Pfeffer & Salancik, 2003). This view – that the manager has the ability to shape the environment, not only be shaped by it – constitutes the originality of the theory compared to other contemporary theories, such as population ecology (Hannah & Freeman, 1975).

Frooman (1999) furthermore emphasized that the organization's relationships with stakeholder can affect the strategies the organization and the stakeholder apply. He proposed four arguments in this regard, as follows:

1) *When the relationship is marked by stakeholder power, the stakeholder will choose a direct withholding strategy to influence the firm.*
2) *When the relationship is marked by firm power, the stakeholder will choose an indirect usage strategy to influence the firm.*
3) *When the relationship is one of high interdependence, the stakeholder will choose a direct usage strategy to influence the firm.*

Table 6.1 Typology of relationships and strategies

		Dependent stakeholder?	
		Yes	*No*
Dependent organization?	*Yes*	Direct compromise as in high interdependence	Direct coercion as in stakeholder power
	No	Indirect compromise as in organization power	Indirect coercion as in low interdependence

Source: Frooman (1999, p. 200).

4) *When the relationship is one of low interdependence, the stakeholder will choose an indirect withholding strategy to influence the firm.* (Frooman, 1999, p. 202).

The consequences of these four arguments are as follows. First, if the organization's dependence on the stakeholder is high, one stakeholder is capable of using a restraining strategy, exercising high-intensity measures (Frooman, 1999). Second, if the organization has dominance over the stakeholder, the stakeholder is only capable of use an indirect usage strategy while searching for alliances with other stakeholders. The stakeholders exercise low-intensity measures. Third, if there are high exchanges between the stakeholder and the organization, the stakeholder aims to use direct usage strategies, implying lower-intensity measures than the direct restraining strategy. Fourth, if the exchange between the stakeholder and the organization is low, the stakeholder uses an indirect restraining strategy to intimidate the resource needed by the organization with measures to balance organization power by cooperating with other stakeholders (Frooman, 1999).

Power. Pfeffer and Salancik (2003) analyzed the sources and consequences of power in interorganizational relations and addressed questions such as the sources of power and dependence and how those who run organizations use their power and manage their dependence. Central to RDT is the argument that dependence leads to power, and power consists the control over vital resources (Ulrich & Barney, 1984; Davis & Cobb, 2010). If one organization is dependent on another, the latter is the one with power. In other words, power is more a structural variable than an attribute of organizations (Frooman & Murrel, 2005; Pfeffer & Salancik, 2003).

According to Casciaro and Piskorski (2005), the notion of resource interdependence is quite vague as it combines a variety of dimensions that should be distinguished. This argument is crucial as it changes the predictions of RDT. The theory traditionally states that a high level of interdependence results in cooperation between firms (by alliances or mergers). Pfeffer and Salancik (2003), however, emphasized that a high-power imbalance in a dyad is connected to a reduced likelihood of creating an alliance as the powerful partner has advantages in an alliance with the weaker partner. Such an alliance would implicate that the powerful partner shares its competitive advantage and gains nothing, diminishing its power and sharing its favorable conditions. However, if the mutual dependence is high, both organizations have good reasons to cooperate (Casciaro & Piskorski, 2005).

Figure 6.1 is an attempt to visualize the relations between the interdependent organizations (A and B), and how the sociopolitical system can exert political and social power over the organization and how market power is the force between the organizations and their competitors. All of these relations are met with strategical maneuvers and the resource interdependence between organizations A and B is considered as an asset leading to power for them both.

Malatesta and Smith (2014) pointed out that RDT's key constructs, such as the power-dependence effect that emerges in diverse interorganizational relationships, are not that easy to measure. Matters evolve and a relationship can be hard to distinguish from a partnership or a joint venture.

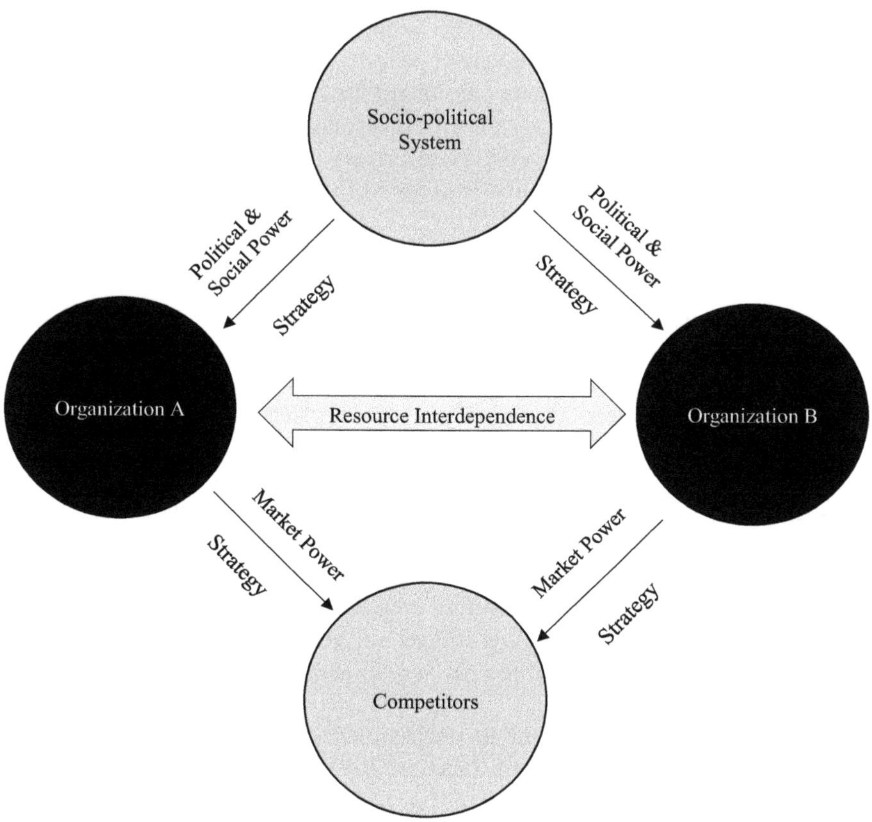

Figure 6.1 Interdependence, strategy options and power.

6.3 The role of the environment

As stated, to accomplish goals, organizations need to acquire resources (Pfeffer & Salancik, 2003). To do so, they have to interact with the environment and collaborate with other organizations to obtain resources. Consequently, no organization is in complete control of its existence. The need to adjust to changed circumstances is as much an external as an internal affair. In other words, organizations' autonomy is limited by their dependence on certain stakeholder groups to sustain certain resource bases. RDT provides a way to understand the connection between the organization and its environment (Hillman et al., 2000; Pfeffer & Salancik, 2003). If a stakeholder group possesses a resource critical to an organization, then the stakeholder group can make valid claims on the organization due to its control of the supply of this vital resource (Frooman, 1999; Pfeffer & Salancik, 2003). The challenge for the organization is to be effective and anticipate external demands within existing patterns of constraints and contingencies (Guo & Acar, 2005).

The environment is considered to be partly activities outside the organization's control (Malatesta & Smith, 2014). Thus, the environment is a system of interdependencies. The focal point of RDT is three environmental features: *concentration*, *munificence* and *interconnectedness*. The first feature refers to the extent to which authority and power are distributed throughout the environment. Munificence indicates the scarcity of critical resources, whereas interconnectedness refers to the extent to which organizations are connected to each other in an overall system. These environmental features work jointly to determine collective dependence (Malatesta & Smith, 2014).

RDT emphasizes that organizations seek to minimize their dependence on other organizations to acquire important resources and change the environment to make those resources available (Hillman et al., 2000; Pfeffer & Salancik, 2003). The theory highlights the following assumptions: (1) organizations favor predictable environments over uncertain ones; (2) organizations favor more permissive than restricted environments; and (3) if possible, organizations endorse strategies to change the environment (Pfeffer & Salancik, 2003).

Organizations furthermore react to changes in the environment at different paces (Pfeffer & Salancik, 2003). In addition, even if most changes in the environment are preceded by hints, these hints may not be monitored or, worse, might be get altered within the organization. Balancing monitoring of the environment is problematic; if the organization monitors everything, it is overwhelmed by information and unable to operate, but if it does not monitor enough, it is not ready to react to changes that might threat its very existence. In either way, it will be pushing daisies in no time.

The organization's contact with its environment determines the information it has about the environment (Pfeffer & Salancik, 2003). People working for an organization, both volunteers and staff members, might serve on board commissions, belong to a variety of clubs and otherwise interact with the environment.

Furthermore, these people may participate in government hearings and so gain knowledge about matters that could influence their activities. Ultimately, it is how the organization interacts with and processes information about the environment that determines its ability to react to external constraints (Pfeffer & Salancik, 2003). It is still important to distinguish between inside and outside directors, as regardless of expertise, the insider director still provides internally focused resources, whereas the outside director provides external resources needed when dealing with external factors (Hillman et al., 2000).

Dependence on the environment leaves organizations with a certain amount of insecurity as those that control resources, and thus have power over the organization may be unreliable partners (Pfeffer & Salancik, 2003; Casciaro & Piskorski, 2005)). It all comes down to the organization's capability to negotiate exchanges and manage changes in the environment. The inability to anticipate or determine the capability and demands of different interest groups, and how these restrain the organization or conflict internally may be the reason why an organization has problems adapting to its environment (Pfeffer & Salancik, 2003). The organization can make crucial administrative errors if it is ignorant of its interdependence or restraints. An organization is effective when it '*responds to the demands from its environment according to its dependence on the various components of the environment*' (Pfeffer & Salancik, 2003, p. 84).

Jones (2007) pointed out that a high level of dependence on a single revenue source, whether the government or foundations, leads to mission drift in organizations. The dependence of private organizations on public grants has faced criticism; Kelly (2007) argued that such dependence compromises organization's legitimacy and causes mission drift as NGOs are compelled to change both their priorities and activities to meet funders' requirements (Bennet & Savanni, 2011). Mission drift might make the activities of organizations drift away from its initial mission and make difficult relations with donors, who may think that organizations are using grants to subsidize government contracts (Jones, 2007). Organizations may also have to use extensive time and resources to abide by the reporting requirements of funders (Choudhury & Ahmed, 2002). In every social undertaking, there is a tension between being more efficient and solving social problems, for instance, in how organizations adapt to the purpose of creating social value as well as economic value (Miller et al., 2012).

Organizations should aim to change their focal point in response to environmental attempts to change organizations (Pfeffer & Salancik, 2003; Casciaro & Piskorski, 2005). Everything organizations do are reactions to their environment, so the focus should be on how to alter the environment to advantage organizations (Pfeffer & Salancik, 2003). The actions of organizations can be changed by altering the circumstances of their environment. If there has been any change in the environment, organizations should focus on analyzing the possibility of other organizations pursuing this change to their advantage as no laws or social values are sacrosanct.

6.4 Strategies to overcome dependence

Only if the organization is able to either expand the quantity of resources or diminish the quantity of competitors for those resources can it change its level of interdependence (Pfeffer & Salancik, 2003). In addition, when the organization stabilizes its access to resources, scarcity of these resources does not diminish – but only moves to other organizations. By forming alliances, joint ventures and mergers, organizations can attempt to overcome dependencies and increase organizational autonomy and legitimacy (Davis & Conn, 2010; Drees & Heugens, 2013; Hillman et al., 2009; Pfeffer & Salancik, 2003; Provan et al., 1980; Sharif & Heugens, 2014). There are also other ways for organizations to acquire power over resource providers. For example, increased size is a possible source of advantages (Davis & Cobb, 2010), while smaller organizations seem to gain more from cooperative exchanges than larger organizations (Das et al., 1998). Alliances seem to form when organizations are mutually dependent, although the organization with some leverage has strategic control (Yan & Gray, 2001). In cases of resource misconduct, Katila et al. (2008) recommended potential resource requirements and defense mechanisms for smaller partners.

The management of an organization has to convince the environment that its activities, beliefs and values are socially acceptable to achieve legitimacy, especially if there are many organizations of different types competing for the same resources or domains (Pfeffer & Salancik, 2003), as in the case of public and private centers in the same city. Legitimacy influences the contest for resources, and public centers might have less difficulty claiming social worth.

Westphal et al. (2006) refined the hypothesis of co-optation, in which representatives of competitors, key suppliers and customers are invited to serve on board as a means of co-optation. Although this hypothesis does not explain the patterns of organizational interlock behavior, Westphal et al. (2006) argued that the mechanism in itself works as suggested by Pfeffer and Salancik (2003), only through less obvious means, such as friendship ties. An organization, though, does not have to maintain more allies than those necessary to uphold of its activities; instead, it needs alliances with those with the right resources and those with a need for the outcomes of the organization (Pfeffer & Salancik, 2003; Casciaro & Piskorski, 2005). Consequently, allies are those defining the activities of the organization. In the case of a change in a coalition, the organization end or change its activities to match its remaining allies.

The organization itself may carry out diversification of its activities to shift its interdependence from a few parties to many (Pfeffer & Salancik, 2003). In doing so, the organization can connect hitherto unconnected environmental segments in a single organization and make them internally interdependent. This, in turn, leads to internal competition, which shifts the interdependence of the focal organization to the segments in the environment (Hillman et al., 2000). However, there is a risk that an extensive collection of environmental segments may lead to managerial difficulties for an organization without sufficient resources. Although this possible multitude of segments may lead to conflicting interests and managerial difficulties, it is also helpful in managing the problems created. When the organization has more demands, any given demand becomes less important (Pfeffer & Salancik, 2003). Scattering the dependency among many segments decreases the organization's need to reply to any given requirement. Furthermore, numerous segments can be satisfied at once when the organization has a more differentiated organizational structure. This is in line with Froelich's (1999) observation of the increasing diversification of revenue strategies within NGOs. It furthermore is consistent with reducing resource dependence and maintaining organizational autonomy (Pfeffer & Salancik, 2003). However, there is also a problem with diversified funding:

> *A greater variety of resource providers typically leads to a corresponding increase in funding criteria and satisfying the criteria of one provider may preclude satisfying another.*
>
> (Froelich, 1999, p. 262)

The subsequent goal conflicts and organizational pressure can be difficult to manage (DiMaggio, 1986; Twombly, 2003) and lead to mission vagueness (Weisbrod, 1998), which is very much in line with the concept of mission drift, as presented in the following chapter (Jones, 2007). While some have found weaknesses in RDT, Davis and Cobb (2010) and Katila et al. (2008) point out that there is evidence of a newfound interest in and scholarly contributions to this theory. '*As long as power plays a part in the conduct of organizational life, RDT will continue to provide insight*' (Davis & Cobb, 2010, p. 40).

6.5 An overview of environmental interdependencies in cultural centers

The respondents perceive their environment as consisting of the audience (the citizens) and stakeholders, such as the municipality, funders and collaborating organizations. According to the experience of the respondents, the environment of the private cultural centers in this study views them positively. Two centers, for instance, have received national prices for their activities, and one does a vast amount of consulting about how to run a cultural center, implying an appreciation of the centers in their society.

Looking at the results from the interviews among the private cultural centers, they seem to be mostly surprisingly negative towards the municipalities. The common view seems to be that the private centers fill quite a void in the cultural field of their communities, but the municipalities do not sufficiently recognize or support this effort. All the cultural centers had some experiences of cooperation with their municipalities. Several respondents emphasize that the interdependence within such cooperation, coupled with complex organizational and administrative arrangements, generates problems as there is insufficient clarity about, for instance, specific job responsibilities. This may be a reason why the cultural centers work towards self-sufficiency, as many respondents proclaim. As Casciaro and Piskorski (2005) highlighted, organizations only maintain alliances with those that have the right resources. The respondents do not state that they want to end interdependency with the municipalities but that they want to diminish the power the municipalities have over them.

Regarding types of resources, this study finds that the municipalities, according to the interview respondents, seem to mostly need legitimacy support from the private centers but are not that dependent on the expertise. The private centers, in turn, are mostly dependent on economic support from the municipalities, but not that dependent on legitimacy support. This mutual dependence (Pfeffer & Salancik, 2003) seems to give valid codes for behavior by both the municipalities and the private centers (Scott, 2014). Even if the interdependency with the municipalities does not seem to be completely satisfactory to the private centers, the boundaries for this collaboration between the public and private sectors do appear to be suitable for both partners (Vickers & Yarrow, 1991) as the interdependency is continued.

The respondents see their position within their community as quite solid and appreciated and thus connected to high legitimacy. This position positively affects their engagement in interorganizational cooperation, as legitimacy is a method to acquire and maintain resources (Suddaby, 2010). However, the status of the private cultural centers may also be a sign of cognitive legitimacy; that is, the local citizens simply might not know of any other way than that of the organization (Suchman, 1995). Except for some cities with both private and public centers, there is not much competition or many alternative actors within the field. The respondents nevertheless emphasize their efforts to focus on what is happening in their communities and how to best respond to it – a successful way to proceed according to Webb (2017).

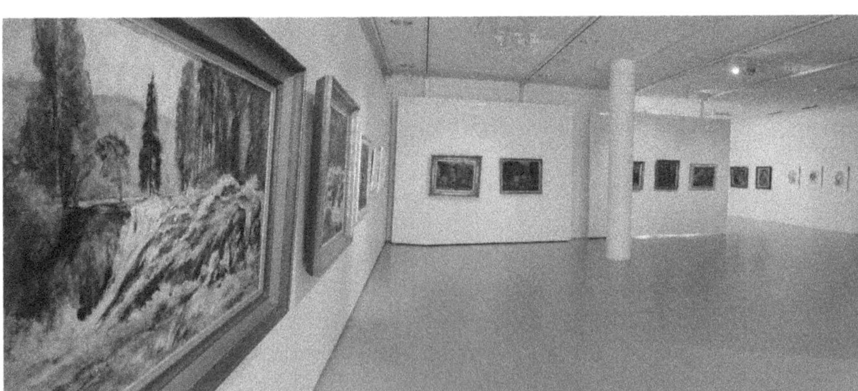

Picture 6.1 The art gallery at cultural center Virta in Imatra, Finland. A photograph by Tuuli Parikka.

The environmental interdependencies also include interorganizational cooperation (Pfeffer & Salancik, 2003). The study findings show that cooperation with other organizations is very important for both private and public cultural centers. It seems as if the centers use their legitimacy as the centers of cultural activities in their communities and aim to efficiently build networks that provide completed artistic content (lower costs than making productions) and receive completed artistic content (more revenue for the centers' own productions), which is in line with the RDT view of networks (Pfeffer & Salancik, 2003). This interorganizational cooperation increases mutual dependence among the cooperating partners, while it empowers cultural centers to create more value for lower costs and increases their legitimacy. In addition, the collective interpretation of this collaboration infuses value into the organizational outcomes (Suddaby, 2010). The collaboration adds to the moral legitimacy of the cultural center, as the center is seen to be doing what they should (Suchman, 1995).

It can appear as if the respondents see a number of weaknesses in the resource dependence of private cultural centers, but at the same time, these dependencies can be regarded as opportunities for the cultural centers to act on. This view is very much in line with Pfeffer and Salancik's (2003) and Casciaro and Piskorski's (2005) argument that organizations use resources gained from external relations as inputs to ensure their survival.

In addition, the respondents circulate a theme of trying to aim for different and new revenue sources as they cannot rely on those they already have; in fact, many complain about the diminishing municipal funding. Examples of such are venue rentals for other than cultural events, alliances and special grants. Thus, the focus on earning more revenue is merely to maintain the current goal of versatile cultural offerings. This is also in line with Pfeffer and Salancik (2003), who emphasized that an organization may diversify its activities to shift its interdependencies from a few parties to many. Doing so moves the focus away from the focal organization itself and enhances the organizational legitimacy (Oliver, 1991).

Additionally, the private cultural centers raise the issue of competition for event audiences with public institutions. Thus, even the concept of piloting in new activities surfaces as a strategical response to competition. This may also be a result of being late adopters as too many actors are looking for the same resources (Leblebici et al., 1991).

The respondents clearly articulate the need for diversified funding sources, from crowdfunding to volunteers. All the private cultural centers aim to have a vast set of revenue streams, an aim not unfamiliar to businesses either. All the cultural centers have a business model that extended beyond offering a venue and cultural activities; restaurants are the most important businesses in this model.

6.6 Resource dependence: the need for diversified funding

This subchapter is aimed at studying whether private cultural centers are dependent on a broad diversity of revenue sources, and thus exhibit more variation than public centers. Public centers are assumed to be dependent mostly on a single revenue sources and to thus exhibit conformity. This study aims to point out that the dependence on diverse revenue sources among private cultural centers, unlike their public counter peers, can lead to heterogeneity. To examine the need of diversified funding, this thesis focuses on the variables presented beneath the hypotheses.

The hypotheses are:

> *H2:* The type of perceived resource interdependence leads to a higher degree of resource diversification in private cultural centers.
>
> *H02:* The type of perceived resource interdependence does not lead to a higher degree of resource diversification in private cultural centers.

The variables used in this construct are:

1) Economic effect/private funding
   (How much do the following things affect your activities: private funding?)
2) Economic effect/voluntary staff
   (How much do the following things affect your activities: volunteer staff?)
3) Effect/funders
   (How do the following entities affect your activities: funders?)
4) Economic effect/crowdfunding
   (How much do the following things affect your activities: crowdfunding?)
5) Economic effect/sponsorship
   (How much do the following things affect your activities: sponsorship?)
6) Economic effect/municipal funding
   (How much do the following things affect your activities: municipal funding?)
7) Do you have own cultural offerings
   (Do you have cultural offerings of your own?)
8) Economic effect/interorganizational cooperation
   (How much do the following things affect your activities: interorganizational cooperation?)

All the variables were based on a 5-point Likert scale.

6.6.1 Factor analysis

The Cronbach's alpha reliability analysis score is only .569, so this study started with exploratory factor analysis, a statistical method that increases the reliability of a scale by identifying inappropriate items that can be removed. Thus, to reduce the amount of information concerning the diversification of resources, exploratory factor analysis was conducted. First, I selected the most important variables (8). Second, rather than relying on the eigenvalue criteria, exploratory factor analysis was performed to identify three dimensions in which resource diversification takes place. Maximum likelihood estimator was used as the extraction method,

Table 6.2 Factor analysis of the need for diversified funding

	Loadings			*Communalities*
	1	*2*	*3*	
Economic effect / private funding?	**0,559**	0,208	0,072	0,360
Economic effect / voluntary staff?	**0,401**	-0,083	0,264	0,238
Effect / funders?	0,093	**0,995**	0,018	0,999
Economic effect / crowdfunding?	**0,633**	0,041	-0,054	0,405
Economic effect / sponsorship?	**0,603**	0,205	0,058	0,409
Economic effect / municipal funding?	0,112	0,266	0,108	0,095
Do you have own cultural offering?	0,072	0,082	**0,994**	0,999
Economic effect / interorganizational cooperation?	0,015	0,131	0,171	0,470

Extraction Method: Maximum Likelihood
Rotation Method: Varimax with Kaiser Normalization.
A rotation converged in 5 iterations.

and these three dimensions were defined as independent of one another (i.e. they were not correlated as the solution was Varimax rotated).

According to Guadagnoli and Velicer (1988), the component pattern for a sample size of 100 is stable if the component contains at least 4 variable loadings of > 0.6, which Table 6.2 presents. Eight questions related to the reasons for diversification of resources were factor analyzed using maximum likelihood analysis with Varimax rotation. The analysis show that the three factors explain 57,64% of the variance for the entire set of variables.

Factor 1 has high loadings for the following items: private funding, volunteer staff, crowdfunding and sponsorship. Hence, the factor is named *private funding* and explains 27.36% of the variance. The second factor derived has high loadings with affect/funders, so it is called *resource focus*. The variance explained by this factor is a further 15.87%. The third factor has high loadings with having one's own cultural offerings, so this factor is named *own resources*. The third factor explains 14.41% of the total variance. Substantively, these results identify three clear patterns of resource diversification among the respondents: (1) the importance of private funding (or not); (2) the importance of resource focus (or not); and (3) the impact of one's own resources (or not).

The communalities of the variables included are rather in between, except for the variables affect/funders and do you have own cultural offerings. This may indicate that the variables chosen for this analysis are only weakly related with each other. As there are only few and weak cross-loadings, it is unlikely that reducing or increasing the number of factors would improve interpretability. Two items, municipal funding and interorganizational cooperation, are still eliminated as they do not contribute to any factor structure and do not meet the minimum criterion of having a primary factor loading of .4 or above.

To meet the assumptions of multinomial logistic regression, some preanalysis needed to be done. Multicollinearity was tested on the six remaining variables, producing VIF values of 1.114–1.378. This means that there are no multicollinearity symptoms. Levene's test of homogeneity of variances was also conducted to test for heteroskedasticity. The obtained values of Sig. variables are between .137 and .804, higher than the recommended level of .05. There is one exception: the variable volunteer staff has a Sig. value of .011, less than the level of .05. Still, as the majority of the variables are higher than the level of .05, it is concluded that there is no heteroscedasticity problem.

6.6.2 *Multinomial logistic regression*

Multinomial logistic regression was performed to model the relationship between the predictors and membership in the four groups (private, public, hybrid centers and governmental organizations). The traditional .05 criterion of statistical significance was employed for all the tests. Adding the predictors to a model containing only the intercept significantly improved the fit between model and data (X2(69, N = 91) = 104.572, Nagelkerke R2 = .755, p = .004). Goodness-of-fit was tested by conducting Pearson (p = .813) and deviance (p = 1.0) tests for the groups. According to both tests, the model is a good fit. As shown in Table 6.2, significant unique contributions are made by *private funding*, *voluntary staff*, *sponsorship* and *do you have own cultural offerings*. *Affect/funders* and *crowdfunding* are the only variables without significant, unique contributions (p = .971; p = .237, respectively).

In Table 6.3, Nagelkerke's R2 of .755 indicates a strong relationship between prediction and grouping. The overall success of predictions is 70.3% (56.3% for private centers, 82.9% for public, 100% for hybrid and 50% for governmental organizations).

Table 6.3 Predictors' unique contributions in multinomial logistic regression (N = 91)

Predictor	*X2*	*df*	*p*
Economic effect / private funding?	18,648	12	0,097
Economic effect /voluntary staff?	45,316	12	0,000
Effect / funders?	4,547	12	0,971
Economic effect / crowdfunding?	11,599	9	0,237
Economic effect / sponsorship?	24,501	12	0,017
Do you have own cultural offering?	33,311	12	0,001

The chi-square statistic is the difference in -2 log-likelihoods between the final model and a reduced model. The reduced model is formed by omitting an effect from the final model. The null hypothesis is that all parameters of that effect are 0.

For private centers relative to public centers (the reference group), the Wald test statistic for the predictor *private funding* on a 3-point Likert is 6.195, with an associated p-value of .013. The regression coefficient for private funding (3) is statistically different from zero for private centers relative to public centers, given that the five other predictors are in the model.

For private centers relative to public centers, the Wald test statistic for the predictor *volunteer staff* on a 2- and 3-point Likert scales (disagree and neither disagree or agree) is 6.671 and 5.978, with associated p-values of .010 and .014. The regression coefficient for voluntary staff (2–3) is statistically different from zero for private centers relative to public centers, given that the five other predictors are in the model.

The other four variables have no significant contributions on Likert scales with any number of points (1–5) for private centers. The other center types have no significant contribution on any predictor. Except for governmental organization relative to public centers, the Wald test statistic for the predictor sponsorship on 1- and 2-point Likert scales are 81.992 and 80.361, with an associated p-value of .000. Public centers are again used as the reference category.

The results of the multinomial logistic regression, therefore, suggest that the null hypotheses can be rejected. The regression coefficient for sponsorship is statistically different from zero for governmental organizations relative to public centers, given that the five other predictors are in the model.

6.7 Environmental interdependencies

This subchapter aims to study whether the cultural centers have large environmental interdependencies. As mentioned in this thesis, organizations are embedded in networks of both interdependencies and social relations. Organizations use resources gained from external relations as inputs to ensure survival. To examine how the cultural centers perceive their interdependencies, this chapter focuses on the variables presented after the hypotheses.

The hypotheses are:

> *H4:* Cultural centers in general have a manageable environmental interdependence.
>
> *H04:* Cultural centers in general do not have a manageable environmental interdependence.

The variables used in this construct are:

1) Interorganizational cooperation?
   (How much do you cooperate with other partners/organizations?)
2) How important is interorganizational cooperation?
   (How important do you describe this cooperation as?)
3) Has cooperation changed in recent years?
   (Has cooperation changed in recent years?)

4) Economical affect/interorganizational cooperation?
   (How much the following things affect your activities: interorganizational cooperation?)

All variables were based on a 5-point Likert scale. Cronbach's alpha was used to establish the internal consistency and reliability of all items. The reliability coefficient values are .717 for these four items. Multicollinearity was tested, and the VIF values are between 1.110 and 2.355. This means that there are no multicollinearity symptoms. Levene's test of homogeneity of variances was also conducted to test for heteroskedasticity. The obtained values of Sig. variables are between .769 and .886, more than the recommended level of .05. It thus is concluded that there is no heteroscedasticity problem.

6.7.1 Multinomial logistic regression

A multinomial logistic regression was performed to model the relationship between the predictors and membership in the four groups (private, public, hybrid centers and governmental organizations). The traditional .05 criterion of statistical significance was employed for all tests. Addition of the predictors to a model that contained only the intercept significantly improved the fit between model and data (X2(42, N = 92) = 52.739; Nagelkerke R2 = .483; p = .124).

Goodness-of-fit was tested by conducting Pearson and deviance tests for the groups. According to the Pearson statistic, the model is a good fit (p = .774), while deviance statistics suggest the same (p = .916). As shown in Table 6.4, no significant unique contributions are made by any of the variables.

Nagelkerke's R2 of .483 indicates a moderate relationship between prediction and grouping. The overall prediction success is 58.7% (60.6% for private centers, 73.2% for public, 33.3% for hybrid and 16.7% for governmental organizations). The Wald criterion demonstrates that none of the variables makes a significant contribution on Likert scales of any points (1–5) for any of the center types. The

Table 6.4 Predictors' unique contributions in multinomial logistic regression (N = 90)

Predictor	*X2*	*df*	*p*
Inter-organizational cooperation?	8,466	19	0,488
How important is the inter-organizational cooperation?	9,633	9	0,381
Has the cooperation changed last year's?	12,609	12	0,398
Economic effect / inter-organizational cooperation?	20,081	12	0,066

The chi-square statistic is the difference in -2 log-likelihoods between the final model and a reduced model. The reduced model is formed by omitting an effect from the final model. The null hypothesis is that all parameters of that effect are 0.

results of the multinomial logistic regression, therefore, suggest that the null hypothesis cannot be rejected.

6.8 Summary and conclusions

As we have noted in this chapter, organizations cannot internally generate all the resources required to sustain their activities and, therefore, must conduct transactions with elements in the environment to secure a stable flow of resources. This is based on the RDT proposed by Pfeffer and Salancik (2003) in 1978. These transactions in turn leads to a dependence on the resource providers. The range of the organization's dependence on specific exchanges needed for its activities, again, determines its vulnerability to extraorganizational influence. The point here is not how many providers the organizations relies on, rather whether the organization has access to the same resources from other sources.

The theory of resource dependence has three main themes to understanding how organizational decision making is constrained by the environment. These are: (1) *interdependency*; (2) *strategic options*; and (3) *power.* These can be seen as three strategical viewpoints on how resource dependence works.

As organizations' autonomy is limited by their dependence on certain stakeholder groups to sustain certain resource bases, we can conclude that the role of the environment is imperative to the organization. The environment is naturally outside the organization's control and functions as a system of interdependencies. Organizations therefore seek to minimize their dependence on other organizations to acquire important resources and change the environment to make those resources available. The organization can make crucial administrative errors if it is ignorant of its interdependence or restraints to the environment. Everything organizations do are reactions to their environment, so the focus should be on how to alter the environment to advantage organizations. If there has been any change in the environment, organizations should focus on analyzing the possibility of other organizations pursuing this change to their advantage.

Only if the organization is able to either expand the quantity of resources or diminish the quantity of competitors for those resources can it change its level of interdependence. By forming alliances, joint ventures and mergers, organizations can attempt to overcome dependencies and increase organizational autonomy and legitimacy. The organization itself may also carry out diversification of its activities to shift its interdependence from a few parties to many.

To examine the need of diversified funding, this chapter examined the following hypotheses together with the qualitative data. The hypotheses regarding the resource diversification were:

H2: The type of perceived resource interdependence leads to a higher degree of resource diversification in private cultural centers.

H02: The type of perceived resource interdependence does not lead to a higher degree of resource diversification in private cultural centers.

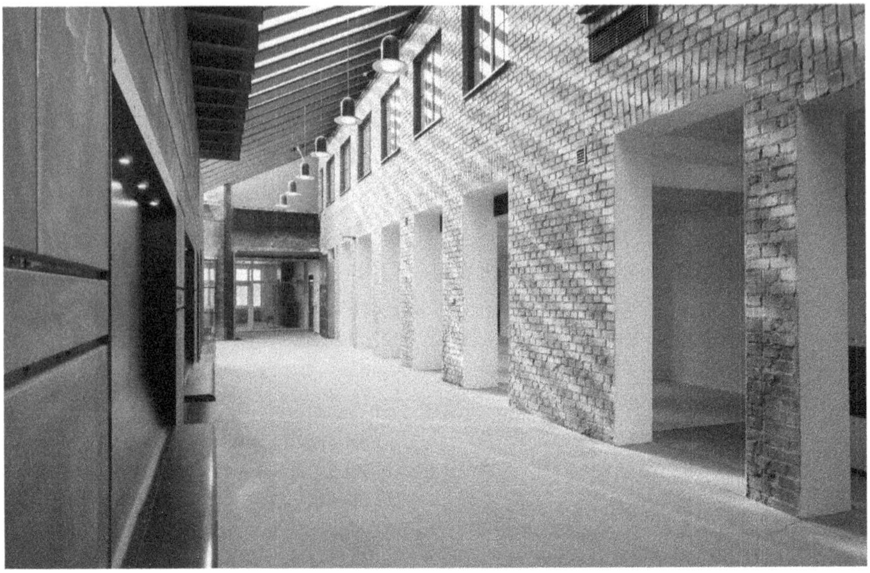

Picture 6.2 The foyer of cultural center Korundi in Rovanniemi, Finland.

The hypotheses regarding the environmental interdependence were:

H4: Cultural centers in general have a manageable environmental interdependence.
H04: Cultural centers in general do not have a manageable environmental interdependence.

The qualitative questions this chapter aimed to focus on are how cultural centers perceive the concept of resource dependence, and how they manage this dependency in practice.

Looking closer at the results from the interviews, we can see how the private cultural centers perceive the environments view on them as positive. Anyway, they still think that collaboration with the municipality is difficult, whereas the opposite applies with other private organizations and henceforth build alliances with these.

When comparing the findings with theory, it appears that the heterogeneity of the available services of the private cultural center, is what grants the center its particular character. In addition, the diversity of funding sources, such as venue rentals, alliances and grants, not only gives private centers economic security but also makes better use of their resources. Adopting different funding sources is how private cultural centers defy the institutional requirements challenging them (see Chapter 5), as suggested in institutional theory (Oliver, 1991). It also strengthens the notion of management in private cultural centers being more active within the scope of RDT (Pfeffer & Salancik, 2003), and less active in public cultural centers within the scope of IT (DiMaggio & Powell, 1983). This also follows the

Table 6.5 Extension of Table 1.1, ownership and control

New Institutional Theory		*Resource Dependence Theory*	
The Public Centers	The Centers maintained by Governmental Companies	The Hybrid Centers	The Private Centers
High Conformity	Moderate Conformity	Moderate Diversity	High Diversity

predictions of strategic options (Pfeffer & Salancik, 2003), in which the manager reduces resource dependence and maintains autonomy by diversifying revenue strategies (Froelich, 1999).

The quantitative findings are hardly surprising and suggest that cultural centers do have significant environmental interdependencies, supporting the qualitative findings. The research material selected and interpreted indicates that no organization is an island, and the core claim of RDT holds: every organization needs to interact with its environment (Pfeffer & Salancik, 2003). The respondents still emphasize the needs to be effective and to foresee external demands, in line with Guo and Acar (2005), who proclaimed that organizations need to do so not to lose control.

The findings on resource dependence allow for assessing the degree of the dependence. This study indicates asymmetrical relationship between public and private organizations, in which private organizations are more dependent on diverse funding sources than public centers. The latter group is mainly dependent on its main funder, the municipality. Diversification of resource dependence can be found among the private cultural centers. This implies that the assumption of this study is correct; the more dependent a cultural center is on a single source of revenue, in this study, the municipality, the higher the degree of conformity it displays. Likewise, the more dependent a cultural center is on diverse revenue source, the higher the degree of diversity it displayed. In other words, the conformity presented by IT (DiMaggio & Powell, 1983) correlates with a single (or a few) source of revenue, whereas the diversity presented by RDT (Pfeffer & Salancik, 2003) correlates with numerous diverse revenue streams.

However, this study could not find accurate measurements to analyze whether public cultural centers exhibit conformity, but much evidence points in that direction. Public centers do primarily depend on municipalities, which also apply most pressure to the centers. Furthermore, the comparison of diversification does find differences in private and public centers. The quantitative data, with smaller SDs in all the main study variables for public centers than private centers, suggest there is more homogeneity among public centers and more heterogeneity among private centers

As we have seen in Chapter 5, IT suggests that organizations wind up in conformity as to both form and performance outcomes (DiMaggio & Powell, 1983), while RDT suggests diversification based on sources of revenue (Pfeffer & Salancik, 2003). This in turn implies that the predictions of high conformity or isomorphism in IT apply mostly to public cultural centers, whereas high diversification in both activities and revenue structures applies to private centers. The remaining two center types are placed on transitional stages between these two extremes and show that centers maintained by government companies tend to exhibit slightly more conformity and hybrid centers slightly more diversity. By extending Table 1.1 in this book, the categorization of the four center types can be interpreted as follows in Table 6.5.

In practice, this implies that the more dependent a cultural center is on a single source of revenue (in this study, the municipality), the higher the degree of conformity it displays. Similarly, the more dependent a cultural center is on multiple revenue sources, the greater diversity it displays. This does not mean that either of the cultural centers has better or worse offering of culture. It is rather an organizational difference. The private centers aim at developing their palette of activities with a vast amount of inventive methods, while the public centers tend to actualize their mission quite statically. When the only tool you have is a hammer, you tend to see every problem as a nail.

For resource scarcity, which seems to be the largest difficulty among private cultural centers, acquiring and allocating resources should be planned ahead, while staying within the frames of the mission statement. The field itself is not lucrative, so exploring the outskirts of the mission statement offers possibilities to gain resources.

References

Bennett, R., & Savani, S. (2011). Surviving mission drift. Nonprofit Management and Leadership, 22(2), pp. 217–231.

Burns, T., & Stalker, G. (1961). *The Management of Innovation.* New York: Oxford University Press.

Casciaro, T., & Piskorski, M. (2005). Power imbalance, mutual dependence, and constraint, absorption: A close look at resource dependence theory. Administrative Science Quarterly, 50, pp. 167–199.

Choudhury, E., & Ahmed, S. (2002). The shifting meaning of governance: Public accountability of third sector organizations in an emergent global regime. International Journal of Public Administration, 25(4), pp. 561–589.

Das, S., Sen, P., & Sengupta, S. (1998). Impact of strategic alliances on firm valuation. Academy of Management Journal, 41(1), pp. 27–41.

Davis, G., & Cobb, J. (2010). Resource dependence theory: Past and future. Em Stanford's Organization Theory Renaissance, 1970–2000. Online: Stanford.

DiMaggio, P. (1986). Introduction. Em P. DiMaggio (Ed.), Nonprofit enterprise and the arts (pp. 3–13). New York: Oxford University Press.

DiMaggio, P., & Powell, W. (1983). The iron cage revisited: Institutional isomorphism and collective rationality in organizational fields. American Sociological Review, 48, pp. 147–160.

Drees, J., & Heugens, P. (2013). Synthesizing and extending resource dependence theory. Journal of Management, 39(6), pp. 1666–1698.

Emerson, R. (1962). Power-Dependence Relations. American Economic Review, 59(3), pp. 314–321.

Froelich, K. A. (1999). Diversification of revenue strategies: Evolving resource dependence in nonprofit organizations. Nonprofit and Voluntary Sector Quarterly, 28(3), pp. 246–268.

Frooman, J. (1999). Stakeholder influence strategies. Academy of Management Review, 24, pp. 191–205.

Frooman, J., & Murrell, R. (2005). Stakeholder influence strategies: The roles of structural and demographic determinants. Business and Society, 44(1), 3–31.

Guadagnoli, E., & Velicer, W. (1988). Relation of sample size to the stability of component patterns. Psychological Bulletin, 103, pp. 265–275.

Guo, C., & Acar, M. (2005). Understanding collaboration among nonprofit organizations: Combining resource dependency, institutional, and network perspectives. Nonprofit and Voluntary Sector Quarterly, 34, p. 340.

Hannan, M., & Freeman, J. (1975). The population ecology of organizations. American Sociological Review, 82(5), pp. 929–964.

Hatch, M. (2013). *Organization Theory: Modern, Symbolic, and Postmodern Perspectives* (3 ed.). Oxford: Oxford University Press.

Hillman, A. (2005). Politicians on the board: Do connections affect the bottom line? Journal of Management, 31, pp. 464–481.

Hillman, A., Cannella, A., & Paetzold, R. (2000). The resource dependence role of corporate directors: Strategic adaptation of board composition in response to environmental change. Journal of Management Studies, 37(2), pp. 235–255.

Hillman, A., Withers, M., & Collins, B. (2009). Resource dependence theory: A review. Journal of Management, 35, pp. 1404–1427.

Jones, M. (2007). The multiple sources of mission drift. Nonprofit and Voluntary Quarterly, 36, pp. 69–86.

Katila, R., Rosenberger, J., & Eisenhardt, K. (2008). Swimming with sharks: Technology ventures, defense mechanisms and corporate relationships. Administrative Science Quarterly, 53, pp. 295–332.

Kelly, J. (2007). Reforming public services in the UK: Bringing in the third sector. Public Administration, 85(4), pp. 1003–1022.

Kingston, C., & Caballero, G. (2009). Comparing theories of institutional change. Journal of Institutional Economics, 5(2), pp. 151–180.

Lawrence, P., & Lorsch, J. (1976). *Organizations and Environment: Managing Differentiation and Integration.* Boston: Harvard Business School Press.

Leblebici, H., Salancik, G., Copay, A., & King, T. (1991). *Institutional change and the transformation of interorganizational fields: An organizational history of the U.S. radio broadcasting industry.* Administrative Science Quarterly, 36, pp. 333–363.

Malatesta, D., & Smith, C. (2014). Lessons from resource dependence theory for contemporary public and nonprofit management. Public Administration Review, 74(1), pp. 14–25.

Meyer, J., & Rowan, B. (1977). Institutionalized organizations: Formal structure as myth and ceremony. The American Journal of Sociology, 83(2), pp. 340–363.

Miller, G., Mcmullen, J., & Vogus, T. (2012). Venturing for others with heart and head: How compassion encourages social entrepreneurship. Academy of Management Review, 37(4), pp. 616–640.

Nienhuser, W. (2008). Resource dependence theory. How well does it explain behavior of organizations. Management Revue, 19(1–2), pp. 9–32.

Oliver, C. (1991). *Strategic responses to institutional processes*. Academy of Management Review, pp. 145–179.
Pfeffer, J., & Salancik, G. (2003). *The External Control of Organizations: A Resource Dependence Perspective*. Stanford, CA: Stanford University Press.
Provan, K., Beyer, J., & Kruytbosch, C. (1980). Environmental linkages and power in resource dependence relations between organizations. Administrative Science Quarterly, 25, pp. 200–225.
Scott, W. (2014). *Institutions and Organizations* (4 ed.). Thousand Oaks, CA: Sage.
Sharif, S., & Yeoh, K. (2014). *Independent directors' resource provision capability in publicly-listed companies*. Corporate Ownership and Control, 11(3), pp. 113–121.
Suchman, M. (1995). *Managing legitimacy: Strategic and institutional approaches*. Academy of Management Review, 20(3), pp. 571–610.
Suddaby, R. (2010). *Challenges for institutional theory*. Journal of Management Inquiry, 19(1), pp. 14–20.
Tausky, C. (1978). *Work Organizations: Major Theoretical Perspectives*. Itasca, IL: F.E. Peacock.
Twombly, E. (2003). What factors affect the entry and exit of nonprofit human service organizations in metropolitan areas? Nonprofit and Voluntary Sector Quarterly, 32(2), pp. 211–235.
Ulrich, D., & Barney, J. (1984). Perspectives in organizations: Resource dependence, efficiency, and population. Academic Management Review, 9, pp. 471–481.
Vickers, J., & Yarrow, G. (1991). Theory construction as disciplined imagination. The Academy of Management Review, 14(4), pp. 516–531.
Webb, D. (2017). Trends in the development and operation of PACs. Em P. Lambert, & R. Williams (Eds.), *Performing Arts Center Management* (pp. 45–62). New York: Routledge.
Weisbrod, B. (1998). The nonprofit mission and its financing. Journal of Policy Analysis and Management, 17, pp. 165–174.
Westphal, J., Boivie, S., & Chong, D. (2006). The strategic impetus for social network ties: Reconstituting broken CEO friendship ties. Strategic Management Journal, 27, pp. 425–445.
Williamson, O. (1975). *Markets and Hierarchies: Analysis and Antitrust Implications*. New York: Free Press.
Williamson, O. (1979). Transaction-cost economics: The governance of contractual relations. Journal of Law and Economics, 22(2), pp. 233–261.
Yan, A., & Gray, B. (2001). Antecedents and effects of parent control in international joint ventures. Journal of Management Studies, 38(3), pp. 393–416.

7 Mission focus and resource strategy management in cultural centers

This chapter will begin with an account of the problem of mission drift that many organizations face while striving merely to survive. Instead of defining what mission focus is, this chapter will focus on what it is not. A part of the problem with mission focus is the difficulty of solving mission-related questions and communicating them across the organization, while making enough revenues to maintain the core focus of displaying a versatile offering of culture. As Paul Bogen (2018, p. 14) puts it in his report on arts and cultural centers in Europe:

> *Far too many Arts/Cultural Centers' do not have a clear, stated vision, mission or values that are produced by all of the key people involved in the organization and are understood and believed in by all of its team and key stakeholders. And if the organization's vision has been produced by and is owned just by its leader, what happens when they depart?*

It seems as if 88% of the European centers had a written mission or vision statement, which would appear as a good result (Bogen, 2018). But only 68% declared that the key people in their organization had a shared, clear understanding of why they existed. With 82% of the centers' CEO's stating that everybody in their organization were clear with the why, only 53% of the staff agreed with this. There seems to be a clear problem with at least communication.

Looking at mission drift through the lenses of resource dependence strategies, which we covered in Chapter 6, some interesting questions emerge. Where is the limit for what an organization can do within the scope of its mission, and who defines it? Better yet, when is it defined accurately?

The hypotheses for the quantitative part of the study are:

H3: The type of perceived strategic options leads to a higher degree of mission drift in private cultural centers.

H03: The type of perceived strategic options does not lead to a higher degree of mission drift in private cultural centers.

As with the earlier chapters, let us start by looking at the theories, or the basics of the concept mission focus and mission drift. Thereafter, we will look upon how cultural centers position themselves in relation to these concepts.

7.1 Mission focus or mission drift?

Ammar (2015) describes a mission statement as one of the building blocks of business. In terms of the content and characteristics of mission statements, Powers (2012) highlights such domains as customer needs, endurance, precision and broad-based coverage as a few of the most important criteria. David et al. (2014) state in turn that every mission statement ought to cover the markets, the range of customers, products or service, philosophy, self- concept, employee care, technology, survival, growth and profitability profile, as well as the public image. Bart and Baetz (1998) point out that mission statements are usually short, simple and straightforward.

Yunus and Weber (2007) however pointed out that for *'businesses it will be difficult to operate with two conflicting goals of profit maximization and social benefit, which ultimately forces their executives (...) to gradually inch toward the profit maximization goal'* (Yunus & Weber, 2007, p. 33). In the academic literature, mission drift is defined as the organizational drift towards the business direction with an underlining of profit-maximization (Doherty et al., 2014; Ebrahim et al., 2014). The term organizational identity *'refers to those core, distinctive, and enduring features unique to an institution'* (Albert & Whetten, 1985, p. 256) and covers *'the shared beliefs of members about the central, enduring and distinctive characteristics of the organization'* (Goldern-Biddle & Rao, 1997, p. 594).

Mission drift, in which an organization deviates from its mission, is commonly defined as a process of organizational change (Jones, 2007). It may occur due to commercial activities and dependence on any dominant funder, such as foundations and the state. While trying to manage diverse revenue sources, private cultural centers may become more resource- than mission-oriented. It has especially been applied to organizations with a social mission, such as nonprofit organizations, social enterprises, hospital and educational bodies. Mission drift is described as a *'focus on profits to the detriment of the social good'* (Battilana et al., 2012, p. 51). This book explores in many chapters the connection between perceived resource dependence and mission drift.

Private cultural centers, both nonprofit and for-profit, pursue nonfinancial goals, such as community commitments and aesthetic goals (Sherer & Suddaby, 2018). They have a clear exposure to mission drift as they aim to fulfil their mission by acquiring a broad range of revenues. At the same time, RDT highlights that diverse dependencies increase independence from the environment (Pfeffer & Salancik, 2003). As a result, identifying mission drift is seldom uncomplicated (Jones, 2007). It may arise when organizations officially change their missions, strategies or objectives, but it can also take place in less visible ways, such as changes to practices of organizational work or to the quality of the services (Weisbrod, 2004). Moreover, the organization may be forced to change its mission as the problems or demands on which it initially focused have changed. It, therefore, may be difficult to distinguish between what is a necessary change and what is mission drift (Bielefeld, 2009).

Weisbrod (1998) emphasized that organizations with flexible mission statements are prone to mission drift from their core services as financially tempting projects appear. These organizations may be tempted to take part in economically stable and politically neutral projects. The goals of the organization and the government may be compatible, but Lipsky and Smith (1989) have nonetheless highlighted that contracting requirements may change the organization's approach to services: *'In essence, they may be forced to conform to standards imposed by contracting policy at the expense of their home-grown notions of what constitutes effective service delivery'* (p. 638).

Bennet (2008) pointed out that a flexible mission may be beneficial and more sustainable for organizations. Although Cairns et al. (2005) argued that mission drift exists, Chew and Osborne (2009) contended that organizations can stay true to their missions even if they display flexibility in organizational operations and structures. Macmillan (2010) furthermore stated that;

> *in the absence of focused empirical research on the maintenance or elasticity of third sector organization missions over time, we are left with some concern about the potential for mission drift, but no clear indication of its prevalence or the causes and consequences of drift.*
>
> (p. 23)

The risk of mission drift is thus deep-rooted in social enterprises (Jeter, 2017). It even seems as if it is inevitable, whether temporary or permanent. It, therefore, is often seen as a spectrum instead of a binary concept.

The concept of mission drift is nevertheless much debated. Sommerfeld and Reisch (2003) found that '*nearly all respondents remarked on how their agencies' programs have become more outcome-based, although their overall mission has not changed*' (p. 312). Chavez et al. (2004), though, has pointed out that public funding has not had negative effects on nonprofit political activity, and organizations with public contracts do not automatically forget their engagement with their mission. Froelich (1999) stated that mission drift might actually be a resource diversification strategy. It may could be interpreted as a conscious strategy to secure the survival and thrival of the organization, a strategy to ensure the continuation of what is done within the frames of the core mission.

7.2 A cultural center viewpoint on mission drift

Being forced to find a variety of resources to maintain a center can shift the focus from the content to the revenues, the very definition of mission drift. Instead of focusing mainly on the artistic content and how the audience perceives it, attention turns to changing the artistic content to increase revenue. This section presents the respondents' view on potential mission drift in their organizations.

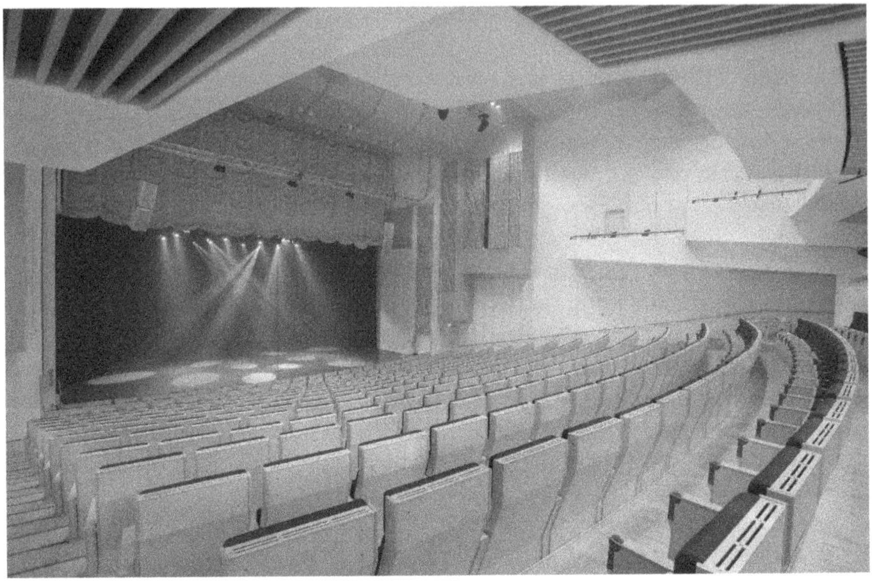

Picture 7.1 The main stage of cultural center Virta in Imatra, Finland.

This becomes evident during the interviews as well. When asked about their mission, most respondents conclude that the artistic content comes first. Whether professionals and amateurs on the stage, movies in the cinema or versatile cultural offerings, it is about what is displayed, not about making profits.

> *It depends on how society works or where we think we could make an effort. [...] We would mostly like to be part of society, that way, and listen and see if there is something we can join. Because, we still see a culture center as a ... there is a such social reasoning behind that we want to contribute something within culture.*
>
> (Respondent H)

Respondents from every center mention that their mission is not to make money from the cultural content but to display art that makes a difference within the community. In fact, some respondents even emphasize their quest to not choose their cultural content based on any expectations to make profits.

> *In short, it is empowering, not precautionary. That is to say, in practice, we search for such program offerings that others do not want, or, in practice, what is not terribly productive in terms of ticketing.*
>
> (Respondent C)

In contrast, the minor possibility of making money on culture is constantly highlighted. As there is, according to the respondents, a marginal chance to make ends meet, so there is no need to aim for commercial success. One respondent even points out that what they do would not be possible to do if the goal was to make profits: '*This would not work if we would have a commercial interest*'. (Respondent Q).

Still, quite a few respondents imply that they have to conform to the rules of business to maintain their centers, although this conformity is never made their main focus. They simply stress that they have to comply with certain rules of business to have any chance of earning revenue.

> *However, the purpose of culture is to understand, that is, it may be a bit too much idealistic to improve the quality of life in the whole community and not so much like an instrument of business. On the other hand, fortunately, there is so little money involved in culture, that it is not yet terribly ... business sharks have not been able to enter cultural field.*
>
> (Respondent O)

Still, this conformity with business approaches takes places through different measures and, in some cases, seems to affect the cultural offerings. A few respondents highlight the strategy of choosing cultural content that balances events expected to generate substantial profits and events that most likely will not generate much profits.

> *We do more business there, in the way we organize concerts where we want people that pay a lot, as in entry, and then we get the money. And then we also have a lot of activities that do not, which in themselves do not give us any income, but they are still there.*
>
> (Respondent P)

The emphasis on the business side serves to make profits to maintain the cultural centers, not to only choose cultural content that makes profits. The respondents indirectly state that they choose to make money on other activities not explicitly directed at their core audience to then be able to provide a variety of cultural content, which is less expensive for the audience.

> *In Europe, they have more, more private houses than here, and then they have often built up as [...] [our center], that you have a B2B side, that rent out spaces and so on, and the idea in most houses is that with the profit that you make [...] You use most of it to make culture or in some way support society.*
>
> (Respondent E)

The cultural centers also aim to make profits on their restaurants, which are considered to be a service for customers and thus not a factor that affects the cultural content negatively. In fact, the main goal of the restaurants is also to be

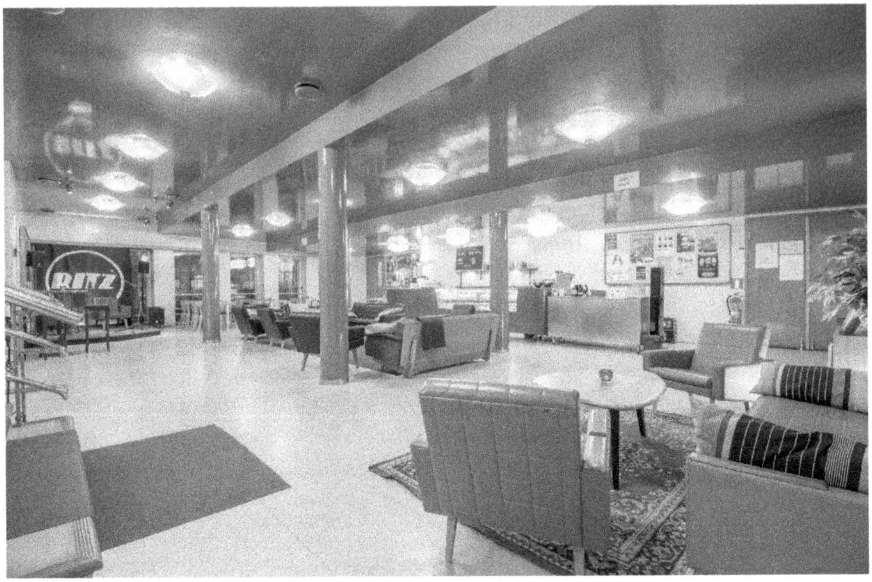

Picture 7.2 The café at cultural center Ritz in Vaasa, Finland. A photograph by Valter Lidsle.

able to make the cultural content less expensive. As one respondent summarized this: '*Alongside the restaurant business, we produce cheap cultural experiences*' (Respondent C). The respondents unanimously dismiss the possibility of mission drift in their cases.

7.3 Resource strategy management

Experiencing the pressure of scarce resources, all the centers feel compelled to develop a palette of revenues that covers their costs. There indeed is a variety of ways of managing this. As one respondent states, '*I guess you have to have some new ways to think about the finances and the other things, that you can keep it as varied as it has been*' (Respondent B). The centers differ quite a bit regarding their solutions to this issue.

One center relies heavily on volunteers, making it possible to arrange events at much lower costs. The idea is to give the volunteers noneconomic rewards (e.g. parties and discounts on tickets to events they do not work) and to offer a community for people who have moved to that area recently. The volunteers are obliged to work on a certain number of events every year and to be on hand if others fail, for instance, due to sickness. All the events the center arranges, around 70% of all events, are solely handled by volunteers. The center also maintains a restaurant during events, which generates revenues for the center. The restaurant is also managed by the volunteers, something they do admit has its complications.

Another center offers a platform for people to propose and develop project ideas and find external financing through the center. This center does not offer job positions to a wide extent but welcomes people who can build up their own employment. It also has a restaurant run by a separate company that donates money to the center's theatre annually.

A third center has built a corporate group around its activities, offering a wide variety of services, from the actual cultural center to an outdoor pool and an ice-skating rink. It offers cultural activities at each venue, so it can share the costs of the employees who manage and market the cultural services they offer (theatre, music and cinema). The center has restaurants at all three sites, which generate money for cultural activities. The same center also does quite a lot of corporate business-to-business events, around 300–400 a year, mainly focused on consulting for other businesses. This activity provides around one-third of its annual budget.

The fourth center has combined a separate information point and a meeting place with its offices. This center offers a wide range of citizen services to the local community, from selling tickets to all kind of events across Finland to providing information on grants application and selling books and CDs. This allows the center to get different revenue sources and still stay within the frame of its mission.

Nearly, all the centers also do all sorts of collaborations with other organizations, giving them opportunities to get some revenue from these projects. These external projects mostly involve the local community and seem to include the centers in their activities in most cases. The projects thus are not only a method to finance salaries but also build on the mission of the centers.

Most centers have a wide range of freelance workers who bring expertise to the center but no monthly wages. This way, the centers can afford to have experts do specific tasks the producers and managers on monthly salaries might not be able to do. These freelancers are always hired for certain projects, so the center can choose which expert is the most suitable for a specific project, instead of having one expert on a monthly salary who must be versatile in a way most people simply are not.

One center tried a new method to finance a new project and collected nearly 1 million euros through crowdfunding. This was a new experience, which the center endorses. It still emphasizes the need to have interesting content as citizens will not support financially a project that is not interesting to them.

> *A very big [...] significance it has in culture and content, as people are taking a stand with their own habits of consumption as to what they want to hear and experience. So, in that sense, it suits cultural projects very well. (...) It is expected to generate returns [...]. I think it's about love for something that you want to support or a progress you want to support.*
>
> (Respondent A)

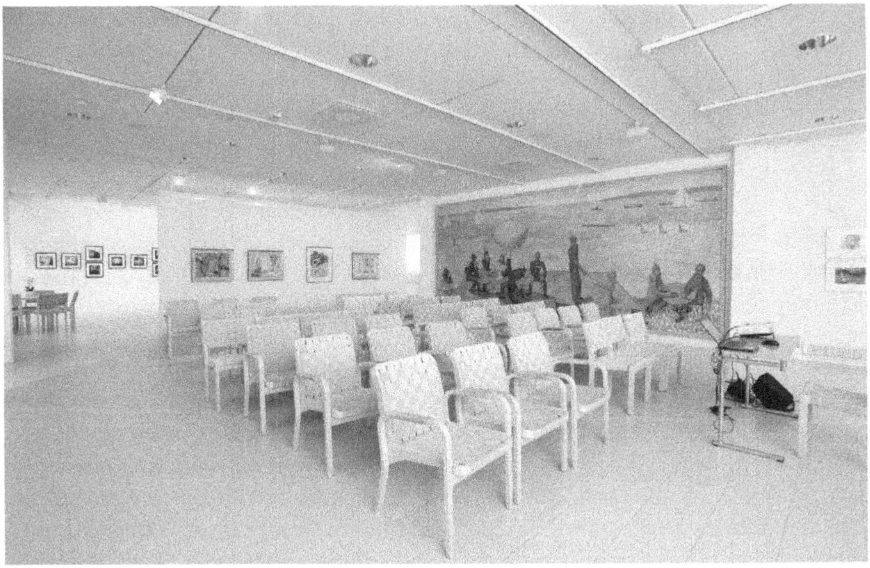

Picture 7.3 An auditorium at the art gallery of cultural center Virta in Imatra, Finland.

Three centers seem to aim to be more self-sufficient. None of the centers appears to think it could ever easily manage without subsidies from the municipality – or especially private funders, for that matter. Instead, these revenues constitute such a small portion of the total budget that all possible regulations and other demands accompanying such subsidies have less significance for their activities.

> *We are constantly talking about our business, the way that we have developed it all the time so that we can, in principle, eventually think that we could do on our own.*
>
> (Respondent P)

The idea seems to be specifically to make each subsidy less important to the overall budget by developing a vast palette of differing subsidies. In this manner, centers can ensure that no one contributor has too much leverage over their activities. Accordingly, the respondents stress their independence in a variety of ways, including being as self-sufficient as possible. *'As it now starts to roll, and we begin to do it in a smart way, then slowly but surely, maybe we'll even be nearly self-sufficient. Absolutely'* (Respondent T).

One respondent has a plan for self-sufficiency: to create a mixture of different subsidies, to aim for box-office hits and to put aside money for a rainy day. This plan includes a measure to build up the budget for events arranged by the center.

> *Thus, the very smartest way to make a cultural home self-sufficient is to have a 20-30-year plan. Look for donations, put away money, and create your own foundation. And, on the other hand, create your own business that may be financed to 20% to 50% with ticket revenues and the other half or 1/4 with sponsorship and external foundations and so forth. Such a mixture is very good.*
>
> (Respondent G)

Furthermore, the respondents seem to enjoy that however they decide to cope with their resource dependencies is a matter of their own decisions. As one respondent states, '*and the funny thing about taking these risks is that it's the association that decides*'. (Respondent P). Most interviewees emphasize that they weigh every decision the cultural center makes according to the resource-saving principle; whatever is being done, there has to be a more cost-effective way to do it. The interviewees do not seem to have any illusions of being avant-garde in a fashion that implies they are alone in their cultural offerings. Most respondents merely stress that whatever their cultural offerings are, they are not anything that has been done in their specific region or, in some cases, even the whole country. The interviewees emphasize that they seek to find more effective ways of doing what they do. As one respondent states:

> *What is done in China is also done here, and we should be able to do it a little bit smarter. That, of course, we are all involved in this global change, but ... that's really fun, it's fun that you do not always do the same thing and keep in mind all the time to get enthusiastic all over again, and it's natural if it comes from the heart.*
>
> (Respondent A)

The overarching theme among the respondents is that they constantly search for more effective ways to do things, more fruitful ways to use the walls they have. Aware of the risks that come with being private, the centers nevertheless pursue efficiency.

> *When you have more risks as a private actor, you have to think about how to get more benefit from this place, how to best use this.*
>
> (Respondent P)

The respondents display very visibly how they compare themselves with public cultural centers. They take pride in being more effective than their counterparts. They may get less subsidies then their public peers, but apparently, they find ways to manage without such public revenues – a necessity, given the circumstances. One respondent vividly puts it:

> *If we think about it, there are eight cultural houses in the Helsinki area that are municipal. They use about 8 million euros in cash, roughly. ... If it is*

> *approximately so, [...] the city's subsidy or contribution is about 1 million euros per house. Then when I'm think about the contribution of the city here, that's 100,000 euros, [...] well, in this sense, we are an effective organization.*
> (Respondent C)

The respondents, however, do acknowledge their interdependencies on many stakeholders, such as the municipality and other organizations. The very core of their activities is ultimately built on external players, such as freelancers, musicians and theatres, and a substantial part of their budget consists of various subsidies.

7.4 A quantitative analysis of mission drift in private cultural centers

This subchapter is aimed at studying whether private cultural centers are subject to mission drift. As stated in this chapter, mission drift occurs when organizations, in this case, private cultural centers, use more resources on getting revenues than on the artistic content displayed in the center (Jones, 2007). To examine mission drift, this subchapter focuses on the variables presented after the hypotheses.

The hypotheses are:

H3: The type of perceived strategic options leads to a higher degree of mission drift in private cultural centers.

H03: The type of perceived strategic options does not lead to a higher degree of mission drift in private cultural centers.

The variables used in this construct are:

1) *How dependent are you on renters?*
   (How dependent are you on external renters?)
2) *More commercial activities*
   (Are your activities primarily commercial?)
3) *Do you choose your cultural offerings on the basis of commercial success?*
   (Do you choose your activities primarily because of commercial success?)
4) *Competition with private sector*
   (Do you feel you have to compete with the private cultural sector?)

All variables were based on a 5-point Likert scale. Cronbach's alpha was used to establish the internal consistency and reliability of all the items. The reliability coefficient values are .744 for these four items. Multicollinearity was tested, and the VIF values are between 1.337 and 1.796. This means that there are no multicollinearity symptoms. Levene's test of homogeneity of variances was also conducted to test for heteroskedasticity. The obtained values of Sig. variables are between .097 and .765, more than the level of .05. It, therefore, is concluded that there is no heteroscedasticity problem.

Table 7.1 Predictors' unique contributions in binomial logistic regression (N = 97)

	B	*Wald*	*p*	*Odds Ratio*
How dependent are you on renters?	–0,61	7,282	0,007	0,544
More commercial activities?	0,477	4,094	0,043	1,611
Do you choose your cultural offering on the basis of commercial success?	0,11	0,197	0,657	1,117
Competition with private cultural sector?	0,167	0,622	0,43	1,181
Constant	–0,681	0,754	0,385	0,506

7.4.1 Binomial logistic regression

A logistic regression was performed to determine the effects on the likelihood of mission drift among the participants (private centers and all the other centers) due to the following variables: *how dependent are you on renters, more commercial activities, do you choose your cultural offerings based on commercial success* and *competition with private cultural sector.* A .05 criterion of statistical significance was employed. Private cultural centers were used as the dependent variable, and all the rest of center types were the referent group.

The logistic regression model is statistically significant ($\chi24$) = 11.143, p = .025 (<0.05). The model explains 15.1% (Nagelkerke R2) of the variance in mission drift. Binary logistic regression indicates that *renter dependency* and *commercial activities* are significant predictors of mission drift in private cultural centers. The other two predictors, *cultural offerings due to commercial success* and *competition with the private cultural sector*, are not significant. *Renter dependency* and *commercial activities* are significant at the 6% level (renter dependency: Wald = 7.282, p = 0.007; commercial activities: Wald = 4.094, p = 0.043). The odds ratio for renter dependency is 0.544 (95% CI: .349–.846), and for commercial activities is 1.611 (95% CI:1.015–2.557). The model correctly predicts 90.8% of other than private centers, and 28.1% of private centers, for an overall percentage correct prediction rate of 70.1%.

Each predictor has five parameters as Likert scale measures. The results of the binary logistic regression, therefore, suggest that the null hypothesis can be rejected.

7.5 Summary and conclusions

Mission statements are generally a short, simple and straightforward covering of the organization's markets, range of customers, products or service, philosophy, self-concept, employee care, technology, survival, growth and profitability profile, as well as the public image. As it seems, mission statements are often not communicated enough among the staff, which in turn increases the possibilities for mission drift. Mission drift could be seen as the opposite to mission focus and may occur due to commercial activities and dependence on any dominant funder. This can happen when organizations officially change their missions, strategies or objectives, but it can also take place in less visible ways, such as changes to practices of organizational work or to the quality of the services. However, it is very hard to identify a mission drift from a normal organizational change.

Private cultural centers, both nonprofit and for-profit, with their pursue of nonfinancial goals (community commitments and aesthetic goals), have a clear exposure to mission drift as they aim to fulfil their mission by acquiring a broad range of revenues.

This chapter focused on the questions where the limit for what an organization can do within the scope of its mission is, and who defines it? Furthermore, when is it defined accurately?

The hypotheses for the quantitative part of the study were:

H3: The type of perceived strategic options leads to a higher degree of mission drift in private cultural centers.

H03: The type of perceived strategic options does not lead to a higher degree of mission drift in private cultural centers.

In terms of balancing the economy with diverse funding sources, the respondents do admit that they seek different funding possibilities, choose some artistic content due to its probability of economic success and incorporate a business side to their palette of activities. As Jones (2007) emphasized, mission drift may occur due to commercial activities. However, there is a unanimous view among the respondents on this resource focus as necessary to be able to display versatile cultural offerings. That is to say, a certain focus on earning more revenue at the expense of the core mission is present, but ultimately it is a means to an end: to be able to actualize the mission of the cultural center. As most respondents said, the cultural field is not a lucrative field, but you can get by if you work for diverse funding.

As concluded by Jeter (2017), the state of mission drift in an organization is inevitable, at least temporarily. If one were to consider merely the quantitative data of this research (Järvinen, 2019), it could be concluded that there is a possibility of mission drift among the private centers as the quantitative findings suggest a heavy dependence on commercial activities and rentals, for instance. Still, the qualitative research, which was undertaken as part of triangulation with the quantitative findings, returned fairly different results. The quantitative results may be accurate in stating what the interview respondents claim: that private cultural centers have to rely heavily on a variety of funding streams. However, as earlier concluded, this does not contradict the ultimate aim to be able to exhibit a variety of cultural offerings. Accomplishing the cultural mission is the foundation of receiving grants, so the respondents at private cultural centers do not feel as that there is any mission drift. As Chong (2008) stated, arts organizations need to be cost effective and aim at diversified funding sources and efficient management structures to secure financial stability without being guided by money. The private cultural centers seem to be doing exactly this – they themselves do define what can be done within the scope of their own mission, and they appear to be aware about how their action affects the mission of their organization, as to the accurate definition of the mission statement.

Still, this does necessarily not exclude the possibility of mission drift. During the interviews, the respondents were aware they were representing their cultural centers and may have been less aware of potential mission drift in their center. They all claim that they can react to new possibilities quickly, which implies a flexible mission statement. According to Weisbrod (2004), such organizations are exposed to risk of mission drift. Furthermore, Froelich (1999) emphasized that resource diversification is per se a level of mission drift.

According to the findings, the key is to balance the activities with such content that helps the organization to survive economically, alongside the core content. As the findings highlight, the cultural field is not lucrative, which implies that the methods to get the funding needed cannot only be those that fit the mission perfectly.

The organizations need to explore the outskirts of their mission to find ways to balance the economy. This suggests that the concept of mission drift is not measurable between different fields and, as Weisbrod (2004) stated, very hard to point out. Despite strong economic pressures, there remains a high commitment to aesthetic integrity. The private cultural centers do not completely abandon their focus on professional and aesthetic quality, even if they are more attentive to the need for economic resources.

Time, as well as surrounding society, tends to alter initial efforts and the organization could very well end up maintaining activities outside its core mission over time. This in turn suggests that mission drift often occurs outside the organizations operating possibilities. Consequently, staying within the frames of the mission requires continuous corrective steps.

References

Albert, S., & Whetten, D.A. (1985). Organizational identity. Research in Organizational Behavior, 7, pp. 263–295.

Ammar, A.A. (2015). The impact of mission statement on performance: An exploratory study in the Jordanian Banking Industry. Journal of Management Policy and Practice, 16(4), pp. 73–87.

Bart, C.K., & Baetz, M.C. (1998). The relationship between mission statements and firm performance: An exploratory studies. The Journal of Management studies, 35(60), pp. 823–853.

Battilana, J., Lee, M., Walker, J., & Dorsey, C. (2012). In search of the hybrid ideal. Stanford Social Innovation Review, 10, pp. 51–55.

Bennett, R. (2008). Marketing of voluntary organizations as contract providers of national and local government welfare services in the UK. Voluntas, 19, pp. 268–269.

Bielefeld, W. (2009). Issues in social enterprise and social entrepreneurship. Journal of Public Affairs in Education, 15(1), pp. 69–86.

Bogen, P. (2018). Stronger arts and cultural organisations for a greater social impact. *Business Models profiling of Cultural Centres & Performing Arts Organisations.* Sweden: Trans Europe Halles, Creative Lenses.

Cairns, B., Harris, M., & Young, P. (2005). Building the capacity of the voluntary non-profit sector: Challenges of theory and practice. International Journal of Public Administration, 28, pp. 869–885.

Chavez, M., Stephens, L., & Galaskiewicz, J. (2004). Does government funding suppress nonprofits' political activity? American Sociological Review, 69(2), pp. 292–316.

Chew, C., & Osborne, P. (2009). *Identifying the factors that influence positioning strategy in UK charitable organisations that provide public services: Towards an integrating model.* Nonprofits and Voluntary Sector Quarterly, 38(1), pp. 29–50.

Chong, D. (2008). *Arts Management* (4 ed.). New York: Routledge.

David, M.A., David, F.A., & David, F.A. (2014). Mission statement theory and practice: A content analysis and new direction. International Journal of Business, Marketing, and Decision Sciences. 7(1), pp. 95–110.

Doherty, B., Haugh, H. and Lyon, F., (2014). Social enterprises as hybrid organizations: A review and research agenda. International Journal of Management Reviews, 16(4), pp. 417–436.

Ebrahim, A., Battilana, J. and Mair, J., (2014). The governance of social enterprises: Mission drift and accountability challenges in hybrid organizations. Research in Organizational Behavior, 34, pp. 81–100.

Froelich, K. A. (1999). Diversification of revenue strategies: Evolving resource dependence in nonprofit organizations. Nonprofit and Voluntary Sector Quarterly, 28(3), pp. 246–268.

Goldern-Biddle, K., & Rao, H. (1997). Breaches in the boardroom: Organizational identity and conflicts of commitment in a nonprofit organization. Organizational Science, 8(6), 593–611.

Jeter, T. (2017). Exploring Mission Drift and Tension in a Nonprofit Work Integration Social Enterprise. Minneapolis: Walden University.

Jones, M. (2007). The multiple sources of mission drift. Nonprofit and Voluntary Quarterly, 36, pp. 69–86.

Järvinen, T. (2019). *The Challengers of Public Cultural Centers.* Helsinki: Unigrafia: Sibelius Academy, University of Arts.

Lipsky, M., & Smith, S. (1989). *Nonprofit organizations, government, and the welfare state.* Political Science Quarterly, 4(104), pp. 625–648.

Macmillian, R. (2010). *The Third Sector Delivering Public Services: An Evidence Review*, Working Paper 20. Acesso em 24 de 4 de 2018, disponível em University of Birmingham: www.birmingham.ac.uk/generic/tsrc/documents/tsrc/working- papers/working-paper-20.pdf

Pfeffer, J., & Salancik, G. (2003). *The External Control of Organizations: A Resource Dependence Perspective.* Stanford, CA: Stanford University Press.

Powers, E.L. (2012). Organizational mission statement guidelines revisited. International Journal of Management & Information Systems, 16(4), pp. 281–290.

Sherer, P., & Suddaby, R. (2018). *Does Resource Diversity Confer Organizational Autonomy? Extending Resource Dependence Theory.* Unpublished Article.

Sommerfeld, D., & Reisch, M. (2003). *The 'Other America' after welfare reform: a view from the nonprofit sector*. Em M. Kilty, & E. Segal (Eds.), *Rediscovering the Other America: The Continuing Crisis of Poverty*. New York: Haworth Press

Weisbrod, B. (1998). The nonprofit mission and its financing. Journal of Policy Analysis and Management, 17, pp. 165–174.

Weisbrod, B. (2004). The pitfalls of profits. Stanford Social Innovation Review, 2(3), pp. 40–47.

Yunus, M., & Weber, K., (2007). *Creating a World Without Poverty – Social Business and the Future of Capitalism*. 1st Edition. New York: PublicAffairs.

8 Quality and profitable cultural centers

As governmental support declines and the competition for grants, donors and sponsor support increases, the cultural organizations should focus on customer development, or quality management, to gain increased ticket sales and thus improved profitability – and in the long run performance (Rentschler et al., 2002). Still, the increasing costs of keeping up the quality will pay itself back with increasing revenues (Crosby, 1980).

As we will find out in this chapter, there is quite a few definitions of the concept of quality. Thus, the definition is as vague as the business model concept (Chapter 3). We will however be focusing on quality management in this chapter in a manner suitable for cultural centers. In the current business literature, quality management is essentially about making organizations fulfill their mission for their stakeholders, which includes everything from improving services, products, systems and processes, to making the whole organization effective (Dahlgaard, 1999). In practice, this means a never ending pursue of excellence: to continuously assure that everything your organization does is within the scope of your mission and that it keeps on improving.

In this chapter, the emphasis will be placed on the importance of establishing ways of working with the core mission of a versatile offering of culture as well as making ends meet in economic terms. The importance of aligning practices to goals that support the strategy will be in focus. Although it might seem as if we have discussed this matter already in earlier chapters, which is partly true, this chapter focuses more on quality. Arts organizations need to be cost-effective and aim to diversify their funding sources and achieve efficiency in management structures in order to ensure financial stability without being guided by money (Chong, 2008). Quality and profitability, however, are not mutually exclusive.

How does the cultural center perceive the concept of quality and how does it reflect in their offering of services? Do they use recognized quality management systems, and to what end? As this is the last chapter in this book before the general conclusion, we will not change the approach; this chapter will begin with a presentation of both concepts and theory, where after a dive into the results of the qualitative study, and a wrap up in a summary and conclusion.

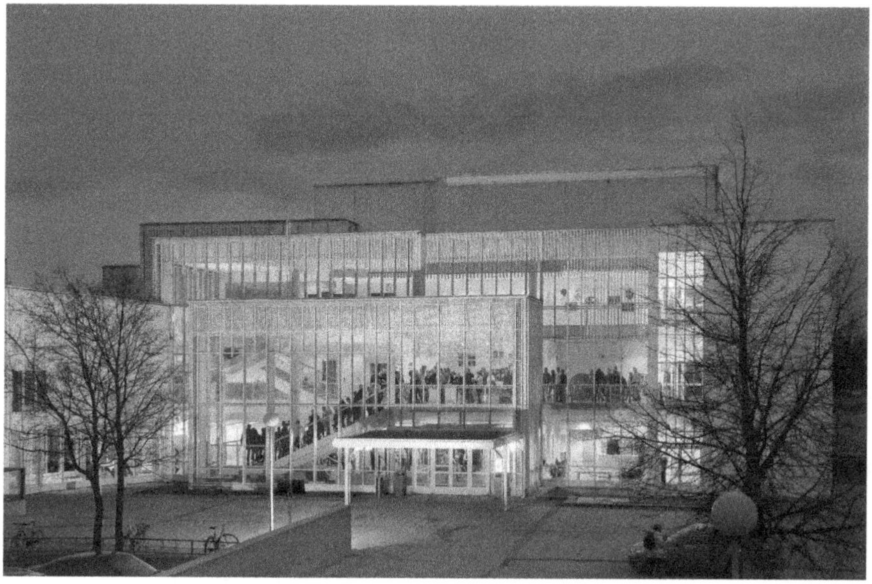

Picture 8.1 The front of cultural center Virta in Imatra, Finland.

8.1 What is quality and quality management?

Some claim that quality can be no more defined than quantified, and others argue that quality is something subjective and determined by individual perspectives (Bobby, 2014; Martin & Stella, 2007; Mishra, 2007; Westerheijden, Stensaker, & Rosa, 2007). The thing with quality is that unlike quantifiable features such as size or value, there is no generally accepted definition (Nanda, 2005). However, quality is typically defined as how good or bad something is (Cambridge Dictionary, 2020). It may also mean a feature of someone or something, something that makes him, her or it different from others or other things – or simply a measurement. When manufacturing products, quality is seen as a measure of excellence – products or services without defects, imperfections and significant variations (Business Dictionary, 2020). It is achieved by rigorous and consistent engagement to fixed standards that in turn bring about consistency of a product to satisfy explicit customer or user demands. Juran (1999) emphasized that quality management consists of three characteristics; quality planning, quality control and quality improvement.

Quality of products and/or services in businesses has however been seen as very important for quite a while (Russell & Taylor, 1995). Before 1951, the concept of quality was primarily associated to products, and the main focus was the degree of *conformity to specialized standards* (Dahlgaard, 1999). Slowly but surely, Juran's term 'fitness for use' took over the debate and transformed the concept of quality to *meeting the requirements of the customers* (Juran, 1951). Instead of *meeting the requirements*, there was an emphasis on *satisfying the customers* (Neely et al., 2005), which has later on turned to *delighting the customers* (Dahlgaard, 1999). Quality is globally seen as a dynamic threshold an organization must meet if they wish to satisfy customers.

Back in 1970s and 1980s, managers began to connect quality to the organizational performance and suddenly quality was a part of the strategic planning process as a way to maintain competitive superiority (Russell & Taylor, 1995). Ever since, there has been an overabundance on theories on quality (e.g. Miller, 1996; Stone-Romero et al., 1997), and the concept of quality has been divided into many branches. According to Juran and Goldfrey (2003), quality is free from imperfections. This would indicate that quality could be measured by for instance the number of defects. Feigenbaum (2004) in turn stated that the cost of quality is the avoidance and the assessment cost. Crosby (1980) goes on to claim that quality is free, which builds on the assumption that the increasing prevention costs will be more than sufficiently covered by increasing revenues, compared to the alternative with decreasing revenues as a result to decreasing prevention costs. As total quality management emerged, the earlier understanding of quality as merely a *conformance to specifications* was even that laid to rest (Powell, 1995). In this very process, the focus was shifted from products with tangible features to everything that was customer-related, with both tangible and intangible features.

Measuring quality has its difficulties in this specific arena; as in any service, there are both tangible and intangible features to quality (Walsch, 1999). As to the tangible features, there are amongst others accessibility, continuity, comfort and price (Bonet & Schargorodsky, 2018). As to the intangible features, one could mention associated social status, prestige or the sensation of the experience. The latter is especially important in arts organizations, but defining quality is still a correlation between different features – both tangible and intangible. All these different interpretations of quality, cost versus benefits, as well as internal and external influences for enhanced performance have been recognized as determinants for cynicism (Wilford, 2007). This is often the case due to organizational search for quick fixes with quality management, which leads to disappointments as such, are not achieved (Hendricks & Singhal, 2000).

Quality management has spread from its original habitat, its industrial origins, to health-care organizations, public institutions, nonprofit organizations and others (Hackman & Wageman, 1995). Still, due to the difficulties in implementing such metrics in other than solely profit-minded organizations, questions have been raised whether quality management really brings more than it takes. On the other hand, in the case of arts organizations with generally quite tight budgets and perhaps even public accountability, evaluation of every undertaking is essential (Anttonen et al., 2016). It might be the best way to guarantee highest efficiency as it helps the leadership in decision-making.

It has been suggested that as the definition of quality is conditional to the situation (van Kemenade et al., 2008), managing quality appears to need different tools, methods as well as ways of thinking too. There is a growing number of different frameworks, or philosophies, for quality management, both universal and custom-made, which are based on self-assessment (Jackson, 2005). These are often variations of, for instance, the Business Excellence model by European Foundation for Quality Management (Ogden & Grigg, 2003). The different quality philosophies used for quality development have been applied very differently in organizations, and it seems as if when one fails, another one is created (Dedhia, 2005). Examples of such philosophies are Total Quality Management (TQM), the ISO management system, Six Sigma and Lean Management. Especially TQM has been very criticized as being a fad without a theoretical foundation (Foley & Zahner, 2009). Others view TQM as an umbrella for different quality systems, which could explain why it has become quite hard to define (Chiarini, 2011). Some even see Six Sigma, ISO 9000 and Lean as pieces of the TQM approach, even if Lean management, originating in Toyota Production Systems, predates TQM (Bergman & Klefsjö, 2010; Dale 1999). Lean Management has nevertheless with its principles, tools and methodologies (that are very similar to those of TQM), lately become one of the leading quality philosophies (Liker, 2011). There are also similarities to TQM to be found in the eight ISO 9000 management principles (Bergman & Klefsjö, 2010). What also applies to all the different philosophies are the vague descriptions (Chiarini, 2011; Dahlgaard & Dahlgaard-Park, 2006; Hensler, 2004; Pettersen, 2009). Let us briefly take a closer look on these four aforementioned examples of quality philosophies.

Total Quality Management (TQM) embodies different features which are promoted by quality philosophers like Deming, Juran and Crosby (Dale, 1999). TQM is all about delivering both high quality services and products no longer reliant on market pressure being the driving force (Weckenmann et al., 2015). Furthermore, with a more holistic approach, TQM aim attention at the engagement of the employees and their relation to leadership (Dahlgaard et al., 1998). The scholars admit there is no single solution appropriate for all applications, rather that the quality management techniques and practices should align with the specific organizations culture, resources and values (Hellsten & Klefsjö, 2000; Melsa, 2009). The main focus of TQM is continuous improvement, management commitment, employee involvement and customer focus.

Six Sigma is in turn considered to be a practice including a set of very effective quality management techniques and principles combining many features from the work of earlier quality practitioners (Pyzdek, 2003). The main goal of Six Sigma is an error-free operational performance, which takes place in practice by improving quality, as well as productivity and financial performance (Franchetti, 2015). The name of this approach comes from the Greek letter sigma (σ), which is used by statisticians when measuring the variability in different processes (Patyal & Maddulety, 2015). Thus, the organizations business performance can be evaluated on a sigma level (Pyzdek, 2003), and in this manner reduce deviations – which is in line with the standard of satisfying the customers (Patyal & Maddulety, 2015).

Lean management focuses on removing nonvalue-added activities, which is thought as being things the customer is not willing to spend money on (Bacoup et al., 2018). This approach also emphasizes the continuous improvement of quality, but also the strength of the process and the products. In addition, it stresses the concept of Just-in-Time, a concept that removes purposeless processes in order to provide a constant flow of products (Ohno, 1988), as well as the concept of perfect quality, HR and visual management to guarantee efficiency within the organization (Liker, 2004). All Lean Management principles are usually customer value-driven, which makes them suitable for a wide range of production and distribution scenarios.

ISO 9000 has since its introduction in 1987 become one of the most acknowledged and coveted quality management systems (Poksinska, 2010). ISO stands for International Organization of Standardization (ISO), founded in 1946 by delegates from 25 countries. With its root in manufacturing industry, ISO 9000 strives to advance organizational development and incites major improvements in the organizations business performance (Schlickman, 2003). Despite starting out in manufacturing, this system is nowadays extensively adopted by a variety of business sectors, containing the service sector. The quality system of ISO 9000 calls attention to the idea where every specific quality system is a result of the aims of a specific organization, as well as its particular products, services and business practices (Poksinska, 2010). These systems require a high level of audited evidence and documentation proving that the expected quality is delivered to the customer.

This presentation of quality management systems is naturally not complete. There are more than 35 established methods developed all around the world for the implementation of performance measuring (Ravelomanantsoa et al., 2010). So, after this brief presentation of four quality management systems (QMS), one could say that they are all in their simplicity differing sets of routines which are meant to systematize and advance the quality of the processes of an organization when offering services, products and other activities (Ponte, 2019). QMS can be helpful when implementing organizational changes or in economic turmoil and may also provide a basis for mutual understanding between people and organizations. When applying quality management in a cultural center, this involves choosing various standards, systems, models and/or tools, which in turn allows the management to focus on customer satisfaction (Álamo Núñez, 1999)

8.2 Profitability

Holding on to quality for yet a while, we could point out that quality is analyzed within equity investing as a selection of measurements created to bring forth the indicators of higher-quality financials in organizations (Hsu et al., 2019). The quality factor portfolios are often assembled in different ways by different providers, with features such as low debt ratio, earnings growth, earnings growth stability or high profitability. It seems indeed as if profitability is one of the most frequent features used in the assembling of quality portfolios (Park et al., 2020). As the aim with this paper is not to examine stock markets nor the other attributes of quality metrics within equity investing, we will simply conclude loosely based on the statements above, that profitability and quality do have a mutual ground.

What exactly is profitability then? Well, it is quite self-explanatory, the capability to earn a profit (Business Dictionary, 2020b). A profit in turn is what is remaining of the organizations revenue after paying all the costs linked to generating the very same income, such as marketing or production costs and so on. Profitability has two sides; revenues and expenses (Park et al., 2020). As explained above, the revenues are the incomes of an organization. In practice, it is the money earned by providing services or selling products. The other side, that is expenses, is the inevitable consequence of the revenues, as generating income does not come without expenses. Profitability is simply the tool by which an organization can monitor the connection between revenues and expenses, in order to understand how the organization is performing and if there is a potential to grow (Park et al., 2020).

There is a connection between quality, costs and profits; high costs generally lead to high service quality, and high service quality in turn leads to high profits (Taylor III & Russell, 1995). By using the organizations resources it can produce both products and services. Resources in turn can be cash, which an organization uses to pay for costs like salaries, marketing, rents and so forth. Although profitability points towards for-profit organizations with one only aim to maximize profits, financial measures may be useful for arts organizations to help them understand their capacity to carry out their mission. (Kim, 2017).

In order to maintain high quality in the organization's performance and to advance business opportunities in a competitive environment, it is of paramount importance to keep up a service quality that make both current and future customers return (Park et al., 2020). Therefore, many organizations invest considerable resources in high-quality service to secure returning customers. The revisits have in turn a close connection to profitability, as it mostly contributes to high economic performance. If this investment in service quality is continuous, it will lead to performance enhancement in the organization (Evanschitzky et al., 2012). There are naturally different approaches to acquiring revisits, one of those being discounted tickets.

It seems as if many nonprofit organizations within arts offer both free and discounted tickets to the audience (Bernstein 2011; Toepler & Wyszomirski 2012). This of course presents a dilemma between developing long-term customers and social responsibility and to retain short-term financial sustainability. It moreover increases the organizations dependence on grants and donations. However, the free-trial opportunity helps bring potential audiences who are interested and can afford to pay but are not yet committed enough to paying for the experience

(Bernstein 2011; Kotler & Scheff 1997; Parker 2012). Further, Moldavanova (2016) and Stazyk et al. (2014) argue that such socially responsible initiatives help nonprofits keep institutional distinctiveness and long-term sustainability, and in a way, profitability.

Earlier studies state, as mentioned above, that service quality has a positive effect on profitability (Raju & Lonial, 2002; Yoo & Park, 2007). Generating profit has a positive effect on performance improvement (Park et al., 2020). An organization that is capable to generate higher profits than its challengers with products or services at a corresponding qualitative nature is superior to these, since its inputs are lower and outputs higher. Quite comparable to operating margins, a larger equity balance equips the organizations with flexibility for maintaining their services even during financial setbacks, and the possibility to grow during better times (Greenlee & Trussel, 2000; Trussel, 2002). In addition, according to Carroll and Stater (2009), financial stability instantly changes the (nonprofit) organizations ability to provide programs or to promote mission awareness.

Over the years, the scholars have gathered a considerable amount of empirical evidence illustrating how diversified revenue streams decrease the financial vulnerability of nonprofit organizations (Carroll & Stater, 2009; Keating et al., 2005; Trussel, 2002). Much like Chapter 6 and resource dependence theory proclaims – through a different angle, though (Pfeffer & Salancik, 2003). But there is likewise empirical evidence of low administrative expenses making the organizations exposed, as it means that they have hardly any costs to discard before diminishing their program budgets, which in turn lessen both the quality and the quantity of their program offerings (Greenlee & Trussel, 2000; Trussel, 2002). Organizations that find themselves under pressure to keep their overhead costs low may also have trouble to aim for a revenue diversification strategy, since keeping up numerous funding streams often comes with administrative burdens (Kim, 2017).

As with one of the central themes in this book, revenue diversification has received the most attention amongst profitability scholars during the past decades (Kim, 2017). The revenue diversification strategy, initially developed from modern portfolio theory (Markowitz, 1952) within the business literature, aims attention at spreading out potential risks and focuses on much of the same issues as resource dependency (Pfeffer & Salancik, 2003). It has been pointed out that arts organizations will presumably perform better with a large revenue diversification and a small donation dependence (Kim, 2017).

The revenue sources of cultural centers are nevertheless more diverse than a few categories can cover; these revenues may consist of individual donations, sponsorship, corporate gifts, foundation grants, government grants and/or contracts, payments for membership, as well as fees for services and goods (Järvinen, 2019). On the top of these, there are also investment interests, rents and sales of inventory, along with many others. It is therefore anything but easy to analyze the profitability of the aforementioned centers. We will still look into how to go about if the measuring of quality and profitability would be of interest in a cultural organization.

8.3 Measurement of both quality and profitability in arts organizations

When measuring value, it is about the relative value of something in relation to something else, a rating of importance, usefulness or general worth (Merriam-Webster Dictionary, 2020). The definition of cultural value is however continually debated and there are no simple answers to the question of its meaning (Carnwath & Brown, 2014). It is commonly characterized trough what it is not, for instance as in the example of not being able to catch the essence of its value within the framework of mainstream economics. Still, arts organizations, just like other productive businesses, couple capital and labor with technology to produce output. Therefore, the need for a quality management system should be no less in them than in other businesses.

Services in the arts field are (or are often seen as) public assets and are therefore considered to be 'market failures' due to, for instance, the differing possibilities to acquire information (Throsby, 2001). Although it is quite easy to measure the opinion of the audience, as the single customer has no problem in forming an opinion, it is much more difficult to develop and maintain a set of indicators that evaluates for instance the sociocultural significance, the artistic value or the public benefit of the activities (Saprykina & Wyler, 2018). The thing when working with cultural services is that success does not necessarily translate into quality. The classical view of the market or a group of experts determining the quality is faulty, as customer satisfaction is not the same as artistic quality, and artistic quality is not the same as customer satisfaction (Saprykina & Wyler, 2018).

During the time, there has been quality management systems, there has also been various suggestion on how to evaluate arts organizations (Baumol & Bowen, 1992; Radbourne et al., 2007; Turbide & Laurin, 2009). These systems (or frameworks) have generally focused on the dichotomy between economic and artistic performance. As you could notice above in Subchapter 8.1, the earlier attention of quality measurement systems was mostly aimed at budgeting systems in order to audit how efficiently the resources were used (Baumol & Bowen, 1992), and later the approaches have focused on multiobjective performance measurement to recognize both artistic and economic performance (Towse, 2001). Gilhespy (1999) suggested that the measuring should focus on quantifying artistic excellence, financial objectives, innovation, public attendance and social cohesion. Turbide and Laurin (2009) in turn proposed six central categories of performance, which are artistic achievement, audit satisfaction, financial management, funder satisfaction, growth and competition, image and reputation and personnel satisfaction. There are of course other studies with comparable approaches but different labels, focusing on both financial data as well as artistic performance and audience satisfaction (see Evans, 2000; Hume & Mort, 2008; Radbourne et al., 2009).

As mentioned, the management accounting literature focused on performance measurement primarily from the profit-oriented perspective (Kaplan & Johnson, 1991). During the 1980s, scholars critiqued the approach of managing by numbers (see Johnson & Kaplan, 1987). Kaplan and Norton (1992) therefore suggested a solution by developing the balanced scorecard concept, which takes into account other indicators than the faulty method of just focusing on profit indicators to measure performance. The balance scorecard (BSC) concept analyzes performance through four perspectives; customers, growth and innovation, internal business-process perspectives, as well as the financial perspective (Kaplan & Norton 1992). The fundament of BSC according to the authors, is that by using four perspectives which are connected to the organizations strategy and contains a mindset of looking forward, the organization has a much better possibility to measure both short- and long-term performance.

Very much alike the SMART model (see Doran, 1981), the performance measures identification in BSC begins from vision and business strategy (Kaplan & Norton 1992). These are then adapted into the four perspectives. The perspective of the customer in turn measures how successful the organization is in satisfying the needs of the customer. The perspective of growth and innovation advances objectives and measures that will stimulate growth and learning within the organization. The perspective of the internal business-process should measure how effective the organization is in meeting the customer needs and making profit. Lastly, the perspective of the financial side is assumed to measure how successful the business is in satisfying the needs of the stakeholders. According to the authors, the BSC model should answer four questions:

1) How do our customers see us?
2) Can we carry on to both improve and create value?
3) What should we get better at?
4) How do we take care of our stakeholders? (Kaplan & Norton 1992).

Regardless of their differences, the aforementioned systems or frameworks (see Subchapter 8.2) are not necessarily contradictory; some of them can be used simultaneously (Ittner et al., 2003). For instance, Six Sigma to improve the organizations key internal processes, and the Balanced Scorecard in turn to manage the organizational strategy. It all comes down to the features and the aims of a specific organization.

There are naturally a variety of indicators available to measure performance in the field of arts (Pignataro, 2011). These are generally developed within a particular subgroup of arts in order to allow for the possibility of diverging features. They are constructed not only to meet a general demand of statistical information, but also to supply valuable information to the supporters of the arts field. In addition to qualitative and quantitative indicators, there are micro- (organizational level) and macro (field level) indicators (Brosio, 1994).

Here are some example indicators emphasized by Saprykina & Wyler (2018, p. 23) when assessing the quality of an arts organization:

8.3.1 Quantitative indicators

- *Financial capacity, budget of the project (attracted state and/or private funds).*
- *Gross revenue from the sale of products and services (including souvenirs and additional services).*
- *Number of partners and activities in the project.*
- *Attendance (viewers, participants, partners).*
- *Total costs for the production of goods and services (basic, additional and servicing).*
- *Time spent by the consumer (a multiplication of the number of people and the time spent at the event).*

8.3.2 Qualitative indicators

- *Polls among all interested stakeholders (consumers, art critics, state representatives, commercial partners, sponsors, public figures and social leaders, mass media outlets, participants in the event – organizers and artists).*
- *Using different platforms: online on the website of events or institutions, social networks, in-depth interviews, focus groups, etc.*

There are many ways to analyze quality and profitability within an organization, and as have been suggested in this chapter, one way is to make use of the different systems already in practice around the world. The multidimensional impact indicators seem to be the best option when measuring arts organizations (Anttonen et al., 2016). It is important to acknowledge that the indicators are a method to organize information on a variety of features of performance, defined by quantification (Pignataro, 2011). But, there still is not anything called 'the performance' of arts organizations or the field of art organizations. The different features of performance that every organization can evaluate will not give a complete picture of the organization, it will merely function as a pointer.

The case might very well be that arts and cultural organizations bring a wide range of benefits to individuals and communities (see Markusen 2014; Toepler & Wyszomirski 2012), that they contribute to economic development and vital community life (see Hayter & Pierce 2009; Markusen & Gadwa 2010; Markusen 2014; Rushton 2013), civic dialogue and social capital (see LeRoux & Bernadska 2014; Stern & Seifert 2009), as well as better educational and health outcomes (see Sowden et al. 2015; Stuckey & Nobel 2010). However, quality management increases the organizations chances to maintain and develop this efficiency and as such provides a long-term perspective, which advances the possibilities for future funding in an arts organization (Anttonen et al., 2016).

8.4 Mixing quality and profitability: a need for diversified funding

The cultural centers have a quite similar view on quality and what they accordingly aim for. As one respondent explained quality:

> *Well, of course it's completely in the viewer's eyes [...] what I myself somehow try to have as a guideline for me, when I choose plays [...] is that if I bring something to Finland, then there must be something ... some point to why I bring them here from abroad. And if it's something new, it's something that's happening right now out in Europe or somewhere else, and something that we are not exactly doing here. I feel that it ... it meets some criteria. [...] So, what I'm looking for are new ways to do theater, or something new in the content, some style of my own or something like that. [...] I feel it gives something, some added value to the performing arts field in Finland, and it's also a profiling thing for the audience.*
>
> (Respondent E)

The respondents thus see quality as something multifaceted; it's about the customer service, the quest for standing out as innovative and as something driving the whole field forward. Quality may be hard to define, but the respondents seem to be rather assured about their own perception of the concept and how they wish to profile their own center accordingly. There appears to be a comprehension about the interplay between quality and profitability, even if the uncertainty of the field leads to an unwillingness to spend too much money on things considered hard to measure as a catalyst on success. They rather see many different revenues than to venture everything on the uncertain revisit of customers due to high quality.

Private cultural centers need to be involved in the region's networks connected to culture. Not only culture is stressed but also business as the centers aim to get earnings through business. Even though self-sufficiency and business earnings are emphasized repeatedly, the importance of businesses not being too market-driven is also highlighted. Private cultural centers must have their own vision about things.

> *We aim to be involved in a living culture, so we can see what works and what is going on. That is how you are directly in contact with the customer base or to anyone who might be interested in coming there [to the cultural centre]. Something allures them there. Often it feels that it is this whole package of different opportunities that you can do there, that make people return.*
>
> (Respondent O)

Most of the respondents preferably stress the need for diversified funding in order for the profitability to match the quest for quality, much in line with both resource dependence theory as well as mission focus. Private cultural centers do not have a single source of revenue on which they can rely, so there is a recognizable need for other revenue. Furthermore, the subsidies private centers receive from the

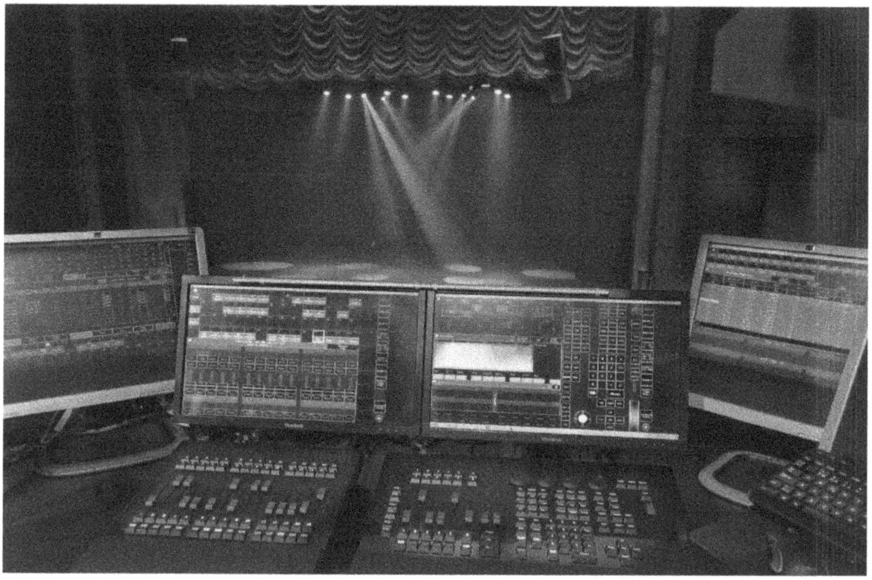

Picture 8.2 The main stage and technique at cultural center Virta in Imatra, Finland.

municipality and the state have to be renegotiated each year. This brings about insecurity as the centers never know what will come in the next year. As one respondent mentioned, a 7% decline in municipal subsidies they received one year might be quite significant. In addition, municipal grants cannot be immediately put to use as project ideas arise as municipal subsidies can only be applied during one period a year. When attaining such subsidies, the centers need to present differing figures of performance – even if these are not comparable to those of the public centers. This brings about the need for measurement of performance, which still seem to be a somewhat unexplored area amongst the centers.

The centers do not think that the economic support from the municipality is sufficient, which in turn could be one reason for the limited measurement. According to one center, it does not get much municipal subsidies at all, and the center that gets most points out that the municipality provides less than 10% of its annual turnover. A third center does not get any direct subsidies, but the municipality supports local producers by giving a day in the private cultural center for free. The sum the municipality pays for a day is less than the ordinary rent but still amounts to about 30,000 euros a year. Furthermore, according to the respondents, there seems to be a trend towards diminishing municipal support: '*Still, the support has now begun to decline. And it is what they have warned about, that they will sink. Fairly clear. Last five years...*' (Respondent E). The thing with such subsidies is, that even if it stands for such a small proportion of the total turnover, they still stand for the very space to do important organizational developments within the cultural centers, as the profitability is scarce and financial stability is dependent on a certain amount of subsidies – however small.

Municipal subsidies are calculated by presenting the quantitative figures of executed activities. This seems to cause discontent among private cultural centers, as quality is hard to measure in such a manner, according to them. For instance, two centers point out that they offer experimental and pioneering theatre, so their expected audiences are not large. Still, afterwards, other municipal theatres and cultural centers put on the same play and manage to get bigger audiences as they have bigger venues and bigger marketing budgets, and the play was already introduced to the community by the smaller private center. This is not to say that the respondents feel they need to change altogether. The concern is more about profitability versus size – are the private cultural centers big enough to compete?

> *I have felt, that it is surprisingly strong this [belief], that a cultural center has to be the size of an institution in order to be a cultural center. However, I myself think that the operator can also be clearly smaller.*
>
> (Respondent L)

The pressure of having to compete with both public cultural institutions and other private, leisure-time competitors simply makes the respondents conscious of the economic reality in which they work. As several respondents mention, they need to figure out what they want to offer audiences, how to do it in a resource-saving way and how to get alternative funding to do so. As Chapter 7 has shown, the mission of displaying arts and culture is at the forefront for the private cultural centers, which equally could be seen as aiming for quality in the service production. As to profitability, the cruel reality is that the centers need to be extremely efficient-even to break-even.

When asked about possible quality management systems, the answers ramble. It becomes clear that there is no sufficient and reoccurring measurement done amongst the centers, other than accounting and follow-up on the number and type of events. Only one of the centers use any recognized quality management system. Some mention external evaluations made every couple of years, but there do not seem to be any consistency between these, and they therefore do not function as follow-ups. Struggling with a continuous resource scarcity, the centers however monitor their economy consistently. Even the smallest changes in the surrounding society or bad decisions about the program of the center could push them into an economic distress, wherefore the monetary evaluation is carried out with greatest accuracy. Whether this economic monitoring really do help them to be more profitable or if it just leaves them with an exaggerated cautiousness is hard to tell.

Although it seems as if the only regular and exhaustive measurement done amongst the cultural centers is of economic sort, there is a surprising number of methods they use which are not among the established systems – much as with the business models (see Chapter 3). The cultural centers are for instance in constant contact with the customers, they are a part of different networks and they do attend in different regional studies on cultural impact, which all give them a quite solid view on the quality of their own center as well – especially as a supplement to the economic follow-up. In other words, the centers mostly have a quite extensive view on how their customer service and cultural offering position itself in qualitative terms, even though they lack established quality management systems. One could even describe their quality management as a form of peer review, as the respondents so reoccurring stress the importance of networks, by which they reflect their own cultural offerings. It still seems as if there is a risk that this form of individual organizational measurement easily becomes an isolated act, performed by single individuals and not shared within a group.

8.5 Summary and conclusions

According to earlier studies, the increasing costs of keeping up the quality will pay itself back with increasing revenues. Quality management will therefore enhance the success of the organization, that is measured in revenues.

Quality as a concept has no general definition, although it is typically defined as how bad or good something is – as a form of a measurement. In product manufacturing, it is the measurement of excellence. Quality has gone through a period of change, starting from its industrial origins with its merely numeric approach to its versatile application in most every form of organization today.

Quality management offers recognized frameworks for the organizations to evaluate their performance these days. Examples of such are the TQM, Six Sigma, Lean management and ISO 9000. However, there are over 35 established methods developed all around the world for the implementation of performance measuring.

Profitability is the capability to earn a profit, or what remains of the revenue after paying all the costs linked to generating the very same income. Profitability is simply the tool by which an organization can monitor the connection between revenues and expenses, in order to understand how the organization is performing and if there is a potential to grow. There is a connection between quality, costs and profits; high costs generally lead to high service quality, and high service quality in turn leads to high profits.

Service quality and revisits are interdependent and of paramount importance for arts organizations. An organization that is capable to generate higher profits than its challengers with products or services at a corresponding qualitative nature is superior to these, since its inputs are lower and outputs higher. There are considerable amount of empirical evidence illustrating how diversified revenue streams decrease the financial vulnerability of nonprofit organizations. Likewise, low administrative expenses make the organizations exposed, as it means that they have hardly any costs to discard before diminishing their program budgets, which in turn lessen both the quality and the quantity of their program offerings.

When measuring quality in arts organizations, it is important to remember that customer satisfaction is not the same as artistic quality, and artistic quality is not the same as customer satisfaction. Although for-profit organization were in the focus initially when the performance measuring started, there has been a shift towards other qualities and organizations. For instance, the balanced scorecard concept, which takes into account other indicators than the faulty method of just focusing on profit indicators to measure performance. It is still important to acknowledge that the different features of performance that every organization can evaluate will not give a complete picture of the organization, it will merely function as a pointer. And as with mostly everything, how you apply the tools is essentially as important as which tools you apply.

This chapter focused on the questions how the cultural centers perceive the concept of quality and how does it reflect in their offering of services, and do they use recognized quality management systems, and to what end? Let us see if we can find some answers to the queries.

The cultural centers do not use established quality management systems in any greater extent. They have a clear view on what quality stands for in their center and aim to form their program accordingly. They find quality to be offering culture and arts that has not been displayed in their region earlier, and that this offering is displayed in a high standard manner. They furthermore emphasize the need to focus on customer service, since this is the way to get revisits, and a measure of quality as well. They need to do some reports on their activities, especially those how get municipal subsidies, but according to the respondents much less than their public peers.

The cultural centers do measure their performance, just not with any established or even fully noted systems – apart from the auditive side. They do interact with their audience and have extensive networks, which in turn frame their own performance in relation to others. Still, there is an imminent danger that this measurement protocol becomes an isolated act that furthermore is not shared within the whole organization. A conclusion is that even if the cultural centers seem to have a fairly good perception of their performance, there is room for improvement.

According to the respondents, the profitability of the centers is really only about balancing revenues with expenses. There is hardly ever any surplus, and if there is, then the balancing will simply happen over a longer period than a fiscal year. Profitability is still very much dependent on the quality, that is customer service and ensuring the uniqueness of the cultural offering.

This chapter helps to explain that without quality there will not be profitability, and without profitability, there will not be quality. Without balancing these two factors, a cultural center will not be able to sustain in a fastmoving economic environment. This chapter has furthermore shown a way to a better market performance and that the expenses for maintaining good quality can be justified.

Hardly surprising, success in an arts organization is mostly measured by the customer. Delivering quality experience, which could be defined as customer care, is something for the whole organization to focus on – it is not only a responsibility of the marketing team, the artists or the management. The most essential elements for success seem to be an organizational engagement to the priority of keeping the customers content, the continuous development and implementation of systems. It is clear that quality alone cannot create growth nor profitability, there simply are other forces at play. Nevertheless, high-quality service does enhance the number of returning customers.

The scholars along with the industry seem to agree that the performance of an organization should be measured by utilizing multiple dimensions of performance.

This in turn has led to a new challenge and that is the concept of drowning in data, as Neely et al. (2002) put it. Performance measurement has still become a routine among all sorts of organizations, although the reality is that you cannot measure everything that you would like to or need to. That is where the quality management systems come into the picture, as it is imperative to choose a few crucial performance measures and use them in a way that they together form an understandable picture of the overall performance of the organization at hand.

We have also seen that all systems have their strengths and weaknesses, which goes to show they cannot get the complete picture. Additionally, as things change the QMS also needs to change. When that happens, it is harder to compare your results to earlier years. However, navigating without any system at all, will most probably leave you lost in the woods.

References

Álamo Núñez, Ed. (1999). *Management of Cultural Facilities*. Manual Atalaya, Apoyo a la Gestion Cultural. Accessed: 18.8.2020. Available at: http://atalayagestioncultural.es/pdf_en/7.7_gestion_de_equipamientos.pdf

Anttonen R., Ateca-Amestoy V., Holopainen K., Johansson T., Jyrämä A., Karkkunen A., Prikk K., Kuznetsova-Bodanovitš K., Luonila M., Kölar J., Plaza B., Pulk K., Pusa, T., Ranczakowska-Ljutjuk A., Sassi M., Stiller I., & Äyväri A., (2016). *Managing art projects with societal impact: study book for students, stakeholders and researchers*. Sibelius Academy Research Report Publications 17. Unigrafia, Helsinki.

Bacoup, P., Michel, C., Habchi, G., & Pralus, M. (2018). From a Quality Management System (QMS) to a Lean Quality Management System (LQMS). The TM Journal, 30(1), pp. 20–42.

Baumol, W.J., & Bowen, W.G. (1992). On the performing arts: The anatomy of their economic problems. In Blaug, M.(Ed.): *The Economics of the Arts*. Aldershot, Gregg Revivals, pp. 218–226.

Bergman, B., & Klefsjö, B. (2010). *Quality from Customer Needs to Customer Satisfaction* (3rd ed.). Lund: Studentlitteratur.

Bernstein, J.S. (2011). *Arts Marketing Insights: The Dynamics of Building and Retaining Performing Arts Audiences*. New York: John Wiley & Sons, Inc.

Bobby, C.L. (2014). *The abcs of building quality cultures for education in a global world*. Paper presented at the International Conference on Quality Assurance, Bangkok, Thailand.

Bonet, L., Schargorodsky, H. (2018). *Theatre Management: Models and Strategies for Cultural Venues*. Elverum (Norway): Kunnskapsverket.

Brosio, G. (1994). The arts industry: Problems of measurement. In: Peacock, A. & Rizzo, I. (Eds). *Cultural Economics and Cultural Policies*. Dordrecht: Kluwer Academic Publishers.

Business Dictionary (2020). *Quality*. Accessed: 12.8.2020. Available at: www.businessdictionary.com/definition/quality.html

Business Dictionary (2020b). *Profitability*. Accessed: 12.8.2020. Available at: www.businessdictionary.com/definition/profitability.html

Cambridge Dictionary (2020). *Quality*. Accessed: 12.8.2020. Available at: https://dictionary.cambridge.org/dictionary/english/quality

Carnwath, J.D. and Brown, A.S. (2014). *Understanding the Value and Impacts of Cultural Experiences*. Manchester, UK: Arts Council England. Accessed: 19.8.2020. Available at: www.artscouncil.org.uk/advice-and guidance/browse-advice-andguidance/understanding-value-and-impacts-cultural- experiences.

Carroll, D., & Stater, K. (2009). Revenue diversification in nonprofit organizations: Does it lead to financial stability? Journal of Public Administration Research and Theory, 19, 947–966.

Chiarini, A. (2011). Japanese total quality control, TQM, Deming's system of profound knowledge, BPR, Lean and Six Sigma – comparison and discussion. International Journal of Lean Six Sigma, 2(4), pp. 332–355.

Chong, D. (2008). Arts Management (4 ed.). New York: Routledge.

Crosby, P.B. (1980). *Quality Is Free: The Art of Making Quality Certain.* New York: Penguin.

Dahlgaard, S.M.P. (1999). The evolution patterns of quality management: some reflections on the quality movement. Total Quality Management, 10(4–5), pp. 473–480.

Dahlgaard, J.J., & Dahlgaard-Park, S.M. (2006). Lean production, Six Sigma quality, TQM and company culture. The TQM Magazine, 18(3), pp. 263–281.

Dahlgaard, J.J., Kristensen, K., & Kanji, G.K. (1998). *Fundamentals of Total Quality Management.* London: Chapman & Hall.

Dale, G.B. (1999). *Managing Quality.* Oxford: Blackwell Scientific Publications.

Dedhia, N.S. (2005). Six Sigma basics. Total Quality Management & Business Excellence, 16(5), pp. 567–574.

Doran, G.T. (1981). There's a S.M.A.R.T. way to write management's goals and objectives. Management Review. 70(11), pp. 35–36.

Evans, G. (2000). Measure for measure: evaluating performance and the arts organisation. Studies in Cultures. Organizations and Societies, 6(2), pp. 243–266.

Evanschitzky, H., Wangenheim, F., & Wunderlich, N.V. (2012). Perils of managing the service profit chain: The role of time lags and feedback loops. Journal of Retailing, 88(3), pp. 356–366.

Feigenbaum, A.V. (2004). *Total Quality Control,* 4th ed. McGraw-Hill Professional.

Foley, K.J., & Zahner, T. (2009). *Creating and Managing the Sustainable Organization: The Stakeholder Way.* Sydney: SAI Global.

Franchetti, M.J. (2015). *Lean Six Sigma for Engineers and Managers: With Applied Case Studies.* Boca Raton, FL: CRC Press.

Gilhespy, I. (1999). Measuring the performance of cultural organizations: A model. International Journal of Arts Management, 2(1), pp. 38–52.

Greenlee, J., & Trussel, J. (2000). Estimating the financial vulnerability of charitable organizations. Nonprofit Management and Leadership, 11, pp. 199–210.

Hackman, J.R., & Wageman, R. (1995). *Total quality management: Empirical, conceptual, and practical issues.* Administrative Science Quarterly, 40, 309–342.

Hayter, C. and Pierce, S.C. (2009). *Arts & the Economy: Using Arts and Culture to Stimulate State Economic Development.* Washington, DC: National Governors Association NGA Center for Best Practices.

Hellsten, U. & Klefsjö, B. (2000). TQM as a management system consisting of values, techniques and tools. TQM Magazine, 12(4), pp. 238–244.

Hendricks, K.B. & Singhal, V.R. (2000). The long-run stock price performance of firms with effective TQM programs as proxied by quality award winners. Management Science, 47(3), pp. 359–368.

Hensler, D. (2004). Why is it difficult to succeed with quality improvements? Measuring Business Excellence, 8(3), pp. 49–54.

Hsu, J., Kalesnik, V. and Kose, E. (2019). What is quality. Financial Analysts Journal.

Hume, M. & Mort, G.S. (2008). Satisfaction in performing arts: The role of value? European Journal of Marketing, 42(3/4), pp. 311–326.

Ittner, C.D., Larcker, D.F., Randall, T. (2003). Performance implications of strategic performance measurement in financial services firms. Accounting, Organizations & Society, 28(7/8), p. 715.

Jackson, A. (2005). Falling from a great height: Principles of good practice in performance measurement and the perils of top down determination of performance indicators. Local Government Studies, 31(1), pp. 21–38.

Järvinen, T. (2019). *The Challengers of Public Cultural Centers*. Helsinki: Unigrafia: Sibelius Academy, University of Arts.

Johnson, H.T., & Kaplan, R.S. (1987). The rise and fall of management accounting. Management Accounting, 68(7), pp. 22–30.

Juran, J.M. (1951). *Quality Control Handbook*. McGraw Hill, New York

Juran, J. (1999). *Quality Control Handbook* (5th ed.). McGraw-Hill, New York.

Juran, M.J., Godfrey, A.B. (2003). *Juran's Quality Handbook,* 5th ed. McGraw-Hill, USA.

Kaplan, R.S., & Johnson, H.T. (1991). *Relevance Lost: The Rise and Fall of Management Accounting*. Boston: Harvard Business School Press.

Kaplan, R.S. & Norton, D.P. (1992). The balanced scorecard – Measures that drive performance. Harvard Business Review, 70(1), pp. 71–79.

Keating, E., Fischer, M., Gordon, T., & Greenlee, J. (2005). Assessing financial vulnerability in the nonprofit sector (Faculty Research Working Paper Series Paper No. 27). Cambridge, MA: Hauser Center for Nonprofit Organizations.

Kim, M. (2017). The relationship of nonprofits' financial health to program outcomes: empirical evidence from nonprofit arts organizations. Nonprofit and Voluntary Sector Quarterly, 46(3), pp. 525–548.

Kotler, P., & Scheff, J. (1997). *Standing Room Only: Strategies for Marketing the Performing Arts.* Cambridge: Harvard Business Press.

LeRoux, K., & Bernadska, A. (2014). Impact of the arts on individual contributions to U.S. civil society. Journal of Civil Society, 10(2), pp. 144–164.

Liker, J. (2004). *The Toyota Way: 14 Management Principles from the World's Greatest Manufacturer*. New York, NY: McGraw-Hill.

Liker, J. (2011). *The Toyota Way to Lean Leadership: Achieving and Sustaining Excellence through Leadership Development*. New York, NY: McGraw-Hill Professional.

Markowitz, H. (1952). Portfolio selection. Journal of Finance, 7(1), pp. 77–91.

Markusen, A. (2014). Creative cities: A ten-year research agenda. Journal of Urban Affairs, 36(s2), pp. 567–589.

Markusen, A., & Gadwa, A. (2010). Arts and culture in urban/regional planning: A review and research agenda. Journal of Planning Education and Research, 29 (3): 379–391.

Martin, M., & Stella, A. (2007). *External Quality Assurance in Higher Education: Making Choices.* Paris, France: United Nations.

Melsa, J.L. (2009). Total Quality Management. In Sage, A.P., Rouse, W.B. (eds.). *Handbook of systems engineering and management. Wiley series in systems engineering and management* (2 ed.). Hoboken, New Jersey: John Wiley & Sons.

Merriam-Webster Dictionary. (2020). *Value*. Archived 2020-06-29 at the Wayback Machine. Accessed 28.8.2020, Available at: www.merriam-webster.com/dictionary/value.

Miller, W.J. (1996). A working definition for total quality management (TQM) researchers. Journal of Quality Management, 1(2), pp. 149–159.

Mishra, S. (2007). *Quality assurance in higher education: An introduction*. Bangalore, India: National Assessment and Accreditation Council.

Moldavanova, A. (2016). Two narratives of intergenerational sustainability: A framework for sustainable thinking. The American Review of Public Administration, 46(5), pp. 526–545.

Nanda, V. (2005). *Quality Management System Handbook for Product Development Companies: A Handbook for Product Development Organizations.* CRC Press, Boca Raton, FL.

Neely, A.D., Adams, C. & Kennerley, M. (2002). *The Performance Prism: the Scorecard for Measuring and Managing Business Success.* Pearson Education Ltd., London, UK.

Neely, A., Gregory, M., & Platts, K. (2005). Performance measurement system design: A literature review and research agenda. International Journal of Operations & Production Management, 25, pp. 1228–1263.

Ogden, S.M., & Grigg, N.P. (2003). The development of sector-based quality assurance standards in the UK: diverging or dovetailing? The TQM Magazine, 15(1), pp. 7–13.

Ohno, T. (1988). *Toyota Production System: Beyond Large-Scale Production.* Portland, OR: Productivity Press.

Park, J., Lee, B.K., & Lim, S. (2020). Quality-driven profitability analysis in service operations. Journal of the Operational Research Society, DOI: 10.1080/01605682.2020.1740624

Parker, S. (2012). *Building Arts Organizations that Build Audiences.* New York: The Wallace Foundation.

Patyal, V.S., & Maddulety, K. (2015). Interrelationship between Total Quality Management and Six Sigma: A review. Global Business Review, 16(6), pp. 1025–1060

Pettersen, J. (2009). Defining lean production: Some conceptual and practical issues. The TQM Journal, 21(2), pp. 127–142.

Pfeffer, J., & Salancik, G. (2003). *The External Control of Organizations.* New York, NY: Harper & Row.

Pignataro, C. (2011). *Performance indicators.* In: Towse, R. (2011). *A Handbook of Cultural Economics. Cheltenham,* UK: Edward Elgar Publishing

Poksinska, B. (2010*). When does ISO 9000 lead to improvement?* International Journal of Productivity and Quality Management, 5(2), pp. 124–136.

Ponte, B. (2019). *Standards, Accreditation Schemes and Quality Management Systems for the Cultural Sector.* Quality for Culture. Creative Commons, White Paper.

Powell, T.C. (1995). Total quality management as competitive advantage: A review and empirical study. Strategic Management Journal 16, pp. 15–37.

Pyzdek, T. (2003). *The Six Sigma Handbook. A Complete Guide for Green Belts, Black Belts, and Managers at All Levels.* New York, NY: McGraw-Hill.

Radbourne, J., Johanson, K., Glow, H., & White, T. (2009). The audience experience: Measuring quality in the performing arts. International Journal of Arts Management, 11(3), pp. 16–29.

Raju, P.S., & Lonial, S.C. (2002). The impact of service quality and marketing on financial performance in the hospital industry: An empirical examination. Journal of Retailing and Consumer Services, 9(6), pp. 335–348.

Ravelomanantsoa, M., Ducq, Y., & Vallespir, B. (2010). Integration of requirements for performance indicator system definition and implementation methods. In: B. Vallespir & T. Alix (Eds.), *APMS 2009, IFIP AICT*, 338, pp. 530–537.

Rentschler, R., Radbourne, J., Carr, R., & Rickard, J. (2002). Relationship marketing, audience retention and performing arts organisations viability. International Journal of Nonprofit and Voluntary Sector Marketing 7 (2), pp. 118–130.

Rushton, M. (2013). *Creative Communities: Art Works in Economic Development.* Washington, DC: Brookings Institution Press.

Russell, R.S., & Taylor, B.W. (1995). *Production and Operations Management: Focusing on Quality and Competitiveness.* Prentice-Hall: Englewood Cliffs, CA.

Saprykina, A. & Wyler, M. (2018). How can one measure the quality and merits of cultural services? Arts Management Quarterly, 128, pp. 18–24.

Schlickman, J.S. (2003). *ISO 9000:2000 Quality Management System Design.* Boston, MA: Artech house,

Sowden, P.T., Clements, L., Redlich, C., & Lewis, C. (2015). Improvisation facilitates divergent thinking and creativity: Realizing a benefit of primary school arts education. Psychology of Aesthetics, Creativity, and the Arts, 9(2), pp. 128–138.

Stazyk, E.C., Moldavanova, A., & Frederickson, H.G. (2014). Sustainability, intergenerational social equity, and the socially responsible organization. Administration & Society, 48(6), pp. 655–682.

Stern, M., & Seifert, S. (2009). *Civic Engagement and the Arts: Issues of Conceptualization and Measurement.* Philadelphia: Animating Democracy.

Stone-Romero, E.F., Stone, D.L., & Grewal, D. (1997). Development of a multidimensional measure of perceived product quality. Journal of Quality Management, 2(1), pp. 87–111.

Stuckey, H.L., and Nobel, J. (2010). The connection between art, healing, and public health: A review of current literature. American Journal of Public Health, 100 (2), pp. 254–263.

Taylor, B.W., III, & Russell, R.S. (1995). *Production and operations management.* Upper Saddle River, NJ: Prentice-Hall.

Throsby, D. (2001). *Economics and Culture.* Cambridge: Cambridge University Press.

Toepler, S., & Wyszomirski, M. (2012). Arts and culture. In: Soloman, L.M. *The state of nonprofit America* (2 ed.), pp. 229–265. Washington, DC: Brookings Institute.

Towse, R. (2001). Quis custodiet? Or managing the management: The case of Royal Opera House, Covent Garden. International Journal of Arts Management, 3(3), pp. 38–50.

Trussel, J. (2002). Revisiting the prediction of financial vulnerability. Nonprofit Management and Leadership, 13, pp. 17–31.

Turbide, J., & Laurin, C. (2009). Performance measurement in the arts sector: The case of performing arts. International Journal of Arts Management, 11(2), pp. 56–70.

Van Kemenade, E., Pupius, M., & Hardjono, T.W. (2008). More value to defining quality. Quality in Higher Education, 14(2), pp. 175–185.

Walsh, M.P. (1999). Toward critical quality. In: Davis, H.T.O., Tavakoli, M., Malek, M. and Neilson, A. (eds.) *Managing Quality: Strategic Issues in Health Care Management.* Hampshire: Ashgate, Aldershot. pp. 41–55.

Weckenmann, A., Akkasoglu, G. & Werner, T. (2015). Quality management – History and trends. The TQM Journal, 27(3), pp. 281–293.

Westerheijden, D. F., Stensaker, B. & Rosa, M. (2007). *Introduction.* In D. Westerheijden, B. Stensaker, & M. Rosa (Eds.), *Quality Assurance in Higher Education* (pp. 1–11). Dordrecht: Springer.

Wilford, S. (2007). The limits of award incentives: The (non-) relationship between awards for quality and organizational performance. Total Quality Management & Business Excellence, 18(3), pp. 333–349.

Yoo, D.K., & Park, J.A. (2007). Perceived service quality: Analyzing relationships among employees, customers, and financial performance. International Journal of Quality & Reliability Management, 24(9), pp. 908–926.

9 Conclusions

This book sought to address challenges cultural centers, independent of what model they represent, may face while staying true to their mission through the jungle of institutional pressures and resource dependencies. This concluding chapter will therefore present some insight into the future directions of management of cultural centers.

9.1 Contributions of this book

The contributions of this book are twofold; the theoretical implications and the managerial implications. Let us start of by focusing on the theoretical aspect.

This book has mainly aimed to further our understanding of the role of resource dependence in institutional change by exploring private cultural centers through a case study and four types of cultural centers in a more general questionnaire. While this research may not have found significant quantitative support for all the themes that emerged in the qualitative phase, the mixture of the findings from the qualitative and quantitative phases still has implications for advancing the conceptualization of the joint resource dependence and institutional pressure phenomena.

IT and RDT are both organizational theories and aim to further understanding of organizations' operational context, with IT presuming an isomorphic approach, and RDT a strategical approach to gain resources. Integrating these theories, as this book has done, shows how a subject can be studied on a broader level. The empirical results linking the effects of resource dependence to a field in change are mixed. In other words, resource dependence and institutional change should be examined jointly to avoid incomplete pictures of the performance of the private cultural centers.

RDT guided this research as it contributed to the why and how of resource diversity, mission drift and organizational interdependencies in the field of cultural centers. RDT focuses on organizational environmental dependence as organizations do not only function through internal decision-making, mission goals or other processes but are equally shaped by resource environments (Pfeffer & Salancik, 2003). All the private cultural centers examined in this study rely on both public and private funders and are notably subject to resource dependency.

IT specifically explains how organizations respond to environmental pressures but overlooks their need for material economic resources. In an empirical context, this study demonstrates a real tension between IT and RDT, in the degree to which the private and public cultural centers differentially prioritize these two forms of pressures. RDT has mostly been employed to examine the use of alliances and collaboration to access to the resources required at a more organizational level. This research, however, suggests that resource dependence alters organizations' interdependencies and strategic responses. A resource dependence threat can transform change agents into driven institutional entrepreneurs. In this case, the actors are eager to set up new logics with disparate connections to legitimacy. Supporting among others, the conclusion of Hambrick et al. (2005), isomorphic pressures can increase or decrease over time.

This book suggests that organizations are not entirely passive as IT proposes and therefore do not necessarily conform to the pressures laid upon them. Nor are organizations complete manipulators, as RDT suggests. The organizations in this study reveal the diverse traits of organizational actors and the nature of the pressures enforced upon them, but they also seem to possess a sort of political power. The private cultural centers can make sense of and change their environment and make strategical choices, including both compliance and resistance. This study does not disagree with earlier views of IT and RDT but expands these views by arguing that these two theories are both complementary and interdependent on many levels, such as when explaining homogeneity, heterogeneity, isomorphism and diversification.

In respect of the concept of business models, the findings suggest that it seems to be acknowledged among the cultural centers, but in practice omitted. However, although the centers do not entirely seem to grasp the concept of business models, there is still always one at play. This book still contributed in clarifying the concept, especially when connected to cultural centers.

Business and arts may be at the opposite ends of the spectrum, but the findings still suggest that the mission of the centers is not to make money from the cultural content but to display art that makes a difference within the community. Nevertheless, there are also notions of having to comply with certain rules of business to have any chance of earning revenue, suggesting a natural balance between the concepts.

Regarding the concept of mission drift, the findings of this study suggest great differences in acquiring the needed resources. This finding, in turn, suggests that the concept of mission drift is not measurable between different fields and, as Weisbrod (2004) stated, is very hard to point out in a specific field or a single organization.

Quality and profitability are as business and arts contrasting. Still, and hardly surprising, the centers seems to have grasped the concept of quality – regarding the cultural offering as well as customer satisfaction. Even if there seem to be some movement between these opposite ends, they do not let profitability steer quality. The balance is still somewhat fragile, as resource scarcity tends to overshadow the profitability. The centers moreover do not use established quality management systems in any greater extent.

The findings of this book furthermore show that private cultural centers are devoted to shaping and reinventing their organizational field. They started out (in Finland) as late adopters of ideas and practices in an institutional field where public cultural centers are the early adopters with authenticated mission statements. Private cultural centers nonetheless have proven to be resilient to isomorphic pressures, confirming that isomorphism also works in reverse. This also seems to be the case elsewhere in the world, where the private initiatives where the early adopters.

In addition to the theoretical contributions, this study has some managerial implications. A number of such implications for private cultural centers arose as the data were analyzed, interpreted, discussed and compared with the existing literature in earlier chapters. This chapter will also summarize these implications.

Two unfolding issues are the differing nature of the institutional environments of the cultural centers and organizations' strategic behavior in this environment. Although this specific study focuses on a Finnish context, the results support some generalizations. These results serve to further our understanding of the effect resource dependence has on institutional change in organization and the practical implications it might present.

Regarding separation of ownership and control, the study findings imply a division of cultural centers into four different groups (private, public, hybrid and governmental organizations), which all have their own specific pressures and strategies. The institutional backgrounds of these center types lead them to act spontaneously in ways seen to serve their own interests without looking after any institutionalized interests in the matter. As stated by Lambert and Williams (2017), it is important to consider the ownership, governance and management structure before founding a new cultural center.

As an organizational strategy and activity, interorganizational cooperation could clearly improve both organization growth and economic stability. Managers should consider interorganizational cooperation as a way to achieve sustainable growth and stability. For resource scarcity, which seems to be the largest difficulty among private cultural centers, acquiring and allocating resources should be planned ahead while staying within the frames of the mission statement. The field itself is not lucrative, so exploring the outskirts of the mission statement offers possibilities to gain resources. Regarding mission drift, managers should stay aware of the balance between focusing on the core content of the mission statement and possibilities to gain resources from activities farther from the core content.

For decision-making, this study implies that driven managers of private cultural centers lean towards different strategies to diversify resource streams and choose a strategic response to institutional pressures. Since private cultural centers may occupy only restricted resources, center managers might be compelled to carry out a set of limited strategies, with very minimal possibilities for alternative action. Furthermore, decision-making seems to be tightly connected to regional

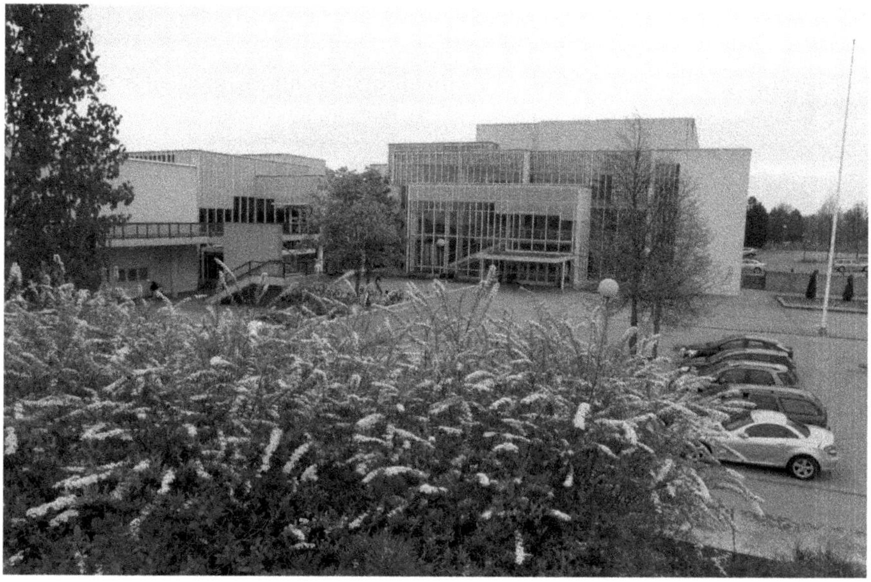

Picture 9.1 The front of cultural center Virta in Imatra, Finland.

needs and expectations. Managers need to know the specifics of the communities where cultural centers are and make decisions accordingly. Regarding change, this important aspect of cultural centers is quite underexplored by earlier research. This book attempted to expand our understanding on this aspect, as institutional change adds to the development of cultural centers in the contexts of Western societies.

9.2 Limitations

Like all studies, this one has limitations that present opportunities for future research. The analysis of the study was restricted to four private cultural centers to more accurately capture issues such as institutional pressures due to resource dependence among private centers. In retrospect, one can admit that interviewing people from all four center types would have presented more versatile data. In addition, the focus on private centers may have presented a bias that, in turn, may have altered the research outcomes.

On a general level, all research designs include compromises due to the practical limits of data collection. The small sample of this study was chosen to allow for rich examination of institutional change within resource dependence. Although this choice increased the probability of fresh and internally valid findings, it did so at the cost of generalizability and external validity. Furthermore, there were very little prior studies on the subject, which complicated the process of carrying out this study. It, therefore, was crucial that the study findings be subjected to rigorous empirical tests.

A comprehensive exploration of how institutional culture, particularly attitudes towards fundraising and revenue generation, has changed would require a broader range of interviews with both private and public centers. This study was limited to identifying the institutional changes the private cultural centers have implemented due to resource dependence, as well as exploring how mission focused they are and if they have a business model. The impact of cultural centers on the local community was left unstudied but could have further elaborated the role of the centers.

The underrepresentation of both hybrid and governmental organization cultural centers is another limitation of this study. The survey sample included mostly public and private centers. Future research could extend this study by giving hybrid and governmental organization centers adequate opportunities to express their perceptions of ongoing institutional changes and resource dependence that may identify a distinctive pattern of novel practices.

Both the data and findings presented by this study were based on a single Western society context (Finland). This may have affected the generalization of the outcomes to other societies. Further research in other Western and non-Western societies is needed to advance the understanding of the influence of resource dependence and institutional pressures in such contexts. The limitations

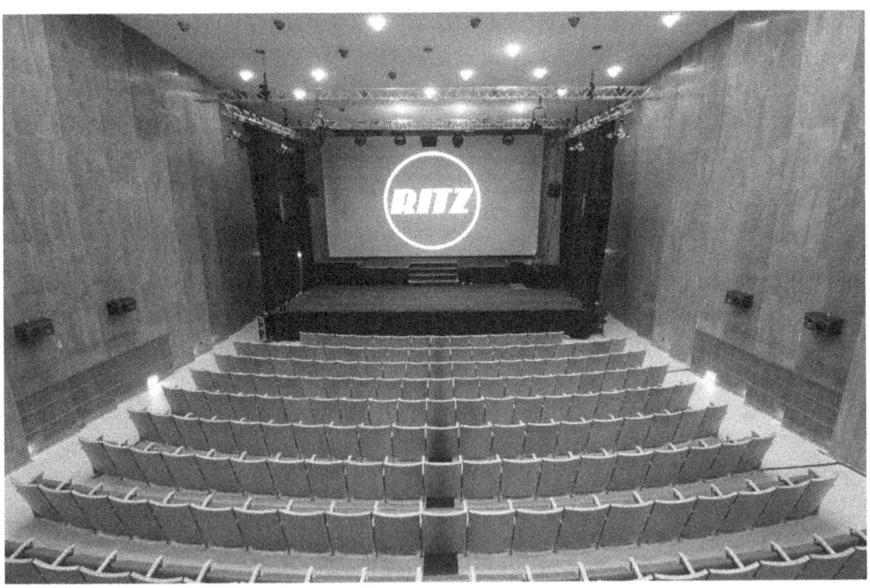

Picture 9.2 The main stage at cultural center Ritz in Vaasa, Finland. A photograph by Valter Lidsle.

discussed in this section do not imply that this study or its findings are insignificant or invalid. The limitations are merely presented for recognition and to emphasize the need for future research.

9.3 Concluding words

The question of the unprofitability of cultural offerings arose more than once during the interviews. Even if the private cultural centers had many successful events, the yearly average of events still seems modest. In fact, the respondents stated that a theatre simply cannot ever reach a profitable level in Finland. Could this unprofitability work somewhat to the benefit of the cultural centers as the low profits most likely decrease the amount of competition?

The balance of traditional cultural center activities and commercial activities is an interesting lateral outcome of this study. How does declining traditional funding affect commercial activity? Does commercial activity diminish efforts devoted to traditional activities? Conversely, does decreased commercial activity lead to more contributions and public funding? Such self-supporting activities could be regarded as a modern form of legitimacy as the resource climate changes. A change towards more transparent business plans, perhaps.

This study implies that managers face many challenges to balance both the content and the economy of private cultural centers. The results furthermore show that current managers seem to have adopted well to the uncertainties of private cultural

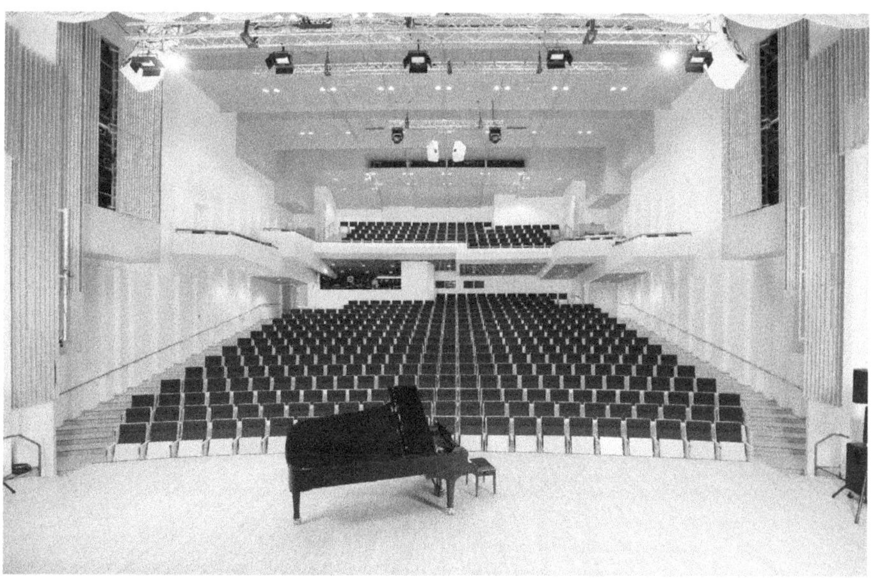

Picture 9.3 The stand at the main stage Karelia at cultural center Virta in Imatra, Finland.

centers within the field of Finnish cultural centers. Managers have adopted a variety of different methods to maintain their centers and reinvented their activities, as well as their resource palettes. But this study also shows that there are much to be done yet.

This book fills a gap in the literature regarding the emerging private cultural centers by showing that their activities are different from those enacted of the other center types. This result highlights the need to focus on the ownership and the control level of cultural centers in future research.

References

Hambrick, D., Finkelstein, S., Cho, T., & Jackson, E. (2005). Isomorphism in reverse: Institutional theory as an explanation for recent increases in intraindustry heterogeneity and managerial discretion. Em B. Staw, & R. Kramer (Eds.), *Research in Organizational Behavior* (Vol. 26, pp. 307–350). Greenwich, CT: JAI Press.

Lambert, P., & Williams, R. (2017). The professionalization of performing arts center management. Em P. Lambert, & R. Williams (Eds.), *Performing Arts Center Management* (pp. 1–19). New York: Routledge.

Pfeffer, J., & Salancik, G. (2003). *The External Control of Organizations: A Resource Dependence Perspective.* Stanford, CA: Stanford University Press.

Weisbrod, B. (2004). The pitfalls of profits. Stanford Social Innovation Review, 2(3), pp. 40–47.

Appendix

Descriptive statistics of the data used in the quantitative analysis

Ownership	*Variables*	*N*	*Min.*	*Max.*	*Mean*	*Std*	*Median*
Private	Changed expectations local inhabitants?	33	1	5	2,76	1,032	3,00
	Changes in the administration?	33	11	5	2,70	1,132	2,00
	Competition with private sector?	33	1	5	3,00	1,295	3,00
	Contest private/public	34	1	5	2,74	1,377	3,00
	Do you choose your cultural offerings on the basis of commercial success?	32	1	5	2,81	1,230	3,00
	Do you have own cultural offerings?	32	1	5	3,59	1,132	4,00
	Economic effect/ crowdfunding?	33	1	4	1,30	0,684	1,00
	Economic effect/ inter-organizational cooperation?	33	1	5	3,39	1,059	4,00
	Economic effect/ municipal funding?	33	1	5	2,76	1,640	2,00
	Economic effect/private funding?	33	1	5	2,88	1,474	3,00
	Economic effect/ sponsorship?	33	1	5	2,18	1,103	2,00
	Economic effect/taxes?	33	1	5	2,88	1,474	3,00
	Economic effect/ voluntary staff?	33	1	5	3,36	1,597	4,00
	Effect/funders?	33	1	5	3,21	1,364	3,00
	Effect/local inhabitants?	33	1	5	3,39	1,321	4,00
	Effect/municipality?	33	1	5	3,00	1,225	3,00
	Effect/state?	33	1	5	2,30	1,403	2,00
	Environmental pressure to change?	33	1	5	2,76	1,226	3,00

Ownership	*Variables*	*N*	*Min.*	*Max.*	*Mean*	*Std*	*Median*
	Has cooperation changed in recent years?	33	1	5	3,00	0,866	3,00
	How dependent are you on renters?	33	1	5	3,36	1,454	4,00
	How important is inter-organizational cooperation?	33	2	5	4,18	0,846	4,00
	Inter-organizational cooperation?	33	2	5	3,85	0,972	4,00
	More commercial activities?	33	1	5	3,09	1,376	4,00
	Need for change?	33	1	5	3,06	1,088	3,00
	Changed expectations local inhabitants?	33	1	5	2,76	1,032	3,00
	Valid N (listwise	31					
Public	Changed expectations local inhabitants?	46	1	5	3,15	0,842	3,00
	Changes in the administration?	42	11	5	2,91	1,213	3,00
	Competition with private sector?	47	1	5	2,45	1,080	2,00
	Contest private/public	5	1	5	1,60	0,894	1,00
	Do you choose your cultural offerings on the basis of commercial success?	46	1	4	2,50	0,960	3,00
	Do you have own cultural offerings?	47	1	5	3,47	1,139	4,00
	Economic effect/ crowdfunding?	42	1	5	1,19	0,505	1,00
	Economic effect/ inter-organizational cooperation?	42	1	5	4,00	0,963	4,00
	Economic effect/ municipal funding?	42	1	5	4,29	1,195	5,00
	Economic effect/private funding?	42	1	5	1,86	1,049	1,50
	Economic effect/ sponsorship?	42	1	4	1,71	0,891	1,50
	Economic effect/taxes?	42	1	4	1,83	0,853	2,00
	Economic effect/ voluntary staff?	42	1	5	2,31	1,115	2,00
	Effect/funders?	41	1	5	3,12	1,249	3,00
	Effect/local inhabitants?	42	1	5	4,02	0,715	3,00
	Effect/municipality?	42	1	5	4,05	1,081	4,00
	Effect/state?	42	1	5	2,62	1,248	2,00
	Environmental pressure to change?	46	1	5	3,30	1,008	3,50

Ownership	*Variables*	*N*	*Min.*	*Max.*	*Mean*	*Std*	*Median*
	Has cooperation changed in recent years?	46	1	5	3,24	0,766	3,00
	How dependent are you on renters?	47	1	5	3,40	1,228	4,00
	How important is inter-organizational cooperation?	42	2	5	4,48	0,809	5,00
	Inter-organizational cooperation?	46	2	5	4,21	0,883	4,00
	More commercial activities?	46	1	5	2,13	1,035	2,00
	Need for change?	42	1	5	3,59	0,884	4,00
	Changed expectations local inhabitants?	42	1	5	3,15	0,842	3,00
	Valid N (listwise	3					
Hybrid	Changed expectations local inhabitants?	9	1	5	2,78	0,667	3,00
	Changes in the administration?	6	1	5	2,78	1,302	3,00
	Competition with private sector?	8	1	5	3,13	1,246	3,00
	Contest private/public	11	1	5	2,91	1,578	4,00
	Do you choose your cultural offerings on the basis of commercial success?	8	1	4	2,25	1,389	2,00
	Do you have own cultural offerings?	8	1	4	3,13	1,356	4,00
	Economic effect/ crowdfunding?	6	1	5	1,17	0,408	1,00
	Economic effect/ inter-organizational cooperation?	6	4	5	4,67	0,516	5,00
	Economic effect/ municipal funding?	6	1	5	3,33	1,862	4,00
	Economic effect/private funding?	6	1	5	3,00	1,673	3,50
	Economic effect/ sponsorship?	6	1	5	2,00	1,673	1,00
	Economic effect/taxes?	6	1	5	3,17	1,329	3,00
	Economic effect/ voluntary staff?	6	1	5	3,00	1,673	2,50
	Effect/funders?	6	1	5	3,33	1,633	3,50
	Effect/local inhabitants?	6	3	5	4,33	0,816	4,50
	Effect/municipality?	6	2	5	4,17	1,169	4,50
	Effect/state?	6	1	5	3,50	1,517	3,50
	Environmental pressure to change?	9	1	5	3,56	1,236	4,00

Ownership	*Variables*	*N*	*Min.*	*Max.*	*Mean*	*Std*	*Median*
	Has cooperation changed in recent years?	9	2	5	3,38	0,916	3,00
	How dependent are you on renters?	8	2	5	4,00	1,069	4,00
	How important is inter-organizational cooperation?	8	4	5	4,50	0,535	4,50
	Inter-organizational cooperation?	8	2	5	4,00	0,926	4,00
	More commercial activities?	6	1	5	3,25	1,753	3,50
	Need for change?	9	1	5	3,00	1,118	3,00
	Changed expectations local inhabitants?	6	1	5	2,78	0,667	3,00
	Valid N (listwise	6					
Governmental company	Changed expectations local inhabitants?	12	2	5	3,55	0,934	4,00
	Changes in the administration?	12	1	4	3,00	1,128	3,00
	Competition with private sector?	12	1	5	3,08	1,564	3,00
	Contest private/public	12	1	5	2,42	1,621	2,00
	Do you choose your cultural offerings on the basis of commercial success?	12	1	4	3,17	0,937	3,00
	Do you have own cultural offerings?	12	1	5	2,42	1,443	2,00
	Economic effect/ crowdfunding?	12	1	5	1,25	0,452	1,00
	Economic effect/ inter-organizational cooperation?	12	1	5	3,33	1,557	3,50
	Economic effect/ municipal funding?	12	1	5	3,75	1,422	4,00
	Economic effect/private funding?	12	1	4	1,67	0,985	1,00
	Economic effect/ sponsorship?	12	1	4	2,17	1,193	2,00
	Economic effect/taxes?	12	1	3	1,58	0,900	1,00
	Economic effect/ voluntary staff?	12	1	5	2,08	1,564	1,00
	Effect/funders?	12	1	5	3,33	1,435	3,50
	Effect/local inhabitants?	12	2	5	3,50	1,087	4,00
	Effect/municipality?	12	2	5	4,00	0,853	4,00
	Effect/state?	12	1	4	2,00	0,853	3,00
	Environmental pressure to change?	12	1	4	3,00	0,953	3,00

Ownership	*Variables*	*N*	*Min.*	*Max.*	*Mean*	*Std*	*Median*
	Has cooperation changed in recent years?	12	2	5	3,58	0,793	4,00
	How dependent are you on renters?	11	1	5	4,82	0,405	5,00
	How important is inter-organizational cooperation?	12	3	5	4,42	0,900	4,00
	Inter-organizational cooperation?	12	2	5	4,08	1,165	4,50
	More commercial activities?	12	2	5	4,08	0,900	4,00
	Need for change?	12	2	5	3,58	1,084	4,00
	Changed expectations local inhabitants?	11	1	5	3,55	0,934	4,00
	Valid N (listwise	9					

Index

For Product Safety Concerns and Information please contact our EU
representative GPSR@taylorandfrancis.com
Taylor & Francis Verlag GmbH, Kaufingerstraße 24, 80331 München, Germany

www.ingramcontent.com/pod-product-compliance
Ingram Content Group UK Ltd.
Pitfield, Milton Keynes, MK11 3LW, UK
UKHW020002200926
475702UK00015B/2437
9780367510237